MW00526885

Backcountry Lawman

THE FLORIDA HISTORY AND CULTURE SERIES

UNIVERSITY PRESS OF FLORIDA

Florida A&M University, Tallahassee
Florida Atlantic University, Boca Raton
Florida Gulf Coast University, Ft. Myers
Florida International University, Miami
Florida State University, Tallahassee
New College of Florida, Sarasota
University of Central Florida, Orlando
University of Florida, Gainesville
University of North Florida, Jacksonville
University of South Florida, Tampa
University of West Florida, Pensacola

Backcountry Lawman

True Stories from a Florida Game Warden

Bob H. Lee

Foreword by Raymond Arsenault and Gary R. Mormino

University Press of Florida

Gainesville · Tallahassee · Tampa · Boca Raton

Pensacola · Orlando · Miami · Jacksonville · Ft. Myers · Sarasota

Library of Congress Cataloging-in-Publication Data
Lee, Bob H.
Backcountry lawman : true stories from a Florida game warden / Bob H. Lee ;
foreword by Raymond Arsenault and Gary Mormino.
p. cm.—(The Florida history and culture series)
Includes bibliographical references and index.
ISBN 978-0-8130-4429-3 (cloth: alk. paper)
ISBN 978-0-8130-6128-3 (pbk.)
1. Lee, Bob H. 2. Game wardens—Florida—Anecdotes. 3. Wildlife conservation—
Florida—Anecdotes. 4. Poaching—Florida—Prevention—Anecdotes. I. Arsenault,
Raymond. II. Mormino, Gary Ross, 1947– III. Title. IV. Series: Florida history and
culture series.
SK354.L44A3 2013
639.909759—dc23
2012031968

The University Press of Florida is the scholarly publishing agency for the State
University System of Florida, comprising Florida A&M University, Florida Atlantic
University, Florida Gulf Coast University, Florida International University, Florida
State University, New College of Florida, University of Central Florida, University of
Florida, University of North Florida, University of South Florida, and University of
West Florida.

University Press of Florida
2046 NE Waldo Road
Suite 2100
Gainesville, FL 32609
http://upress.ufl.edu

To Karen, for her patience and grace, and to our son, Jason

Contents

Foreword

Backcountry Lawman is the latest volume in a series devoted to the study of Florida history and culture. During the past half century, the burgeoning population and increased national and international visibility of Florida have sparked a great deal of popular interest in the state's past, present, and future. As the favorite destination of countless tourists and as the new home for millions of retirees and transplants, modern Florida has become a demographic, political, and cultural bellwether. Florida has also emerged as a popular subject and setting for scholars and writers. The Florida History and Culture Series provides an attractive and accessible format for Florida-related books. From killer hurricanes to disputed elections, from tales of the Everglades to profiles of Sunbelt cities, the topics covered by the more than forty books published so far represent a broad spectrum of regional history and culture.

The University Press of Florida is committed to the creation of an eclectic but carefully crafted set of books that will provide the field of Florida studies with a new focus and that will encourage Florida researchers and writers to consider the broader implications and context of their work. The series includes standard academic monographs as well as works of synthesis, memoirs, and anthologies. And while the series features books of historical interest, authors researching Florida's environment, politics, literature, and popular or material culture are encouraged to submit their manuscripts as well. Each book offers a distinct personality and voice, but the ultimate goal of the series is to foster a sense of community and collaboration among Florida scholars.

In *Backcountry Lawman*, Lt. Bob H. Lee (ret.) revisits his three decades as a fish and wildlife law enforcement officer in northeast Florida. From 1977 to 2007, he patrolled the waters and environs of the St. Johns River region, chasing and arresting poachers and other lawbreakers, and frequently encountering danger and intrigue along the way. Nine years ago the Florida History and Culture Series published Stuart B. McIver's riveting account of the life and death of an earlier game warden, *Death in the Everglades: The Murder of Guy Bradley, America's First Martyr to Environmentalism*. Now we return to this fascinating and generally hidden slice of Florida culture, to the experiences of a more recent game warden, one who fortunately lived to tell the tales of his harrowing occupation.

Lee's considerable skills as a law enforcement officer are more than matched by his obvious gifts of shrewd observation and idiomatic narrative. He is a born storyteller with a flair for anecdotal insight and raw candor. He introduces us to an almost fantastical cast of characters, reconstructing their experiences with wit and a hard-earned perspective of the realities of life on both sides of the law. Literally and figuratively taking us into the backwaters of the St. Johns and the back roads of nearby Putnam County, he examines the "old-school poacher" culture of men like Roger Gunter, the master of the illegal art of "monkey-fishing" (using an electrical charge to catch freshwater catfish), as well as the heroism and eccentric antics of wardens such as Guy "Gator" Banks and Hank Starling. There are "cackling" bass fishermen, poachers on motorcycles, and much more in this original and fascinating memoir, enough grit and gator lore to satisfy even the most ardent student of Florida's wild history of endangered creatures and the wardens entrusted to protect them.

Raymond Arsenault and Gary R. Mormino
Series Editors

Author's Notes

A Word on Characters and Dialogue

The stories I chose to write about were selected from my experiences as a water patrol officer on the St. Johns River and later as a patrol supervisor over three counties in northeast Florida. My research included recorded interviews with the officers I formerly worked with, two prosecutors, and the most notorious poacher in Putnam County, Roger Gunter.

Descriptions of poachers other than Gunter will have a fictitious name (unless they have passed away) and an altered physical description. The dialogue used here represents my recollection of events and of those I interviewed, except for certain direct quotes taken from the transcripts of the Amtrak environmental trial. I made minor adjustments to timelines and geographic locations and condensed storylines to provide a better sense of narrative flow. In a few cases, I've taken the liberty of using composite characters. This was done to protect me. I still live in Putnam County, the primary setting for this book.

Lastly, all fish and wildlife officers are referred to as "game wardens." This form of address is widely recognized throughout the United States and internationally as the accepted generic name for conservation law enforcement officers.

Florida's Conservation Law Enforcement Agencies

Understanding the complete history of Florida's conservation law enforcement agencies can be like untangling a ball of knotted twine. To spare the reader, I offer this brief summary.

The Game and Fresh Water Fish Commission (GFC)—the agency I originally began with in 1977—had constitutional authority to pass laws for the protection of freshwater fish and wildlife, overseen by a five-member commission or policy-forming board. This process was efficient and worked well for the protection of the species under consideration. Best of all, it required no review or approval from the Florida legislature.

Concurrently, the Florida Marine Patrol—under the Florida Marine Fisheries Commission—was in charge of protecting coastal areas and marine species (saltwater fish, sea turtles, and manatees). They had no constitutional authority to pass laws. Instead, they had to go through the arduous procedure of submitting new laws to the legislature for final approval and passage. This process was open to influence by special-interest groups like the commercial fishing lobby and proved to be an inefficient and unwieldy system.

On July 1, 1999, the two agencies merged under the constitutional umbrella of the GFC to form the Florida Fish and Wildlife Conservation Commission (FWC). Overnight, this brand-new supersized conservation agency led the nation in the number of conservation law enforcement officers employed by any one state—700–plus. All have full police powers and statewide jurisdiction. (The agency as a whole has 1,900–plus employees; the rest work in different divisions responsible for research and management of Florida's diverse wildlife and public wildlife management areas.)

The mission of FWC's Law Enforcement Division is to provide protection to residents and visitors who enjoy Florida's natural resources, while enforcing resource protection and boating safety laws in the woods and on the waters of the state. FWC officers cooperate with other law enforcement agencies providing homeland security and are among the first on the scene to help when natural disasters occur because of their specialized equipment to access remote, hard-to-reach locations.

The St. Johns River and Putnam County

Follow Hwy. 17/100 west, up the nearly mile-long span of the Memorial Bridge toward Palatka, and the landscape drops away to reveal Putnam County's finest asset: the broad, shimmering expanse of the St. Johns River.

The river divides Putnam County, population 74,364, into two uneven halves. While technically part of the county, it remains a world unto itself. This is big water, 310 miles in total length and much of it an intracoastal waterway. Wider sections along the lower reaches broaden to three miles and could be mistaken for parts of the Mississippi River.

The river flows north (most rivers in the United States flow south) at the agonizingly slow rate of one-third of a mile per hour, with a drop of only thirty feet from its headwaters in the marshes of Indian River County in central Florida to its outflow into the Atlantic Ocean, near the seaport city of Jacksonville. Tidal influences from the Atlantic affect the river well south (upstream) of Palatka, Putnam County's seat, where one might have to study a patch of floating water hyacinths to figure out which way the current flows.

With a citizen poverty rate of about 25 percent and easy access to 822 square miles of public wilderness tracts, private hunting leases, farmlands, cattle ranches, and watercourses rich in game and fish, Putnam County was and still is one of the premier areas in the state to catch hard-core poachers.

If ever there was an ideal place for a game warden to make a living, this county would be as close as one could come.

Welcome to my home.

Introduction

Danger can come in many forms. Take the night I crept through the overhanging branches of a ligustrum hedge. The air was calm, peaceful even, as I parted the dense foliage and stepped out onto the manicured front yard of a palatial home in Welaka, a quaint fishing town bordering a high bluff overlooking the St. Johns River. Blinded by the interior lamp lights of a well-lit living room ahead, I could see nothing of the lawn in front of me.

My plan: to quietly sneak past the home and down to the river, where—according to an informant—a man was illegally catching fish on the end of his dock with an electrified dip net. The device received power by way of an extension cord plugged into a 110-volt receptacle.

I looked forward to the moment I could lay hands on him. It would mean instant bragging rights at our semiannual regional meetings, where unusual poaching cases garnered the most recognition.

Back then I was twenty-four, with little experience, but one hell of a lot of enthusiasm. I wanted to catch this guy so bad I could taste it.

I took one more step and the ground disappeared beneath me. Suddenly, I was in freefall. I immediately stretched my legs and arms out like a skydiver. My first, brief thought was that I had fallen into an old well. But in the next millisecond, I realized this made no sense. A well is only about a yard across. Whatever I had fallen into was much wider.

I crashed into the ground, my left cheek split open on a sharp rock. I lay there stunned in the pitch-black. I took stock of my body parts and realized that, thankfully, nothing was broken. The flashlight I'd been carrying had been knocked loose in the fall. With both hands, I felt around for it until my fingers wrapped around the cool aluminum body. Flicking the switch on illuminated a freshly dug pit about six feet deep and ten feet wide, for what purpose I hadn't a clue.

I wasn't too concerned about what had happened until I cocked my head to the right. Poking out of the ground next to my eye was a two-foot section of steel rebar that stood perfectly straight and permanently cast into a piece of buried concrete. Had my head been just six inches to the right, the half-inch-diameter steel rod would have cleanly pierced my right eye socket and punched out through the back of my skull. And that's how I would have been found when the sun came up, like a mounted butterfly pinned to cardboard backing.

The hand of death had taken a swipe at me and I'd survived. Whether it was due to fate, divine guidance, or both, I didn't know. But my education had begun. I was learning to expect the unexpected when navigating through the night without lights.

Oh, and by the time I crawled out of the hole and stumbled down to the dock, the electric fisherman had returned to the house. I walked away empty-handed.

*   *   *

A lot has been written about the day-to-day dangers that game wardens face, mostly due to the sheer volume of armed hunters and poachers they encounter. While it's true that a good number of wardens have been injured or killed in shooting incidents, we also seem to do a pretty good job of doing ourselves in. Stalking those who commit wildlife crimes can be a dicey business.

1

Meeting the Enemy

Northeast Florida's most notorious "monkey-fisherman," Roger Gunter, sits down for an interview with his former law enforcement nemesis: Me.

*   *   *

In my thirty years as a game warden in northeast Florida, I ran across hundreds of poachers. Illegal hunting and fishing—be it birds, deer, striped bass, or alligators—are part of this state's rich history, and have an outlaw appeal that can't be quelled by law enforcement. Having worked as both a game warden and a patrol supervisor, I've chased hunters on foot, through swamps, across lakes, down miles of rivers. But of all the types of poachers I chased, the most elusive and peculiar were devotees of the practice called "monkey-fishing."

For many years, and particularly during the 1960s, 1970s, and early 1980s, the practice of illegally catching freshwater catfish using an electrical charge was a big problem for wardens of the then Florida Game and Fresh Water Fish Commission (GFC). And nowhere was monkey-fishing a bigger business than in the commercial fishing towns of Welaka and Georgetown, on the St. Johns River in Putnam County.

Monkey-fishing, by its nature, is a private act. It's usually done under the cover of darkness, or during daylight in a remote creek. It can be financially quite rewarding for residents of poor communities and offers more than a little charge of excitement to the fishermen. The sight of hundreds of catfish rising to the surface in a desperate attempt to escape electrical currents applied along sandy river bottoms has for years attracted—even addicted—wayward commercial fishermen. And those who practiced monkey-fishing created a colorful history that will forever remain a part of St. Johns River lore. Most were hard-core poachers who did not surrender willingly to my siren and blue light. In fact, just about every time I tried to catch one, they'd end up leading me on a hellish boat chase.

Without question, the worst was Roger Gunter, a man who had, and still has, the well-deserved reputation for being just a little bit crazy. Gunter is sixty-nine now, but back then he was Putnam County's most notorious outlaw, an old-school poacher who caught and killed gators, deer, and fish with utter disregard for the law. A true profiteer at the expense of wildlife, Gunter was the ultimate prize for any game warden; in his thirty years of monkey-fishing, he'd never been caught for that offense.

Gunter didn't fare as well when it came to deer and ducks. He was caught a handful of times for hunting violations, happily walking out of court with a dismissal or a small fine. Back then, folks at the courthouse regarded Gunter's game-law foibles as merely an amusement.

Toward the end of my career, I thought it would be interesting to sit down with this notorious poacher and possibly even write about him. Gunter disagreed. For five years, I asked him to sit for an interview, but as long as I worked at the Florida Fish and Wildlife Conservation Commission, he flat refused. "I've got too many secrets, Cat," he told me. (Gunter calls everyone "Cat"; it's easier than remembering names.)

But a month before I was scheduled to retire in September 2007, he finally changed his mind. "I'll talk to you," he told me. "But only after you've officially retired." Then he paused for moment to consider what he might be in for and added, "I need to know. Can I be arrested for anything I've done in the past?" I assured him that the statute of limitations protected him from being prosecuted for any of his old wildlife crimes.

A couple of months later on a warm October afternoon, I met with Gunter at his home ten miles southwest of Palatka. We'd agreed on a one o'clock meeting, and when I drove into his yard right at one, he was waiting for me outside, pacing.

Gunter may have been nervous, but he was also busy. The morning before our meeting, he cast-netted shiners for the owner of a commercial fishpond, where the expensive bass bait was raised to sell at bait shops and fish camps. By four o'clock that afternoon, he'd be perched in a tree stand waiting to kill a deer with a bow and arrow. It was the tail end of archery season, when the bucks go into rut, dropping their guard to chase does in heat. Gunter had his eye on one with a monster rack and hoped to kill it that evening.

Over the years, Gunter's work as a poacher provided a solid supplemental income to his salary at the Georgia-Pacific Paper Mill in Palatka, where he worked for thirty-seven years, the last five years as a supervisor. But his life as an outlaw had a motive deeper than money. Part of it was how he was raised—Gunter shot his father full of birdshot when he was just nine years old, trying to defend himself against the old man's drunken antics—but he was also deeply in tune with nature.

Gunter's life revolved around the sun, the moon, and the tides. He started putting food on the table for his ma and pa when he was just a child. He hunted barefoot until he was forty years old. He nearly died from the bends in 1978 while deep-sea diving in the Atlantic Ocean, an incident that left him with some paralysis in both legs. (Though he can walk fine, he says you could stick a pin in either leg and he wouldn't feel it.) He survived being bitten by water moccasins—twice. And everything he shot went into a cook pot. Squirrel brains, and the tongue, were a delicacy. And though he's nearly seventy today, nothing has changed. Gunter still hunts or fishes every day, depending on the season. And he doesn't feel particularly constrained by the laws of man.

I hadn't seen my old foe for a couple of years, but he still looked the same. He wore dull-green rubber boots, faded blue jeans, and a brand-new sleeveless camouflage shirt (he knew I would be taking his picture), topped off with a boonie hat on his bald head.

We shook hands. As an ice-breaker, I asked him if he had any deer antlers. "Oh, yeah," he answered in the loud raspy voice of the partially deaf. "I got me some deer antlers. You want to see them?"

Together, we walked up three wooden steps to a large screened-in porch fronting his double-wide mobile home. Inside, the ceiling was literally covered with deer antlers, their racks nailed to the plywood by their sawed-off skull caps. Dangling from the antler tines were rattlesnake rattles, suspended by tiny white strings like so many Christmas ornaments. One rattle had an astounding sixteen buttons—one for each time the massive snake had shed its skin. On the far wall were more deer racks, jammed side by side in two long rows.

Lying haphazardly among the antlers were several "William Tell" arrows, the result of practice shots where one arrow pierces the nock of another, embedding into the shaft as it splits apart. Other arrows were from deer kills, the dark-brown stains of dried blood still visible. There were also a dozen turkey feet and thick, black beards of large gobblers mixed in with the other souvenirs.

Among the trophies, I spotted one that was personally very familiar. Hanging from a piece of bare wire, twirling slowly in the breeze, was a bright-yellow license plate. It was the tag off an old GFC vehicle—no doubt a special prize for this notorious poacher.

We walked outside again and sat at a dark-green picnic table in the shade of a live oak tree. I snuck a quick look around. I couldn't help it—old habits die hard. In one sweep of my eyes, I saw a small grove of well-tended grapefruit trees, a couple of tin-roofed sheds, some steel (leg-hold) traps, an airboat, a tree stand, a motorcycle, bows and spearguns, an aluminum boat, a camouflaged all-terrain vehicle, a four-wheel drive truck, and two German shepherds in an enclosed pen.

The mental snapshot I took away was of a man who kept his equipment in order. Three decades of chasing poachers had taught me that the more organized a guy was, the less likely we were to catch him. Gunter was very organized.

In all my years of chasing Roger Gunter, I never expected to be facing him across a picnic table. I also never expected to see a softer side of the man. But Gunter seemed relaxed, even unguarded. When an

Roger Gunter shows the author a homemade rheostat he fashioned for his monkey-fishing machine (electric shocking device), 2007.

ash-gray cat jumped onto the picnic table, the professional poacher stroked it lightly with one hand and cooed, "How's kitty doing today?"

Gunter's arms—a little too long for his body—rested comfortably on the table. Originally a fair-skinned redhead, his daily exposure to the sun had given his skin the look of swarthy offshore sailor. His sleeveless shirt fully exposed the tattoo of the Eighty-Second Airborne on his left arm. In the past, he'd often peppered his conversations with military terms like "recon," one of his favorites. In Gunter's world, that meant scouting to see if the game wardens were hiding nearby.

I pulled a digital recorder from my shirt pocket, laid it on the table between us, and pressed "record." This was the moment I'd been waiting for.

"Roger," I began.

"I'm a professional," he broke in, tapping his fingertips against his chest for emphasis. "I'm not like a lot of these guys you've caught that weren't paying attention to what they were doing and didn't take precautions."

In the late 1950s, Gunter recalled, he began killing gators "on a regular basis" and selling their hides. It was a pretty good living until some of his buddies got arrested by federal agents up in Georgia, he said. "So I had to quit that. It was about that time my daddy-in-law showed me this little machine that shocked fish."

The monkey-fishing device is actually made from an antique telephone magneto, or generator, used to power hand-crank telephones (used from the late nineteenth century up through World War II). The magneto is strapped to a board, along with a small electric motor, and the two are connected with a rubber shaft. When the electric motor is hooked up to a 12-volt car battery, it spins the magneto, generating an electrical current—up to 110 volts. (Early versions of the device used the hand crank from the old telephones to generate electricity, a frenetic cranking that some thought resembled a nineteenth-century organ grinder with his performing monkey—hence the name "monkey-fishing.")

Monkey-fishermen like Gunter attach two insulated wires to the magneto's outlet terminals and strip their ends to bare copper. The wires are dropped over opposite gunwales (sides) of a boat, leaving them suspended a few feet below the hull. Water becomes the electric conduit between the wires' copper tips, and any catfish swimming in the vicinity are shocked. The charge isn't strong enough to affect scaled fish like bass or bream, but slick-skinned catfish can't resist it. They bolt toward the surface in an effort to escape the stinging current and bob there until the fisherman is ready to scoop them up with dip nets. (Interestingly, the electrical charge has little effect when the water temperature falls below 70 degrees Fahrenheit, thereby relegating this form of fishing to the summer months.)

"I started out with reed poles," Gunter told me, "but graduated to aluminum handles." He drilled holes in the tubes to make them sink faster if law enforcement showed up, but the metal poles were strong and could take the strain of repeated dipping. Gunter's were as long as fourteen feet with a bent net to make scooping easier. In one

Six hundred pounds of catfish seized in a monkey-fishing (electric fish shocking) case by the author. The fish were donated to the Putnam County Sheriff's Department, 1978.

night of fishing, Gunter boasted, he could "fill five or six boxes with fish"—about 500 to 600 pounds—"before my arms gave out."

Fishing with electricity is undeniably effective. Fish researchers still use the method to count fish populations in a section of river or when they need samples for testing. To catch scaled fish, they use stronger electrical currents, typically from gas-powered generators. But using electricity for recreational fishing is explicitly prohibited by state law.

The law echoes other game laws that value "fair chase." Deer can't be shot at night, turkeys can't be killed over bait, and freshwater fish can't be taken by electricity. The laws are designed to encourage sportsman to use skill, not tricks, to catch their prey, and to prevent the use of instruments that can seriously diminish a species. For some, the laws are a deterrent. For men like Gunter, they're a challenge.

Anyone who has monkey-fished for very long will end up in a boat chase with a game warden. Gunter was no exception. His boat chases on the river are legendary, and include the longest boat chase in St. Johns River history. It began at two o'clock in the morning on the Wekiva River near Sanford, and ended fifty minutes later in Lake George—nearly forty miles away.

In the end, Gunter and the man who'd been driving the boat gave the slip to the officers who had been chasing them. But it wasn't without a price. The driver had half his face torn off when they drove through a shiner lift net doing sixty miles per hour with their lights out.

"I had to take him to a clinic to get him stitched up," recalled Roger when I asked him about it. "He was messed up pretty good. I kind of took it easy after that for a while. That was a wild ride, even for me."

Even before that accident, Gunter was careful. He spooked easily, closing up his operation at the mere hint of a lawman. And like a master chess player, he was always thinking three moves ahead.

"I always liked to fish by myself," Gunter told me. "I didn't want to split the profits with anyone, and there was less chance of someone pimping me out. And I never went to the same spot more than two times in a row. Sometimes I'd drive thirty miles north and fish, and the next night I'd go thirty miles south. I had machines hid all up and down the river in old .50 caliber military ammo cans. I'd hide them behind old tree stumps and at points and in coves along the river. But I'd never bring the machine or the nets into the boat ramp. I always loaded out clean. I knew you couldn't make a case on me just because I had a bulkhead full of fish."

Solo fishing meant more profit for Gunter, but also more risk. A lot of monkey-fishermen used a rheostat made from a door spring to adjust the electric motor's revolutions. By experimenting with different motor speeds, a fisherman found the perfect charge level to shock the fish just right. The trick was to try to get the fish to where they weren't too agitated, making them easier to dip up.

Gunter used a rheostat, too, but he got into serious trouble one night when he was testing the current. "I've been electrocuted a lot while I been monkey-fishing—it just happens," said Gunter. "But nothing like the morning I was up in Clark's Creek, north of Bost-wick. It was about 3:00 a.m., and I was by myself. One of the wires was hanging off the side of the boat into the water. The other one I took in my right hand and put it under the water so my thumb was on the copper tip. And my left hand was fiddling with the rheostat trying to get the charge right. I could feel it tingling. The muscles in my arm would tense and relax according to how I was adjusting it. When the current felt right to me I'd leave the rheostat on that setting. That's how I controlled the fish and kept them from skipping away. The goal was to have them roll around at the surface where they were easy to dip up."

But this time, Gunter said, something went wrong. "A wave hit my boat and knocked my hand up out of the water. Let me tell ya, that's when I knew what it felt like to be a light bulb. I'd just become the conductor for the electric current. The whole right side of my body froze up. I couldn't move. My chest had constricted and I could hardly breathe. I really thought I was going to die right there because I couldn't open my hand. After about thirty seconds, I managed to rock forward and get my hand back in the water, where I could turn the wire loose. Let me tell ya, I tore the Budweiser up after that. I sat down and drank me three or four in a row. It took me about two hours to get right."

By the late 1980s, monkey-fishing was pretty much a thing of the past. A state law was passed early in that decade making it a third-degree felony to flee a law enforcement officer on the water, so mon-key-fishermen were more easily deterred. Finding remote creeks has become more difficult as north Florida has grown. And the demand for catfish has been all but gutted by commercial catfish farms, which can deliver perfectly sized fish on demand, reducing the need for wild-caught catfish.

The last case I can remember handling was one my officers made in 2004—on the Ocklawaha River in Putnam County—involving two brothers, aged fifty and sixty. Interestingly, I had caught the same two men in almost the exact same spot twenty-five years before.

Like most monkey-fishermen caught by law enforcement, they were charged with second-degree misdemeanors, which carry a maximum

The monkey-fishing machine (electric shocking device) along with the boat the author sits in were seized as evidence, 1978.

penalty of a five-hundred-dollar fine, sixty days in jail, and forfeiture of the equipment.

The monkey-fishing era may be over, but it will never be forgotten by those who lived it—on either side of the law.

"Monkey-fishing is the most fun thing I've ever done," Gunter told me. "It's more addictive than sex, drugs, or booze. I can remember times when I'd be sitting at a bar with a good-looking gal on each side of me, just relaxing and enjoying a beer. And then I'd get to thinking about burning those fish up. Well, I'd just jump up right then and go. There's nothing else like it."

*   *   *

Author's Note: Please consider this a primer on monkey-fishing and Roger Gunter. Both will be key topics in later chapters.

2

How I Became a Game Warden

On what seemed like an idyllic summer day, my dad and I were swimming in Lake Saddleback, a small freshwater lake behind our home in the community of Lutz, thirteen miles north of Tampa. Dad was farther out than me, about chest-deep, when he let out a god-awful shout, "Sonofabitch! Run, run, an alligator just bit me!"

He rushed toward shore with an alacrity and speed that I'd never seen before. His legs and knees worked furiously, pushing up a white frothy wake like the prow of a battleship going aground. When he came abreast of me, he snatched me up by one arm and hauled me out with him. I can remember skimming across the surface like a water ski. In no time, we stood on a strip of sugar-sand beach that lined the water's edge of our lawn. Bent over, Dad grabbed his sides, gasping for air. Aquatic wind sprints weren't his strong suit.

"Where did it bite you?" I asked, breathless, and feeling safe and curious at the same time, now that we both stood on solid ground. If it was bloody, I wanted to see it. Of course, I would have never wished ill upon my father, but at the age of nine, I wasn't about to pass up on the opportunity to see mangled flesh, either.

Dad turned his right heel up to show me an inch-long gash with a narrow stream of bright-red blood dripping down the sole of his foot. "Wow," I said, peering down for a closer look. "So you really think that's a gator bite?"

"Looks like I got lucky—he only snagged me with one tooth. I doubt he's very big; let's see if he comes up."

Sure enough, five minutes later the bony snout and hooded eyes of a seven-foot gator surfaced. Lying stationary, he eyed us from about twenty yards away with what I can only describe as keen disappointment.

Apparently, Dad had been too fleet of foot to allow the beast more than one chomp. There's nothing quite like a one-on-one encounter with a throwback to the dinosaur era to inspire feats of great athleticism.

"Come on up to the house, son. I know how to take care of that alligator." I followed behind as we weaved our way through moss-cloaked cypress trees that dotted our backyard and up to the modest wood-frame house my mom and dad had built in 1952, a year before I was born. The area we lived in had a few homes nearby with even fewer kids my age to play with. I wanted action. That gator needed to die.

My hope was that Dad would grab the .22 caliber rifle and shoot the gator. Instead, he picked up the receiver on our rotary telephone and dialed up the then Game and Fresh Water Fish Commission (GFC). For the moment, I would miss out on the thrill of a vicarious gator hunt.

Two nights later, the headlights of a GFC patrol car—towing a small fiberglass boat—swept down the palm-lined, crushed-shell driveway to our home. Two game wardens stepped out, shook hands with my father, and explained—with the quiet confidence of professional hunters—how they would kill the gator that had attacked him. In fact, they would shoot all of them that they could find in the six- to eight-foot range to be sure they got the right one. They invited us to sit and watch from the shore if we liked.

Oh, yes, I liked that idea very much.

We sat on a bench made with a thin marble slab laid across two cinder blocks. Tree frogs chorused nearby, while mosquitoes buzzed us with abandon. We idly slapped at them as we watched the wardens prepare their gear. The show was about to begin, and I had a ringside seat.

Lake Saddleback is thirty-one acres in size and shaped like a saddle-bag with a narrow cut between two odd-shaped lakes ringed with lily pads and purple-flowered pickerel weed. It had been dredged to provide fill for the homes around it, leaving holes fifteen to twenty feet deep—plenty of water for more than a few gators to lurk about.

The wardens never cranked the small outboard engine attached to their craft. Instead, they paddled out wearing headlamps attached to wires that dangled to 6-volt batteries belted to their waists. The bow man used one paddle to move the boat along real quiet-like. The light played back and forth, and then the beam locked onto a gator right in front of them: the saurian eyes shone like embers of burning coal against the ink-black night.

One warden held a light steady, while the other shouldered a lever-action .30–30 rifle and sighted down the barrel. The lake was calm now, complete silence during that brief period of time—no longer than the pause at half breath—when a rifleman takes up the trigger slack.

Boom!

The skull cap exploded, blasted into the night on a geyser of water, and for a fraction of a second, I could see the white bone glisten from what was left inside the gator's head. Then it sank. A long-handled gaff slapped into the water, and the gator was dragged over the gunwale and into the boat with a meaty thunk. Without a murmur, the men continued across the lake.

By midnight, the wardens had finished their work. Three gators lay lined up neatly next to one another on the dew-soaked grass by the shore. Each one measured between six and eight feet. The wardens wielded sharp knives, blades glinting under battery-powered lights, as they skinned them, every stroke a study in efficiency until three white-fleshed carcasses remained. The hides were rolled up double-handed—like a sleeping bag—secured with a thin line, and then placed into a cooler with ice.

One of the officers walked over to me, a closed hand held out in front of him. He smiled. "Here, son, hold out your hand. I've got something for you."

I opened my palm and in dropped three shiny .30–30 shell casings. "Thanks, thanks a lot," I stammered, momentarily stunned by the gravity of these gifts. I brought the empty hulls up to my nose and inhaled, wafting in the scent of freshly burnt gunpowder. "What a wonderful odor," I thought.

The smell meshed with what had become my favorite pastime back then, making homemade gunpowder, which resulted in patches of our backyard being blown up into plumes of gray-black smoke. My parents kept a tight rein on me growing up, but when it came to explosives, Dad thought it perfectly fine that I should be schooled in the ancient Chinese art. Oh, what fond memories I have of my youth.

The gift of spent cartridge casings, mere pieces of empty machined brass, had no monetary value. But to me, they captured everything about that night, the vivid wonderful memories of the green-and-tan uniformed officers who had confidently gone about the business of killing dangerous reptiles. While I was too young then to think about a career, those images stuck to the inside of my brain like a postage stamp. I would never forget them.

*　　*　　*

Twelve years later—March 1975. I was twenty-one years old and about to graduate from the University of South Florida with a bachelor of arts degree in criminal justice. In three months I would need to decide what career path I should take. I knew it would be in law enforcement and was inclined toward choosing the GFC. They were the only agency that seemed to fit my criteria of the perfect job: catch bad guys and work in the outdoors.

By this time, I had been a hardware store clerk, sporting goods manager, truck driver, coffin builder, pest-control eradicator, carpenter's helper, karate instructor, and drywall finisher. In short, I had an appreciation and respect for blue-collar work. While these jobs were all honorable ways of making a living, I wanted more. But most of all, I desperately wanted to avoid an eight-to-five job, where I imagined myself enslaved in a cookie-cutter, man-made cubicle, trapped behind a desk, and surrounded by four blank walls painted an insipid color designed to boost employee spirits. That would not do. I needed to be free. I wanted to see the sun, the moon, or the stars over my head when I went to work.

Still, I wondered if the statewide agency responsible for the protection of Florida's freshwater fish and wildlife would be a good fit for me. From the outside looking in, it appeared ideal, yet I remained skeptical, thinking there might be hidden problems that could only be ferreted out by being in the know. I needed to pull the curtain back and see how they conducted business behind the scenes.

Good fortune allowed me to do just that by way of an internship with the GFC during my last quarter of college. The twelve-week ride-along program, I reasoned, would be enough time to figure out if this would be a good career choice for me.

I worked with wardens in Hillsborough, Pinellas, Polk, Pasco, and Hernando Counties, in west central Florida. This was semitropical flatland country, sprinkled with cow pastures and cypress heads, phosphate pits and spreading oak hammocks juxtaposed against the huge urban sprawls of Lakeland, Tampa, St. Petersburg, and Clearwater. We patrolled what few sections of rural land there were left, swatted mosquitoes, rode horseback, and worked stakeouts for poachers night-hunting deer.

Great fun. But one experience in particular during my tour with them clinched my decision to hire on.

On a muggy Saturday afternoon, while riding with Warden David Gaines, we checked a dirt boat ramp along a remote section of the Hillsborough River. An old pickup truck was parked there, tailgate down. David found parallel grooves in the mud near the water's edge and explained how the men in the truck had dragged an aluminum johnboat out and launched it at that spot. It looked like it hadn't been long ago, given the still-wet drops of muddy water that had splashed up from their bare feet and onto marsh grass that grew along the shoreline.

"They may be up to something," he said. "If they are, they won't come back in until late tonight. Let's go eat. I need to chat up Susie down at the café anyway. I haven't seen her in a few days."

David was single, with movie-star good looks and an easy grin. Women swooned in his presence. In fact, earlier that day, while driving down Interstate 75 toward Tampa in his patrol car, two blondes in a blue Corvette pulled alongside, one holding a piece of paper up against the passenger window with a phone number scribbled on it in big block writing. "Hey, Bob, if you don't mind, how about jotting down that number for me? I'm kind of busy right now," said David, reveling in the moment as he waved back at the women. Dumbfounded, I dutifully noted the phone number—some guys were blessed.

We left the ramp, ate dinner, and returned an hour later. It was "good dark" (thirty minutes after sunset, or when iron rifle sights cease to be visible) by then, and the truck was still there. David hid the patrol car in a thicket of tangled oak saplings a hundred yards away. After we walked a little ways from the car, he stopped. "Hold up a minute," he said. "Let me check to make sure it's hid good." He shuffled from side to side as he shined his flashlight beam at different angles into the head-high brush in front of where the car was hidden. "I'm checking to see if any part of my car shines through these bushes," he explained. "If the guys we're after see a reflection in their spotlight while they're coming into the ramp, they might spook and throw all the evidence overboard and possibly run. Things always go smoother when you can take them by surprise."

I couldn't see how the chrome or reflectors would have shown much anyway. David had permanently covered everything that could shine with either flat-black paint or electrician's tape. At the time, I thought he was simply being overcautious, but I would later learn that this type of check was routine.

We settled in to wait, hidden behind some wax myrtle bushes that grew near the water's edge. Bullfrogs croaked, treefrogs sang, and the mosquitoes dove at us relentlessly—typical Florida lowlands in the summer. We slapped those mosquitoes brave enough to swim through a thick coating of DEET—the chemical in insect spray responsible for repelling the pesky critters. The stinky gunk was powerful enough to melt the plastic of my watchband, so I figured it must be good. I prayed, though, that it wouldn't affect the chromosomal count of my firstborn.

Pow! . . . Pow! Pow! Pow! Pow!

"Twenty-two caliber," whispered David.

I checked the luminescent dial on my watch. Eleven o'clock. "So what do we do now?" I asked.

"We wait. But for a little extra insurance, I'm going to get the riot shotgun and let you hold it in case things don't turn out well. Rack it one time if trouble starts. That always gets their attention."

I swallowed hard. "Are you sure it's OK for me to hold the shotgun? I'm not a certified law enforcement officer."

"Well, do you think that will make any difference if they shoot me and you're standing there without a gun?" said David, with an intensity I hadn't heard before. "In the last three years alone, we've had two wardens shot and killed by deer poachers,[1] and I don't want to be the next statistic and neither do you."

"Uh . . . good point."

Reality set in now with a huge surge of adrenalin. "This must be what it feels like to mainline heroin," I told myself. "And these guys get paid to do this."

In that one brief moment, the small-bore rifle shots, echoing from around a bend deep downriver in the dead of night, had shoved me into the real world—this wasn't a cop show on television. We didn't have a clue who was in the boat, what they were shooting at, or if they would break bad when they came to shore.

I was totally switched on.

By midnight, the glow of a sharp white light lit up the foliage along one bank a quarter mile downriver. Then it would disappear and suddenly blip back on for a few seconds. "They're sweeping a handheld Q-beam spotlight up and down the riverbank," explained David. "That's why it only lights up one spot for a few moments. In game warden jargon, we call it 'working a light.'"

"What do you think they're after?"

"No telling, maybe gators, possibly shooting at largemouth bass. We won't know for sure until the boat comes to shore."

---

1. On Sunday, November 5, 1972, Sergeant Harry Charles Chapin was shot and killed while attempting to arrest poaching suspects for hunting at night. On May 3, 1974, Warden Danese Byron Crowder was shot and killed in Lafayette County while attempting to apprehend a man for deer poaching. After a brief chase, the man stopped and shot Crowder in the stomach and back with a .243 caliber rifle. The suspect was sentenced to life and was denied parole in 1998.

The vessel noiselessly nudged toward us, only the slap of an errant paddle marring the stillness of the night. Finally, they were right in front of us. I could see five men in the dim back-glow of the spotlight, seated in what I guessed to be a twelve-foot aluminum johnboat with only a few inches of freeboard. My heart was slamming the walls of my chest. I'd had four years of karate at the university and had experienced adrenalin surges before, but this was a purer kind of rush, more visceral. David and I were the hunters, and they were the prey. Yes.

David switched on his flashlight and pointed the beam directly into the eyes of our suspects. "State Wildlife Officer. Shut your spotlight off and put your hands on top of your head."

Their light snapped out. A dutiful cry of "Yes, sir" chorused from their mouths.

"I want everyone to step out of the boat one at a time, starting with the first man nearest the bow. Don't any of you pick up the rifle. Just leave it in the boat."

One at a time each man stepped out onto the grassy bank. When the third man lifted his foot out of the boat, the bow rose up (picture a seesaw after one person jumps off); with no counterbalance, the stern started to sink and the remaining two men began to lower their arms, ready to tread water.

"Keep your hands up," encouraged David. "Up, up, up, up."

These were big, beefy boys who had not missed many breakfasts. Each one would have topped the scales at an easy 250. "Yes, sir, but we're sinking."

"I don't care if you sink. Keep those hands on top of your head." I couldn't see David's face, but I imagined right about now he had a smile from ear to ear, enjoying one of those rare moments in the field that can only be experienced. The bow angled up sharply, and the stern slowly went down, *glug, glug, glug,* until it touched bottom. The men stood with water up to their chests, eyes wide, not knowing exactly what they should do next.

"Well, now that you've sunk your boat," said Gaines, with a chuckle, "go ahead and step out of it and wade up to shore."

Once we had all of the men sorted out and frisked for weapons, I dragged the boat on up to the shoreline, pulled the plug, and retrieved the water-soaked rifle and light.

Our intrepid weekend warriors, by their own admission, were attempting to illegally shoot bass, but had difficulty with the refraction of light, which makes an underwater object appear to be higher in the water than it really is, thus causing the person aiming to overshoot. The only way to compensate for it is to aim under the target. (We didn't tell them that the more expert fish poachers fit a balloon over an extended muzzle and stick it down underwater next to the fish.)

The men were issued notice-to-appear citations in criminal court for attempting to take wildlife with a gun and light at night and sent on their way. We kept the rifle and spotlight for evidence.

"So what do you think?" asked Gaines, as we watched the taillights of the pickup truck disappear around a turn in the road and behind a copse of trees.

"I'm filling out my application tomorrow."

*   *   *

November 1977, northeast Florida. I stood on a narrow wooden dock by the Shell Harbor Boat Ramp on the St. Johns River, windbreaker zipped up to guard against a chilly northeast breeze. I was dressed in civilian clothes, nervously waiting to meet Bob Raulerson, my field training officer. I could finally call myself a State Wildlife Officer, although I wouldn't graduate from the state law enforcement academy until December of that year.

I'd been assigned to a newly formed river crew of six men whose primary objective was to quell the illegal commercial fishing that had become rampant on the river. Our area of patrol stretched for more than one hundred miles from Green Cove Springs in the north to Sanford in the south, with very little overlap in patrol zones.

I was there on weekend break to look for a place my wife and I could rent in south Putnam County. My supervisor suggested I take an hour out to meet with Raulerson, who happened to be on river patrol that day. I was every bit the rookie and didn't know what to expect.

I heard the boat before I saw it. The high-pitched whine of a big outboard wrung out for all it was worth heading south, upriver, and then the tone became throatier as it whipped around a bend a mile to the north. A rooster tail shot twenty feet into the air behind an olive-green, low-profile hull with a red dot centered above the boat's outline. Sixty seconds later, my field training officer smartly pulled the throttle back and idled up to the dock.

"So what do you think of my red stocking cap?" said Raulerson, pointing to the top of his head with a crooked grin.

"Well . . . looks good to me." I needed to make a good impression. I wasn't about to tell him his candy apple–red hat, all scrunched up at an odd angle, looked goofy as hell. No way. Not to mention that wearing it was a uniform violation.

"You're probably wondering about the stocking cap. Listen, we do whatever it takes to stay warm out here. The brass stays away from the river when it's cold. Trust me when I tell you that they only come out to work with us during the summer months, and even then it's darn seldom. How about a boat ride?"

"Sure."

"You might as well get used to this boat; it will be assigned to you in six weeks."

"Why is that?"

"I'll be taking a sergeant's position down on Lake Okeechobee when your training cycle is finished." He handed me an olive-green life vest. "Make sure you zip that up tight."

I stepped into the boat and sat down in a bucket seat mounted low to the deck, opposite from Raulerson's station behind the starboard side console. All I had to do to touch the river was drop my left hand over the side and it was right there, twelve inches down. Not an altogether safe feeling.

Raulerson twisted around in his seat to face me: "Now let me tell you a little about this boat. The fiberglass hull is eighteen feet long and made by a company called Old Timer located near Orlando. It's used mostly as a commercial fishing vessel on the St. Johns River and Lake Okeechobee. Everyone on the river refers to this style of boat as a 'skipjack.' Yankees think we're talking about the skipjacks used on the Chesapeake Bay in Maryland for oyster fishing. We're not. This hull configuration is different. The high-angled bow can ride through a heavy lake chop without nose-diving, and the low gunnels from midship to stern make it easy for giant fish traps, called hoop nets, to be rolled into the boat. Of course, we don't commercial fish, but we do check a lot of nets and traps to make sure they're in compliance with design specifications, so this style of hull works out well for us too."

Raulerson cranked the engine and nudged the throttle forward, letting the boat idle away from the dock. He continued his lecture: "You'll see where the engine cowling says 200 horsepower Johnson. It's not. Now don't tell any of our supervisors this, but I had some special work done to it by a friend of mine who runs an outboard repair shop and also races boats. He removed the 200 powerhead and replaced it with a 235 and took off the flame arrester to give it more air. I've got a twenty-eight-inch chopper prop pushing the hull with the engine jacked up as high as it will go. This setup makes it a bit slow coming up on plane, but the payoff comes later when it's opened up. You ready?"

"Let's go." I looked around for something to hold onto. There was nothing, no handrails, no way to brace myself other than to grab hold of the rounded gunwale with my left hand and hope for the best.

He shoved the throttle forward. The boat eased ahead a few feet before it hesitated, propeller whining as it thirstily sucked in enough water to gain a solid purchase. Then we catapulted forward and I felt my cheeks pull back, flapping like a sheet on a windy day. I remembered the old film clips of astronauts being tested to see how many G-forces they could withstand in a centrifuge, where their facial muscles took on grotesque distortions as they were spun round and round, and wondered if I resembled one of them about now.

Raulerson leaned in toward me and hollered over the engine roar, "You see how the hull is up, floating on a cushion of air." He took one hand off of the steering wheel and flattened it, palm down, to mimic how the hull was behaving, drifting a few inches from one side to the other with only a few feet of the stern down in the water.

"Yes," I shouted back, with spittle flying out the side of my mouth.

"We call this 'walking the dog.' It means we're at top-end speed, about seventy. Now listen carefully: Never attempt a sharp turn when it's in this attitude and never yank the throttle back suddenly at this speed. You'll regret it."

Mesmerized as I was by the scary sensation that the hull might become airborne at any moment, the thought of making a turn or suddenly slowing down would have been the furthest thing from my mind had I been driving. I only wanted to survive.

"I have a low windshield on this boat," continued Raulerson, "which means I catch the full wind blast in my eyes. The trick to driving this way is you got to angle your face into the wind and let the tears blow back across both eyes—keeps them from drying out." He settled back into his seat and gave me that cockeyed grin again.

I wondered if he was all there.

Secretly, though, when I left my field training officer that day, I was practically giddy to know I would be assigned—according to Raulerson—the fastest patrol boat in the agency at that time. And I would later find out that I would need every ounce of speed the boat could deliver. A difference of only one to two miles per hour can define the winner in a boat chase.

But before I could engage in the sport of a high-speed boat pursuit, I would first have to learn the most important rule of good boatmanship—how to keep my patrol craft afloat.

3

Midnight Ride on
a Six-Gallon Gas Can

Before I became a game warden I'd never been on the St. Johns River, or in a high-speed, 200-horsepower skipjack patrol boat, or in a body of freshwater much larger than the tiny lake I'd grown up on near Tampa. The extent of my waterborne experiences was limited to captaining a ten-foot aluminum johnboat with a tiller-steered, four-horsepower Evinrude outboard. I'd been a good swimmer, though, successfully completing the Senior Lifesaving Course at the age of sixteen. Work as a lifeguard never did come my way, but skills learned from that course would not go to waste in my new position as a full-time water patrol officer.

So it was on July 1, 1978, at about good dark, that I began a silent—lights out—drift below Rodman Dam on the Ocklawaha River. The sluggish current carried my eighteen-foot Old Timer patrol boat downstream toward its confluence with the St. Johns River at the leisurely pace of one mile per hour. I would never make it to the St. Johns in one night—a distance of about ten miles—but I could easily complete half that distance by the end of my shift at three the next morning.

The excitement in this form of patrol was in not knowing what lay around the next bend. I could meet head to head with a boatload of electric fishermen, an illegal fish trapper, or a grizzled old gator hunter at any moment. Any of these options offered an unprecedented opportunity for some good sport.

Why else would a young man wearing a badge and a gun be out here alone, in a remote river swamp, without backup, in a radio-traffic dead zone with no way to communicate with anyone? The situation suited me perfectly. All I ever wanted out of this job was to experience a little outdoor adventure.

I manned the boat from atop a wedge-shaped raised platform in the bow, armed with an eight-foot oar to steer around and push away from deadhead logs and fallen trees. These gnarly obstructions would appear out of the gloom as darker silhouettes, barely visible against a backdrop of filtered starlight that slipped between the overhanging tree canopies.

By midnight I'd completed a three-hour drift, and to my great disappointment no one seemed to be out. I hadn't heard any outboard motors or seen any suspicious spotlights shining around the next curve. Indeed, it had been a pleasant, though uneventful, night with only the bellow of an occasional bullfrog to keep me company—until I heard a faint trickle of water.

I froze, straining to detect the origin of this seemingly benign sound. Then I slowly turned, until I faced the transom of my boat. The noise came from the bilge. As I stared into the night, my stomach tightened at the realization that something was very wrong. None of the storage compartments were visible, which on any other night would appear as faint shapes in the starlight. Tonight, the interior of my boat was a solid ink-black.

I stepped down off the forward deck and splashed into water. By the time I made it to the stern, the water was knee-deep and rising fast. Two more inches and it would reach the transom cap, where the surface of the river would equalize with the water inside the hull. That brief distance—just a shallow gap between thumb and forefinger—represented all of the time I had left until my boat sank.

My headlamp and flashlight were both underwater, and there was no time to look for them. Instead, I had to quickly figure out why my boat was taking on water. There were really only two choices: either the drain plug had popped out, or there was a crack in the hull. My bet was on the drain plug.

I settled down into the water and immersed myself until I was on my hands and knees near the stern. With my head tipped to the side for air, I stretched out my fingers, blindly probing the back corner of the bilge until I found the drain plug hole. With a gentle push, I slid one finger all the way through the smooth brass opening.

The plug was gone.

I jammed a second finger into the hole to staunch the incoming flow of water. With my free hand, I frantically felt for the spare drain plug I always kept in the bottom of the bilge. That hasty search produced greasy sticks, leaves, and acorns—typical bilge litter—but no drain plug. And now the water level inside the hull was one inch from the transom cap and creeping higher.

I kept the fingers of my right hand jammed in the drain hole, and stretched out with my left hand to the control panel and flipped on the bilge pump switch. The pump started up with a satisfying hum, spewing water back into the river.

At that moment I was flooded with relief and felt much better about my prospects for getting out of the mini-drama I had suddenly found myself caught up in. With my fingers pretty well corking the drain hole, I knew the water being pumped out would greatly exceed what little water seeped back in.

By now, however, the stern had settled dangerously low into the river. Any tipping or rocking of the hull would put the transom under, causing it to sink. "I just need to remain still," I told myself, "and let the bilge pump do its work."

The pump's flow rate was 750 gallons per hour. That's a lot of water, and I was confident within thirty to forty-five minutes my problems would be over. Once enough water was pumped out, I'd have time to look for the spare drain plug. And if I couldn't find it, I could always fashion a temporary plug out of an old towel I kept in one of the forward compartments. It was just a matter of time.

A few seconds passed before my newfound confidence was suddenly shattered. The bilge pump's steady hum had turned to a roar as it started bouncing all around the bilge.

The hose had come off.

The pump was now recirculating water inside the boat, which left me in a real dilemma. If I pulled my hand out of the drain plug hole—even for a few seconds—the incoming rush of water would put the boat under. There was simply no time to reattach the hose to the pump. It takes two hands, and I needed three.

By now, the water level inside the boat was nearly to the top of the transom. My time had run out.

I yanked my fingers out of the drain plug hole and scrambled into the driver's seat, turned the ignition key, and shoved the throttle forward. I hoped to generate enough forward momentum to force the hull up onto a nearby bank. The 200 Johnson turned over and stayed alive for five brief seconds before stalling out with a sputter. My last-ditch effort to prevent a sinking had only made matters worse. Those few turns of the propeller blades had perfectly positioned my boat over a thirty-foot-deep hole.

The transom sank below the river's surface with the bow up, pointed into the night sky at an angle that became steeper with every passing second. I crawled across the storage compartments and up to the bow, where I reached up as high as I could, fumbling in the dark, while I tied the bow line off to a tree limb along with my briefcase. "There," I thought, "no matter what happens now I'll be able to find my boat. But more important, I'll have saved the paperwork."

Even though I'd only been on the job for nine months, I was already thinking like a senior civil servant. At the age of twenty-four, I wasn't concerned about my own safety so much as I was about what my sergeant would think if the paperwork was destroyed.

As the bow inched higher, I was forced to lean into the deck at an increasingly steep angle to keep from falling out. Then, like a seesaw that had come to a perfect balance, the boat steadied.

I used those precious few moments to figure out what to do next. My options were limited: stay with the boat, strike out through the swamp on foot without a light, or swim out. My assessment was sharply interrupted by the sound of a deflating balloon erupting out of the dark. Air rushing out from underneath the motor's cowling had just sounded my vessel's death knell. The air pocket inside the cowling had been the only thing keeping my boat from going under.

I dropped my head and sighed, thinking, "This really sucks." It was a private moment of catharsis, one that I believed aptly summed up my present situation.

It was time to go.

I zipped up my life vest, grabbed a spare six-gallon gas tank, and jumped into the water just as my boat tilted vertical and slid straight down toward the bottom of the Ocklawaha River.

I held onto the gas tank with my right hand while treading water with my left. As my boat was drawn deeper into the water, a familiar sound was left in its place. It was reminiscent of a child sucking through a straw to get that last bit of milkshake from the bottom of a cup. You knew that when the sucking stopped, it would all be gone— and now, so was my boat!

Survival experts say when people are thrown into an unknown situation they search back through their memories, grasping for past experiences that they can apply to the current problem. And while I didn't realize it at the time, that was exactly what I did.

But I only had to go back two days, to a conversation I had had with a senior officer. During a night chase on Lake Okeechobee, his patrol boat had flipped while he was eight miles from shore. A six-gallon gas tank had been tossed out of the boat along with him. He'd found the tank to be remarkably buoyant and a great aid in swimming back to land. He insisted that if my boat ever sank, I should make sure to grab one. I never for one minute believed I would have the opportunity to test his advice, but here I was, bobbing along like a big green sea turtle.

I shoved the gas tank up under my chest for added buoyancy. The combined benefits of life vest and tank together pushed my head and shoulders out of the water. Those few inches of added height made a lot of difference in comfort and in being able to detect any dangerous situations that might lie ahead. Poisonous snakes and alligators I couldn't see, but at least I could avoid bumping into the overhanging limbs of wax myrtle bushes, where vicious hornets built their nests.

I used a shortened breaststroke to guide me around numerous trees that had fallen into the creek. As I brushed past their long, leafy branches, it occurred to me they were very likely the cause of my predicament. Earlier, while I'd been floating along in my boat, a stray branch must have brushed up against the stern, snagged the drain plug's lever, and pulled it out.

As the current carried me downstream, I started to think about where I was and who I'd been trying to catch.

*   *   *

The Ocklawaha River, colloquially known as the Creek, meanders through a vast hardwood swamp carpeted with poison ivy, teeming with water moccasins, and thick with alligators. This is a swamp wilderness, where some of the largest gators in the Northern Hemisphere reside. The real brutes measure thirteen-plus feet and weigh in at more than eight hundred pounds. This was the section of river in which I found myself. At five feet ten inches tall and weighing in at 173 pounds, I would have been a mere appetizer had any of these beasts wanted a nighttime snack.

The Creek runs for seventy-four miles along the northern and western boundary of the Ocala National Forest in northeast Florida before emptying into the St. Johns River near the fishing town of Welaka, in Putnam County. Paralleling the main run is a maze of side creeks that wind back and forth through the swamp and occasionally tie back into the Ocklawaha. Many of them are just wide enough for a small boat to maneuver through. They are secretive stretches of water, their seclusion all the more attractive to the locals, who found them inviting places to get into mischief.

During the summer of 1978, the summer I was summarily immersed into the tepid waters of the Ocklawaha, fish poaching had been rampant. The target of this illegal activity was catfish. Thousands upon thousands of channel and white cats swarmed through the Ocklawaha River on their annual spawning run during the late spring and early summer. They are the tastiest of these bewhiskered fish and preferred table fare by restaurants because of their firm white meat, unlike the butter cat and speckled cat, which have a deep red meat of lesser quality.

The outlaw commercial fishermen who pursued these catfish were professional poachers whose favorite method for procuring them was by electric shocking, better known as "monkey-fishing" in these parts. In just four hours of fishing, teams typically made up of two men to the boat could scoop up six hundred pounds of catfish using long-handled dip nets. Boat chases were a common occurrence between the game wardens and the monkey-fishermen, who often drove sinister-looking, flat-bottomed wooden boats painted flat black and powered by excessively large outboard engines.

By the time I started working in Putnam County, strategies for catching monkey-fishermen had long been established by those who came before me. And one of the most popular and successful ways of catching them was to work one of the tributaries that flowed into the St. Johns River. Here, the likelihood of getting close to them was greater than in open water. This was critically important because they usually threw the evidence overboard before they ran. If the game warden wasn't close enough to throw a marker buoy on top of the splash made by the illegal equipment, then he was out of luck. No evidence retrieved meant no court case.

The Ocklawaha River was often clear, which made recovery of any tossed evidence an easier job. Patrolling through its primordial swamps had quickly become a favorite of mine, as I'd already been successful in catching a few of these electric fish poachers unawares.

One of the tactics used when working a creek was to start far up-stream, shut the engine off, and drift downstream with the current while listening for running outboard motors. If an engine was heard, the warden would crank his motor and try to slip up as close as he could before turning on his blue lights and attempting to make a vessel stop. This was the tactic I had chosen on the night my boat sank.

One Hour Later

The running splash of the big gator got my attention. I couldn't see him in the dark but felt his wake as I was left rocking in his backwash, clinging tightly to my metal gas can with renewed vigor. He had launched off a bank somewhere in front of me, apparently spooked when I drifted around a bend.

There were hundreds of gators in this creek. But this was the first one of any size that had bolted right in front of me.

All of my senses were popping now. I tried not to imagine what would happen if he got hold of me, but a subconscious image kept bursting through. It was like a B-grade movie trailer on constant rewind that I couldn't stop no matter how hard I tried: The gator dove deep, then circled around and came up behind me, pushing forward with great speed as his jaws opened and then closed, locking down on my thigh. Instantly, he went into a death roll, spinning and spinning and spinning until my leg was ripped from its socket, leaving a stream of blood and flesh and pulp behind as he swam back to his lair.

My resolve began to weaken. I could have swum over to the bank, crawled up on the muddy shore and waited until daylight for the first fisherman to come by and pick me up. But I was hardheaded, young, and apparently not very bright. So I stayed the course and continued with my plan for self-rescue. Looking back thirty-plus years after this event, I can't help but wonder, "What was I thinking?"

There was another factor, though, that made my choice to drift down the creek attractive. I knew I wouldn't have to spend all night in these waters. Luckily, my boat had sunk a mile and a half upstream from the only two hard-soil landings on this stretch of the Ocklawaha.

The next few minutes passed with an occasional readjustment of my gas can so it wouldn't slip out from underneath me. Off to my right, I scanned a ragged line of dark tree canopies framed against a slate-gray horizon—searching for any change in elevation. As I was swept into the next turn, the silhouette abruptly shot up. Ahead was Reidy's Bluff,[1] a thirty-foot wall of sugar sand, saw palmetto, and scrub oaks at the northernmost border of the Ocala National Forest. I looked up at the campsite, searching for any signs of habitation. But it was silent and dark.

---

1. Known today as Davenport Landing, a primitive campsite operated by the U.S. Forest Service.

Farther downstream, though, I could hear the blare of country music and raucous laughter coming from Davenport Landing.[2] Davenport was an easier run by water than a circuitous hike through the pinewoods so I continued to let the current carry me downstream. If I hadn't been devoured by now, I reasoned, what were the chances of that happening in the last quarter mile?

Fifteen minutes later I floated up to a narrow strip of shoreline that emitted a pearl-like glow in the ambient starlight. It was a white-sand beach—the landing site for Davenport Landing. From here, the ground sloped up to a campfire, where I heard the voices of several men talking.

I stepped out of the water and parked my gas can on the shoreline. I climbed a narrow footpath up to the campsite. The trail broke out into a flat, sandy clearing where four men squatted on sawed-off logs, their faces half-lit, half-dark behind the flickering flames of a robust fire. One of them kicked at a log, igniting a shower of sparks. I stood still for a minute to study them. They were thoroughly drunk and enjoying the moment, believing they were alone in this remote wilderness comprising 388,480 acres of government land.

I stepped into the circle of firelight. River water ran off my uniform in small rivulets, collecting into puddles around my leather boots. I hadn't shucked anything when I went into the water. I was still wearing my gun belt, along with a Smith & Wesson .357 Magnum revolver holstered to my side.

Alcohol has a tendency to create tunnel vision, and the men still didn't notice me standing right in front of them. They were plastered.

Finally, I said, "State Wildlife Officer. How are you all doing?"

They swung their faces toward me with that "deer in the headlight" expression, momentarily startled. After a long pause, one of them carefully asked, "Who . . . are . . . you?"

"I am a State Wildlife Officer."

Then another said, "So you're what, a game warden?"

---

2. The Davenport Landing referred to in this story is now known as the Davenport Landing Historic Site. Back in 1978, it was open for primitive camping. Today, it can only be accessed by footpath or boat.

"Yes, my boat sank, and I drifted down the creek to get here."

"Hey," he barked out in a cotton-mouthed drawl, "You know what?"

"No, what?"

"Shit happens," he chuckled, and they all raised a beer.

I nodded my head, "Well, guys, I can't argue with that."

4

Patience

There were three rapid knocks on my front door. It was ten o'clock, on a clear night in late January, and whoever was waiting outside of my home had stopped by unannounced. That was not entirely unexpected in my line of work. But still, I was a little wary as I swung the door open to face a man whom I'd never met before. One hand was behind my back, grasping a .357 magnum revolver.

He stood in the glow of the porch light, wearing muddy rubber boots, blue jeans, and a tattered camouflage hunting jacket. He had the manner of a man who was comfortable in the woods. The orange plastic dog collars clipped to his waist belt, along with a 6-volt battery and headlamp, told me the kind of hunter he was.

"I've had it," he said.

"What are you upset about?"

"These assholes running steel traps—one of my coon hounds got his paw mangled in a trap last week over near Georgetown, and it cost me $250 in vet bills. Earlier tonight, I found another trap-line in the river swamp a couple hundred yards south of the Ft. Gates Ferry. You," he said, pointing a long, lonely finger at me, "need to do something about it."

"I can handle it. Let me get a pencil and paper, and you can draw me a map of where the traps are located."

I was excited. I finally had an informant. It felt like an important milestone had been reached in my brief career as a game warden. For the eighteen months I'd worked in Putnam County, the "locals" had stonewalled me. They'd proven to be a close-mouthed lot who resented game wardens for infringing on their way of life. They regarded us with the same disdain as a lowly palmetto bug (a giant cockroach, to those from the North).

The coon hunter had a steady hand. He drew Ft. Gates Ferry Rd. with two parallel lines, and sketched in the river to frame up the general area for me to look. Next, he added a dotted line to represent a woods trail that I should follow to find the traps. This trail meandered to the south, away from Ferry Rd.

He handed the notepad back to me.

"The man running these traps is named Bert," he said. "Sometimes his dad checks them when he has to work. They'll park at a new home construction site a quarter mile from the trap-line. Bert's father-in-law happens to be the builder." He touched the map with his finger to show me the location. "I don't know what time he checks them. But most people run them in the early morning or late evening."

"And that," I thought, "is the problem with working a stakeout on steel traps." Fur trappers could run their traps at any time throughout the day, not just in the morning or evening. The ensuing wait can be long, tedious, and, at times, quite grueling.

* * *

The use of steel-jawed leg-hold traps, or simply "steel traps," is a prickly and contentious subject. By some accounts, it is an archaic and brutal practice that should be better left as a historic footnote in modern society, much like the medieval dungeons and torture chambers of Europe.

The most strident opposition comes from the Humane Society and other animal-rights groups, who argue that these traps are unbelievably cruel. Photographs on their websites show defenseless animals in varying states of distress, or even dead, after being caught in the jaws of a leg-hold trap.

In 1974, Florida became the first state to outlaw steel (leg-hold) traps. Welded fence staples (*trap in foreground*) make for an unusually cruel device.

Here in Florida I have witnessed similar scenes, where raccoons caught by one leg have eaten at it for days until they finally succumbed to shock and died. These gruesome discoveries were not a pretty sight.

I've always been an advocate for hunting and trapping, but I also believe that animals deserve a clean death free from undue misery and suffering. So while my personal ideology may be conflicted, the law in Florida is not.

To be fair, though, the use of steel traps is an important part of our American heritage. After all, it was the fur trappers who first explored the untamed wilderness in the nether regions of what is now the United States.

The majority of states, along with Canada, still allow the use of steel traps, which fosters traditional-style trapping as it was first done in North America 350 years ago. It also provides an important part-time livelihood for more than one hundred thousand fur trappers in North America.

In 1974, Florida was the first state to ban the use of steel traps by regulation of what was then the Game and Fresh Water Fish Commission. Several more states have since followed suit.

The only legal way to trap furbearers—otter, bobcat, opossum, beaver, and raccoon—in Florida is by the use of live traps shaped like a rectangular box and made of wire mesh, or by the use of snares.

Florida has never been associated with a lot of trapping because of its warm climate, which makes for a poor-quality pelt compared to northern areas of the country. Interestingly, the correlation between climate and fur quality has been shown within Florida, too. In the early 1960s, otter hides from south Florida fetched $5.50 a pelt, while those from northern counties brought $13.00.

When I first started working Putnam County, in December 1977, there were about fifty part-time fur trappers and a couple of wholesale hide buyers. Over the next five years, the market would collapse. The only trapping left would be mainly for raccoons, and then more for their meat than the hides.

*　　*　　*

Around noon on the following day, I slipped into the river swamp south of Ft. Gates Ferry to scout it out. I stepped from tree roots to limbs to stumps so none of my tracks were left behind in the mud. Occasionally I'd turn around to check my backtrail, to make certain I hadn't made a mistake and left even a scuff mark behind. That seemingly insignificant piece of sign would be enough to tip off a keen-eyed trapper that someone had passed through his area. And like a deer winding a hunter, he'd spook and never come back.

I patiently worked my way toward the river until I came to a small game trail. It wove a hand-wide muddy path through the cypress balls and needles and the leaf litter of red maple and sweet gum trees.

I stayed to one side while I cycled my gaze from the ground, to the far distance, and back to the ground again. After I'd traveled fifty yards, something ahead looked out of place. The angles were wrong. Dead branches leaned against the trunk of a tree to form a makeshift tunnel underneath. As I inched closer, I could see the outline of a steel trap with its jaws spread wide open, lying flat on the ground in the shadows beneath the branches. A few leaves had been sprinkled onto the pan, or triggering mechanism, of the trap. The rust-colored metal melded naturally to the background of brown leaves and moist mud. Several feet of chain connected the trap to a drag stick that would prevent an animal from running off.

The stacked branches were intended to funnel the animal into the trap—along with an open can of fresh sardines strategically placed nearby. That tasty treat would lure the next raccoon ambling by onto the trap, his lucky find ending with a metallic *whap!*

I continued along the path and found another trap, followed by yet another. They were spaced about thirty yards apart and ran for about an eighth of a mile. All of the sets were designed in a similar fashion, making it relatively easy to find the rest.

And this was usually the case, whether it was illegal steel traps, fish traps, or marijuana grow sites. Human nature thrives on consistency, making the job of a game warden a bit easier if that one trait is kept in mind. It is also a weakness many poachers have. The hardest part has always been finding the first one.

Before I left, I'd need to build a blind near one of the traps so I could watch the trapper undetected. Looking out toward the river, I saw a palmetto-covered tussock. It was a shallow mound of humus that rose up from the swamp floor, about thirty yards from the nearest trap.

"Perfect," I told myself.

I walked into the middle of the plants and got busy, cutting out an open area with my pocketknife. Next I scraped up all of the dead palmetto thatch and limbs and leaves and shoved them off to one side. My hiding place was now soundproof. No matter how I moved, there would be no crackling of tiny limbs or the crunch of dried leaves to give me away.

I walked back to the closest trap, turned around, and checked for any gaps in the blind that would allow someone from that position to spot me. There were a couple of small breaks that still bothered me. I went back and plugged the holes with some of the palmetto fans I had trimmed earlier. I left the swamp the same way I'd come in.

The next morning was dark, still, and cold when I settled into my hide about a half hour before sunrise. It was just above freezing, and the high humidity gave the cold a harsh bite. I was layered in heavy winter clothing that included a pair of hip waders. The water level in the swamp could fluctuate by a couple of feet depending on whether or not a northeast wind was blowing, and the waders offered good insurance in case of a sudden weather change. A plastic raincoat spread out on the ground provided a barrier against the damp soil.

Before settling into my blind, I'd thrown the nearest trap and then raked all around it with a stick to make it look like an animal had escaped. This was a simple ruse designed to get the trapper to put his hands on the trap and reset it by spreading the jaws back open. I needed to witness this act before I could charge him with illegal use of the device.

Delicate shafts of first light broke cleanly through the trees. With the first glow of morning came the drone of big outboards. Bass boats, fast and sleek, streaked south toward Lake George—a 46,000-acre bulge in the St. Johns River. This was the largemouth bass bedding season, prime time to wrestle a wall hanger from the thick carpets of eel grass that hugged the big lake's shoreline.

First light was also the best time for someone to come and work the traps, especially if they had a day job. I scanned the swamp to the southeast, in the direction of the new homesite. I focused far instead of near. This is how the first glimpse of a person can be detected, an elbow or a knee, the roundness of a shoulder, or a patch of clothing with just a touch of shine from sun reflection. It was all about the lines and angles and color contrasts that didn't fit against the natural background. That's what I was looking for as I cast my eyes back and forth between the trees.

By nine o'clock, I relaxed and broke out a four-hundred-page novel, a police procedural. I didn't know how long I could stand to read about another lawman in the throes of constant excitement when I had none, but at least it gave me a way to pass the time.

By eleven, I was counting squirrels. In midwinter they come off the high ground and into the swamp. The acorn mast had rotted away, and they were now intent on devouring the red maple buds that had begun to bloom. When noontime arrived, I reached into my backpack and pulled out a ham-and-cheese sandwich, potato chips, and a bottle of water. This seemingly insignificant event would most likely be the highlight of my day.

I stretched lunch out as long as I could, then looked up through barren tree canopies to patches of a clear blue sky and checked the sun's position. I willed it to move faster. Ever so slowly and ever so gradually, it followed a steady arc toward the western horizon, first 1:00 p.m., then 3:00, and finally 5:00. It was time to pay closer attention. But the clock continued to tick long into the fading light, until it was almost dark. I made up my mind to give it five more minutes and then leave.

Snap.

I heard the limb break before I saw him. It was really too dark to make him out until he was at the sprung trap. He silhouetted as a big man in the gloom of twilight. I suspected he was the father of Bert, the twenty-two-year-old man who was supposed to be running these traps.

He walked right by the trap, turned around, and headed back in the direction he'd come from. He couldn't see well enough to tell that the trap was shut. "Twelve hours for naught," I thought. "Oh, well."

I eased out of my blind and left the swamp the same way I'd come in.

Day two started much like the preceding one. It was clear, though, by nine thirty, the wind had started to pick up, blowing the Spanish moss in long, gray wisps like an old man's beard. The sun crept across the sky in an agonizingly slow arc until it finally hovered as a giant orange ball above the horizon. It was five o'clock.

I took off my winter jacket just in case there was an unexpected turn of events. Bert was in a lot better shape than his dad.

The sun had settled well behind the trees, and the gloom of twilight begun, when Bert walked down the trail. He was lean, no body fat, and a little under six feet. He wore a checkered, long-sleeved flannel shirt, blue jeans, and knee-high rubber boots. He carried a hand axe for bopping coons in the head. He leaned the axe against a cypress tree, then knelt down next to the thrown trap and began to squeeze the springs with both hands to open the jaws.

I stood up. All of Bert's attention was focused on the trap, as it should have been. One slip and he could end up with a crushed pinky.

"State Wildlife Officer," I said, in a firm voice. "Don't move."

He looked up at me for just a second. That's when I saw the blank expression on his face that had become all too familiar.

"Don't do it!" I shouted.

He spun around and began running pell-mell through the swamp. Clods of mud flew from his boots as he dodged cypress knees, hooking right, then left, and right again, as he deftly avoided the knee-high shin busters. I started after him but was having a hard time of it, even though I was a hard-core runner back then.

My muscles had grown stiff, lying on the cool, damp earth for twelve hours. My choice in footwear also made for an awkward, stumbling gait. Running in hip waders was a bitch.

He fell, then I fell, as we tripped over fallen logs and dead branches scattered all across the swamp floor. We dodged shallow pools of water with soft mud bottoms that we would have sunk waist-deep in had we stepped there. In between tripping and falling, I kept an eye on a large blown-down tree that was blocking my suspect's path.

With no break in stride, he barreled straight for it and jumped. He placed both hands on the topside of the tree's trunk, while he whipped his hips and legs up and over in a clean vault to the other side. I took the less challenging route, diving headfirst under it, and slid out the other side in a shower of mud. I scrambled to my feet and pushed on, slipping and sliding my way ahead.

Trying to catch Bert now had become a fleeting dream. He was running on pure adrenalin that was fueling a blistering pace. The best I could hope to do was to keep him in sight.

The terrain was changing fast as we ran out of the swamp and up a shallow slope into a thicket of twisted oak and crooked wood. He plowed into it, pulling apart the brush with first one hand and then the other as he carved a path through the formidable undergrowth.

I was twenty yards behind him when I hit the thicket, chafing my hands and arms and face as I furiously peeled back the stiff wood to force a trail. Then we broke out into an open grassy area, where the new home was under construction. Bert was running straight toward the foundation's wooden form, head erect, arms pumping like an Olympic sprinter.

And that's when everything seemed to slow down for me. Perhaps it was a premonition that fate was about to deal me a lucky hand. Suddenly, I had become aware of everyone and everything around me, like in a slow-motion film.

A cement truck was up ahead to my left. The driver was holding a green garden hose in one hand as he washed out the dump chute. Construction workers were at the far end of the form, busy with their trowels as they put the finishing touches to a freshly poured slab of concrete. Off to my right was the foreman—my suspect's father-in-law—frantically waving his hands, as his mouth opened and closed, shouting spirited warnings for his son-in-law to stay away from the home's delicate foundation.

It was at that moment that I realized the answer to a question that had been niggling at me during the whole foot chase. Why was Bert running?

After all, this wasn't the crime of the century. The answer, I believed, was because he didn't think I knew who he was. And now he was just three steps from the form. Before he could adjust his course to tack around it, I sucked in a lung full of air and bellowed out, "Bert, halt!"

Bert snapped his head around, eyes wide in surprise. Two steps, then one more, and his right toe hooked the wooden form. He tripped, falling into the cement soup with flailing arms and skidding feet as he desperately windmilled, trying to find reverse.

But it was too late.

He carved an impressive, torpedo-like groove in the wet cement before sliding to a stop. He stood up and shook himself off like a dog that had rolled in the mud. Then he walked up to me with his hands outstretched. He'd had enough.

"Turn around," I said.

I cuffed Bert and walked him over to the guy with the water hose, who sprayed him off as best he could.

I grabbed Bert under one arm and marched him off to my patrol truck hidden in the Welaka State Forest, a half mile away.

Sometimes it's better to be lucky than good.

5

Running over Vernon Bennett

Dreams of my favorite Lazy Boy recliner came in fitful spurts. Every time I shifted, my eyelids would flutter open and bring me back to the stark reality that I was curled up in the cramped bottom of a dew-soaked patrol boat. Of the many nights I'd spent on water patrol, I'd yet to discover a position conducive to real rest.

The interior of my eighteen-foot Old Timer was utilitarian to a fault. No factory built-in cushions or chairs, only hard fiberglass with stiff, sharp angles. And I wouldn't expect anything more out of a commercial fishing vessel originally designed to work catfish traps.

Still, some degree of comfort would have been nice given the long hours I spent on waterborne stakeouts. A bedding of life vests provided some relief, though, as I lay against the side of my boat, arms crossed, lolling in and out of the fog of sleep. Two more hours and I'd be heading home.

It was three in the morning on a Wednesday in September, and I'd yet to hear or see another vessel as I drifted with my lights out in the southern end of Crescent Lake. It looked like this shift would turn out to be a dud.

What I didn't know was that another set of eyes watched the lake too. He didn't want to be seen by anyone. The good ones never did.

*   *   *

Crescent Lake is shaped roughly like a banana drawn in crayon by a four-year-old, with a few bumps here and there. It is wedged into the southeastern corner of Putnam County and ranges north and south for thirteen miles, with an odd turn to the east at its south, or bottom, end. Here, the tea-stained waters of Haw Creek flow into the 15,960-acre lake, draining much of the lowland marsh and palmetto flatwoods of Flagler County. The north end purges into Dunns Creek, which snakes northwest for five miles through a hardwood floodplain before it empties into the St. Johns River.

The "narrows," as the locals like to call them, lay out from the mouth of Haw Creek. Thirty feet deep in the center, with lily pads along the edges, this area teemed with catfish during the summer months in the late 1970s and early 1980s. Monkey-fishermen would visit this spot once or twice a week during the wee hours of the morning. And any area favored by these electric poachers quickly became a favorite of mine.

There were also other commercial fishermen who fished the area with hoop nets, wire fish traps, and trotlines. But for the most part, they stuck to catching catfish, which were legal to harvest with these devices.

On this night, my thoughts were centered on catching a monkey-fisherman. I'd arrived at the southern end of Crescent Lake a few minutes after midnight. I shut my patrol boat down in open water—two miles out from the narrows—so I could watch them undetected.

*   *   *

The raspy squawk of a great blue heron perked me up. Wading birds are normally reclusive at night unless something spooks them. I scooted up higher against the side of my boat to better focus on whatever had alarmed the bird.

Then another sound, a faint drone, casually slipped across the lake's still waters from the south. Curious, I pushed aside a plastic raincoat that had been protecting me from the morning dampness and stood up. Cupping both hands to my ears, I turned my head slowly from side to side, straining to get a better read on what I'd heard. At first, I thought it might be a water pump kicking on at one of the homes dotting the lake's southern shoreline. But the more I listened, the more I became convinced it didn't fit any of the noises associated with a dwelling in the early morning.

I studied the shore, letting my eyes trace the uneven shapes of the dark tree line against a gray-black, star-speckled sky. Then I lowered my gaze to where I guessed the shoreline edge should be. I scanned back and forth for some clue to the origin of what I'd heard. But only the twinkling of house lights, partially obscured by the branches of leafy trees, shone back at me.

The sound seemed to be coming from the vicinity of Vernon Bennett's house. The sun-bleached, wood-frame structure with a high-peaked tin roof had withstood more than five decades of nor'easters that would rip down the lake's full length during the fall months. It stood out from the newer, less weathered homes and was an easily recognized landmark for daytime boaters.

Bennett, sixty-two years old then, had commercial-fished the lake his entire life. He kept to himself, didn't visit the bars, and, most important, he didn't talk. At least he didn't talk to the people who talked to me. Many poachers, like most conventional criminals, eventually get caught because they couldn't keep their mouths shut.

I'd met him only twice in the five years I'd worked the river and Crescent Lake. On both occasions, he'd been unfailingly polite. His thinking, I imagined, was that if he was nice to me, perhaps I'd pay more attention to those fishermen who enjoyed getting me riled up. It was the "squeaky wheel gets the grease" strategy, and it often worked for the fishermen smart enough to employ it. Human nature dictates that extroverted law enforcement officers will gravitate to those who challenge them. I was no exception.

Bennett had lines of fish traps scattered throughout the south end of Crescent. The traps were made from plastic-coated wire mesh, formed into a double-funnel cylinder about six feet long and two feet across. One end opened into the first funnel, where the fish entered. From there they'd naturally swim forward through the second funnel, where a restrictive device made from a cone-shaped throat of tight twine closed in behind them, sealing off all avenues of escape.

To empty a trap, all the fisherman had to do was open a square wire door in the back end and shake the fish out. Then a bait bag of soybean cake was dropped through the opening, the door closed, and the trap placed back into the water, where it would sink to the bottom.

Bennett liked to run multiple traps off one main line. The main line would be up to a hundred yards long and anchored at either end to the bottom with a couple of cinder blocks. Short drop lines of eight to ten feet would be tied to single traps, the other end tied to the main line.

By picking up the main line, Bennett could work his way along it— hand over hand—until he reached a drop line and haul up a trap. Running traps set in tandem was far more efficient than motoring from one individually set trap to the next.

On the occasions I'd checked Bennett, he'd had only catfish in the boat. During these inspections, he'd done nothing to make me suspicious, like throw game fish overboard as I approached. The only other thing I knew about Bennett was that he'd never been caught poaching.

*   *   *

I stuck my right thumb out in front of me and sighted across its blurred silhouette at the noise, as if I was looking down a rifle barrel at the front sight. I needed to figure out if it was moving. The sound slowly passed by my thumb, heading east along the shoreline. It had to be a small outboard engine, the driver, exceptionally cautious. The vessel was blacked out with no navigation lights displayed.

I picked up the rain jacket and laid it across the lid of a sopping-wet storage compartment and sat down. I needed to sort out what was happening because this guy was up to no good.

The engine noise got progressively louder as the boat made a turn due north. If it stayed on this track, it would pass within a hundred yards of me. I prayed he wouldn't change course and head my way. The game would be up then, and whatever he planned to do would be ruined if he spotted me.

I lifted up the fiberglass lid to the storage compartment and pulled out a pair of 7 × 50 binoculars. My forefinger turned the center dial, slowly bringing into focus the profile of a long, dark shape chugging across the lake at the speed of a fast walk. The engine shut off a hundred yards due east of me.

I suspected it was Bennett and that he'd stopped at one of his trap lines. Most likely he planned to run traps set to catch speckled perch, a freshwater game fish illegal to harvest by commercial methods.

I reminded myself that there must be a very good reason why Bennett had never been caught. By what I could tell so far, the old man was crafty as hell. I'd need to be very careful, my timing flawless, if I hoped to catch him with any fish in the boat.

Tactically, though, I was in an excellent position. We were separated by the length of one football field, and Bennett was in a boat I could outrun on foot had we been on dry land.

"This ought to go pretty well," I told myself.

We were about a mile from the nearest shore, and I couldn't help but wonder how he'd found those traps in the dark. There were no landmarks out here, such as channel markers or pilings or tall trees, to use as a reference point.

The only thing I could figure was that he must have run a course based on some primitive form of landmark triangulation. It would be impossible for him to have stopped at the precise location of an unmarked trap line at night without using some method to navigate by.

I imagined myself in his position and figured his triangulations could have been based on lining up two different sets of lights on the horizon. In looking back northwest toward Crescent City—on the lake's southwest shore—I could see where a house light in the foreground could be lined up with a red beacon atop a radio tower in the far distance. He only needed to do this twice at offsetting angles. When both sets of the two lights were aligned, he'd be on the exact spot.

The binocular lens formed a round frame for the scene before me, dimly lit by the ambient starlight. The dark, blurry image of someone rose up in the boat, followed by the splash of a trap drag, and then thumping, with the resonance of a hard object against wood. The blur bent over, leaned back, and dragged up a long, dark shape the height of a man into the boat. The sounds of fish flopping on a wooden deck soon followed.

An hour passed and he still hadn't turned on a light, not even a dim penlight to help him see. He'd done this before. It was how he made his living.

The engine cranked up with a coarse thrum. The long, black blur that was his boat headed on a path straight to his home. He would pass within fifty yards of my position.

My plan was to let him come to me. The primary concern was to make sure I didn't run him over. A boat powered by a 200-horsepower outboard can close the gap with a slow-moving vessel mighty quick. I'd be cautious, yet ready if he started throwing fish overboard. I laid a hand-sized, orange plastic throw buoy, wrapped with twine and a flat piece of lead, on the deck by my feet.

I started my engine as he passed by, eased the shifter into forward gear, and pushed down lightly on the foot throttle pedal. The bow rose up, plowing through the water at about eight to ten miles per hour. Thirty yards from the boat, I flipped on my headlamp and emergency light, illuminating Bennett in a brilliant white cone and sharp blue flashes.

He was wearing black plastic bib rain slicker pants and a white T-shirt, his hair was tussled, but his eyes were clear and alert. He wasn't shaken up in the least. He released the tiller of an ancient outboard and calmly walked to the middle of his eighteen-foot cypress-wood boat. He began heaving sacks of speckled perch overboard, weighted with pieces of concrete block. The fish scales shone like bright white mica in the headlamp beam. One sack went into the water with a splash off the starboard side of his boat, followed by another. I was closing slowly on his port side.

"State Wildlife Officer," I shouted. "Stop throwing those fish overboard and sit down!"

He ignored me, of course, and chunked another fifty-pound bag of fish into the water. I was worried that by the time I reached him, all the evidence would be resting on the lake bottom.

Five seconds before I reached his boat, I decided on a hasty strategy: bump the gunwale and knock him off balance. At the very least,

I expected to recover one bag of fish. It seemed like a good idea at the time.

I plowed straight ahead and sighted across the pointy bow of my boat, and aimed it directly at Bennett. I expected to come to a stop when the hull of my boat touched his gunwale. Instead, the prow rode up over the top of the old cypress boat and steamrolled right over Bennett. I'd failed to factor in the smooth, perfectly rounded curve of my prow, wet and slick with spray, coming into contact with a gunwale that had only a foot of freeboard. Bennett vanished out of sight without a sound; he was trapped underwater, sandwiched between my keel and his boat.

"Oh, shit!" I yelled, and yanked back on the gear-shift handle, throwing the engine into neutral. At least if the prop did hit him, it wouldn't cut him to pieces. The engine's foot thudded into the side of Bennett's boat and jerked me to a stop. My patrol boat had settled crossways on top of his boat, sinking it. I tossed the throw buoy out to mark our location.

In those brief moments, two thoughts flashed simultaneously through my head: the old man was dead, and I'd be fired.

I needed to find Bennett. Fast. Maybe he was still alive. I wondered how long he could hold his breath underwater. Not very long, I concluded.

I leapt out of my seat and ran to the center of my boat. He had to be somewhere underneath the middle section of my hull. I leaned over the starboard side and peered down into brown, translucent water with my headlight beam.

Nothing.

"Jesus Christ," I told myself, "if I don't see him on the other side I'll be thoroughly screwed." I jumped over to the port side. The collar of a white T-shirt flapped in the unsettled water two feet beneath the surface. I grabbed a double handful of cotton cloth and hauled Bennett out from underneath my boat. Spitting and sputtering, he gasped, choking for pure, fresh air.

It felt like I'd just dodged a heat-seeking missile. I could finally breathe regularly again. Bennett would live to catch more fish, and I would still have a job. I hoped.

I held Bennett up by the nape of his T-shirt so he could get his wits about him. My boat still lay crossways on top of his. The only part of his vessel showing above the waterline was the top half of the rounded cowling from a 5-horsepower, 1950s outboard motor.

Remarkably, Bennett had yet to say a word. I was braced for a deluge of expletives ranging from my family heritage to my resemblance to the hind end of a donkey. But he continued to sit quietly on the flat board center seat.

"Mister Bennett, are you OK?" I asked.

"I'm fine."

I noticed a small cut on his face and asked him again, "Are you sure you're OK?"

"Yep," he replied matter-of-factly, as if this happened every night.

He was incredibly mild-mannered for a man who'd just been water-pancaked. "Listen," I said, "I'm sorry I ran you over, but you just wouldn't stop throwing those fish. The next time a law enforcement officer tells you to stop, you really need to stop." He looked at me with tired eyes—like, *Do you think you could give me a break here?*

"OK," I said, in a change of tack, "this is what we're going to do. I'm going to start my engine and slowly back away from your boat. Then I'll help you get bailed out and going again."

Bennett stared into the night, nonplussed—like, *Oh well, these things sometimes happen.*

I backed my patrol boat away. The old cypress boat popped up like a cork, with about three inches of the gunwales showing above the surface. A couple hundred gallons of water sloshed back and forth inside the homemade vessel.

Bennett grabbed the handle of a snow shovel—a standard tool used for shoveling large quantities of fish—and started bailing out his boat, one scoopful at a time.

I tied us off, so we were rafted together. Then I got in his boat and gently pried the shovel loose from his hands and said, "Listen Mister Bennett, I'll bail out your boat, you just sit down and relax. You've been through enough for one night."

He shrugged wearily and sat down on the driver's seat.

Forty-five minutes later, I had the boat emptied of water. The clean

A chunk of cinder block placed in the bottom of a mesh bag or cloth sack is the quickest way to sink a load of illegally trapped game fish, early 1980s.

deck glistened under the glare of my headlight. Incredibly, Bennett had managed to toss every sack of perch over the side. The situation reminded me of a quarterback who sees the blitz coming and realizes he will be crushed within the next fraction of a second, yet somehow manages to throw the ball for a touchdown.

"Mister Bennett, do you think that old motor will crank?"

"Probably."

"Why don't you give it a try?"

He yanked the cord a few times, and it coughed, sputtered, and finally fired off. "Go ahead and shut it back down," I said. "We still have some business to attend to. I'm going to try dragging for a few minutes to see if I can snag one of those bags of fish you threw overboard. You just sit there and take it easy."

"OK."

The marker buoy floated ten yards away. I uncoiled seventy-five feet of ⁵⁄₁₆-inch braided nylon line tied to a five-pound trap drag. The drag was made using a piece of steel bar with four quarter-inch steel rods welded on one end. The tip of each rod was bent into a half circle, kind of like a grappling hook. If the drag was pulled over a line or webbed mesh bag like the type Bennett had thrown overboard, it would easily snag. So long as the puller kept tension on the line, the item caught could be brought up to the surface.

I threw to one side of the marker, letting the drag sink straight to the bottom before retrieving it. Nothing. I tried to the opposite side of the marker. Nothing. On the third toss, I felt the drag hang up with a nice spongy feel. If it had been a log, it wouldn't have budged. I dragged the object up to the side of the boat. It was one of the webbed mesh bags bulging with speckled perch. Bending over, I ran my fingers through the webbing, tightened my grip, leaned back, and rolled it into the boat. I cast for a few more minutes and dragged up a second bag of fish. The combined weight of both bags would later total 115 pounds.

Feeling better now, I turned to Bennett and told him: "I'm going to charge you with two counts: The first one will be for operating a motor vessel without navigation lights, the second for taking freshwater game fish by an illegal method. I could seize your boat, but I think you've been through enough misery for one morning. You can head on back to your house after I issue you the citations."

"All right," he said.

I suspected a lawsuit might be coming my way so I wanted to appear as something of a humanitarian if I ended up in court. It probably wouldn't help, but I thought it was worth a try. I issued the citations and watched him putter away into the night.

The headlines in the *Crescent City Courier* later that week—dated September, 9, 1981—exclaimed in a big, bold font, "Fisherman Charged: Boat Ramming Was Accident, Says Officer."

Thankfully, I never did hear any more from Bennett, a decent man who graciously decided not to press a lawsuit against me. He was a class act who understood how the game was played.

When you're caught, you're caught.

6

Night Poaching on a Motorcycle

My former career in wildlife law enforcement was an exceptionally lucky one. Others have been lost to poachers' bullets, drownings, and high-speed pursuits. But my career, while dicey at times, seemed to duck the darker moments that some of my peers unluckily encountered—until one night, when I found myself taking what I thought for a moment was my last truck ride.

On that night, my fate would rest in the hands of Warden Wilbur Holdridge, a twenty-two-year veteran and one of the most talented at driving "black," or without lights. We were partnered together in one truck, while Wardens Tommy Shearer and Bruce Hamlin worked out of another one. As a team, we would try to catch Roger Gunter, a cagey and elusive outlaw who night-hunted deer with abandon.

We'd received a tip that he and a friend—I'll call him Johnny Wright—planned to meet at Gunter's single-wide mobile home shortly after their three-to-eleven evening shift ended at the Georgia-Pacific Paper Mill in Palatka. Then they'd hop on a motorcycle and ride into the woods to shoot a deer.

October 27, 1982, Putnam County

Night sounds surrounded Wilbur and me as we sat atop the hood of his patrol truck. In the far distance, a cow lowed, somewhere a metal screen door banged shut, and tractor-trailer rigs rumbled over the Cross Florida Barge Canal Bridge a mile to our east. County Road 310 was only a stone's throw away, bathed in the glow of a full moon, while we watched, hidden in an oak scrub thicket.

"Listen," said Wilbur, with a quiet authority tempered by an easy southern drawl. "It sounds like a truck coming."

I glanced at my watch. The luminescent hands showed 11:20 p.m. "That would be about right," I said. "Their mill shift ends at eleven, so twenty minutes would give them enough time to make it this far."

I could hear the truck clearly now. The singsong pattern of badly worn off-road tires rang out as it whipped around a curve to our east. Headlamp beams swept through the trees, creating a cascade of deep shadows. Gradually, the tire noise became less noticeable. I started to get antsy. The truck was slowing down.

Deceleration continued until a black Chevy 4 × 4 pickup rolled to a stop right in front of us. The engine shut off, along with the lights.

"It looks like Wright's truck," I whispered. "What do you think he's up to?"

"I'm not sure. Watch him close, while I get ready." Wilbur quietly slid to the ground, walked around to the driver's door of our patrol truck—a 1979 Dodge Ramcharger—and pulled it open. The truck body lurched as he stepped up on the floorboard, stretching his six-foot-two, 240-pound frame above the rooftop for a better view. If we had to make a hurried traffic stop, all Wilbur had to do was drop down into the driver's seat and fire off the engine.

In his early teens, Wilbur worked on his aunt's 3,000-acre dairy farm in Daytona Beach and broke wild horses for her whenever she needed it. The rodeo circuit never interested him much, but he remained a cowboy at heart and worked his own herd on his free time. Wilbur was never much of a boat man, but he loved the woods and loved to hunt, a good combination for a game warden whose regular patrol beat was the pine forests and hardwood hammocks of Flagler County. By this time in his career he'd caught hundreds of night hunters, had a couple of dozen pursuits, and been involved in one shooting incident.

I brought a pair of 7-power binoculars up to my eyes, elbows on top of knees to steady them. The driver sat alone in the cab, head and shoulders silhouetted against a bright moonscape. He leaned over to the passenger door and rolled the window down. Then he shouldered a scoped rifle and pointed it out the open window and beyond to a power line right-of-way cleared of vegetation.

"It's a darn good thing we happen to be on the opposite side of his truck," I said, muttering the words softly under my breath.

"I'd be hunting me a big tree to hide behind if I was on that side of the road," said Wilbur, as he leaned over the roof to talk to me. "It's either that or we'd have to announce ourselves, and I'd hate to blow this detail because we had the bad luck to end up in his crosshairs. I hope he sees a deer to shoot so we can wrap this up early."

Wilbur and I were thinking the same thing: "No crime had been committed yet." We needed to see the driver shine a spotlight while in possession of a firearm, or kill a deer, before we could charge him with illegally hunting at night.

"I don't know if we're going to get that lucky," I said.

After a couple of minutes, the driver put the rifle down, cranked his engine, and sped off, the tire noise fading into the still night.

"I think Wright stopped on a whim," I said. "Roger's way too cautious. He'd never hunt from a road."

"I agree," said Wilbur. "I bet Roger would be some kind of mad if he knew his buddy had pulled a stunt like that."

Our truck radio crackled, "Wright just drove up to the Gunters' place in a black Chevy," said Tommy Shearer. He was working off a handheld radio as was his partner, Bruce Hamlin. Both men had walked away from their patrol truck and were now on foot, hidden in a clump of brush across the highway from Gunter's trailer. They were about two miles from us.

"Ten-four," I replied.

Fifteen minutes later the radio squelch broke again: "Gunter just showed up," said Tommy. "You guys didn't see him because he came in from the other end of 310. We heard him stop his motorcycle at every gate checking for tire sign. We hid our truck before the dew fell, so hopefully he missed ours."

Roger Gunter

Gunter walked out of the mill gates at 11:00 p.m., climbed on his motorcycle, and headed for home. He leaned into the handlebars, feeling the rush of cool air against his face, winding up the 750 Kawasaki for the ten-mile ride.

On this night, he took a detour from his normal route. Gunter, forty-three, didn't leave anything to chance. "Taking precautions," as he liked to say, and doing "recon work" near the area he planned to hunt had kept him one step ahead of the law for most of his life.

Something else, though, niggled at Gunter's mind: Johnny Wright, the fella he planned to hunt with that night, had a "mouth on him." Gunter was worried that Wright may have slipped up and said something to the wrong person. "I got to be real careful," he told himself.

Instead of taking State Road 19 south through Palatka, to 310 and home, he choose a route south through the town of Interlachen on County Road 315 to 310. After he passed Hansen's Bait Shop, he slowed down, pulling into every side road, where he stopped to wiggle the handlebars back and forth, illuminating the sand and grass in the harsh white glare of the bike's headlight.

Tires rolling across dew-covered ground leave a distinct trail of moist debris, mostly bits of damp dirt, along with crushed leaves, broken pine needles, and other woody detritus. If Gunter found this type of transfer sign, he'd take a closer look, to see if it was one way "in" or "in and out." If the sign was "in"—only—it meant a game warden truck was likely hidden around the corner out of sight.

Satisfied that this three-mile section of highway was clear, Gunter went on to the house. He'd told Wright before they left the mill to check 310 coming in from the east. He still couldn't shake the feeling of unease, though. It was as if a tiny invisible man sat on his shoulder whispering into his ear, "He's a screw-up." At the same time, Gunter kind of felt sorry for Wright, twenty-four, who had declared he wanted to "kill a deer real bad," or at least get some meat.

Gunter wheeled his bike into the front yard. Wright leaned lazily against his truck, hands in his pockets, listening to Led Zeppelin rock it out from a radio inside the cab.

Tools of a serial poacher. At one time, Roger Gunter killed fifty to sixty deer a year—many of them at night or out of season. The author counted more than one hundred notches—each one for a dead deer—in the stock of this Remington .270 caliber Model 700 bolt-action rifle, 2007.

"Shut that thing off," said Gunter. "You should be listening for the man instead of that crap."

"You're late."

"You damn right I'm late. I checked all of 310 to the west. Did you check everything coming in from the east?"

"Yeah, sure."

"I hope so. Are you ready to go?"

"Yup."

"I'll get my gear."

Gunter came out of the trailer wearing a military rucksack, with a bolt-action .243 caliber high-powered rifle slung over one shoulder. Attached to his belt was a 6-volt battery with wires stringing to a small chrome lens headlight tucked away in a cloth waist pouch. Wright wore the same headlight rig. Only Gunter carried a gun. Both men wore camouflage jackets buttoned up over sleeveless T-shirts with the neck cut out by a knife in a ragged, deep vee. Just like inner-city gangs used distinctive colored clothing to identify members, so did Gunter and the loosely knit group of rogues who poached with him.

Gunter climbed on the bike while Wright settled in behind. They cruised out of the dirt driveway and onto the highway heading east.

Wardens Tommy Shearer and Bruce Hamlin

The two wardens sat side by side under dense cover as they watched the Kawasaki's taillight disappear around a curve. Tommy leaned in toward Bruce: "OK, they've left to hunt. Try to find a place to hide right next to the trailer. Call me when you figure out what they brought back." Tommy was schooling Bruce, who was a rookie with only five days in the field. Even though Bruce had previously worked as a K-9 deputy for a central Florida sheriff's department, the strategy for catching game violators was foreign to him.

"I think it's going to be hard to find a good hiding spot near his trailer," said Bruce, scanning the front yard with his binoculars. "All the fruit trees are trimmed up, even the shrubs are cleared out underneath."

"Hide under the trailer then."

"Got it."

Bruce started to get up when Tommy tugged his arm. He had one final piece of advice: "Just remember, if you hear a shot, it doesn't mean they'll bring the deer back to the trailer. They may leave it in the woods to pick up later. We don't want to jump them unless we know they've got a deer."

Bruce climbed over the fence and darted across the road to the edge of Gunter's driveway. A metal panel gate leaned open into the yard. As he walked through, a cur dog ran out from underneath a bush growling. Bruce froze. He was trapped in the open with nowhere to hide. The whole detail could be blown in the next few moments if someone stuck their head out of the trailer's front door.

"Here, boy," coaxed Bruce, kneeling down with one hand outstretched. "Come here. Come on now. It's OK." The mottled black-and-white dog raised its head, cocking it to one side, trying to figure out if the dark-clad person was friend or foe. Finally, he wagged his tail and came over for a pet. "Good boy. See, we're going to get on just fine," said Bruce, caressing the dog's head and neck with long, smooth strokes. "Let's you and me see if we can find a good place to lie down."

Bruce crept into the backyard and crawled underneath the mobile home. He wriggled across stale dirt, to the back side of the metal steps leading to the front door, figuring this was as good a spot as he would find to watch the two poachers when they returned.

Gunter and Wright Shine for Deer

Gunter drove for a couple of minutes before turning north onto a dirt lane that cut straight through a flat, grassy field. After a quarter mile he picked up a two-rut track that wound through a thin stand of turkey oaks. The terrain gradually changed as it melded into a mature live oak hammock where a heavy acorn mast lay on the ground. He ran the bike off into a palmetto patch, laying it down inside the thick, green fronds.

The men had entered a section of land that measured a mile by a mile, exactly 640 acres. Decades earlier, the property had been divided into a subdivision named Kenilworth and sold off as "investment property" to naïve northerners in postage-stamp lots of .07 of an acre. What the buyers didn't realize until it was too late was that their Sunshine State properties were woefully undersized for the county's minimum building codes. The land remained vacant, unfenced, and full of game, an enticement poachers like Gunter found hard to resist.

"You shine," whispered Gunter. "If we use two lights they'll wash each other out. It makes it harder to see the eyes."

"OK," said Wright.

Gunter drew the bolt back and chambered a round. Wright reached up to the elastic band running around his forehead and fumbled for a moment before his fingers found the small plastic switch under the lamp and pushed it on. The yellow-white glow leaped away from his forehead revealing the trunks of coarse-barked old-growth oaks layered with Spanish moss, and a landscape void of any understory. The park-like terrain was perfect for illuminating deer.

The two men slipped through the hammock, careful to stay on a sandy path that dulled the sound of their footsteps to a soft scrunch. Gunter trailed behind Wright, tracking the headlamp's beam. They'd walked a quarter mile when Gunter eased up behind Wright and tapped him lightly on the shoulder. "Move your light back to the right," he whispered. As Wright swept the light, it came to rest on the trunk of a thick oak, easily five feet in diameter. "Hold it there," said Gunter.

"I don't see anything."

"Just wait. I think I saw a tail flip."

Two minutes passed. Then an eight-point buck came out from behind the tree, paused, and lifted its head. It was only seventy feet away. The naturally brown eyes—now turned to twin orbs of bright metallic green—stared curiously into the incandescent light.

Gunter eased the gun to his shoulder.

Booomm!

"Jesus Christ!" shouted Wright. "At least you could have warned me."

"He was too close. Follow me," said Gunter, heading away from the still-thrashing deer. The animal would die in a minute. Heart shots were always that way.

"Why don't we go get the deer?"

"No, we got to take precautions first." He led Wright to the edge of the clearing and into a copse of crooked wood. Gunter flattened his hands, motioning for his partner to squat down. "Shut your light off. We'll wait here a few minutes. We're close enough to the highway we can hear their tires roaring if they decide to come in after us."

"What? You think they're watching us?"

"No, but you got to take precautions."

Fifteen minutes later, Gunter flicked on his headlamp. Wright did the same. Both men worked silently in shadows cast by the high-arched, interwoven tree canopies.

They dragged the animal over to a low-hanging limb. Gunter laid his backpack on the ground and removed two ⅜-inch-diameter hemp ropes. He threw both ropes over the limb and secured them about two feet apart. He bent down and cut a three-inch slit above the hock of each hind leg. They lifted one leg head-high and tied it off to one rope, then did the same to the other leg.

Eighteen minutes later, the deer was stripped of its hide and cleaned of its meat. What hung before them was a bloody rib cage, barely attached at the hip sockets by the femurs. The shoulders had been cut off, along with the backstrap, tenderloin, and hams. All the meat was placed into white plastic garbage bags and stuffed into the rucksack. Gunter cinched the top flap down and shouldered the pack, along with his rifle. He dragged the carcass into the bushes, covering it with dead limbs and palmetto fans. Both men walked back to the bike. It was now three in the morning.

Gunter sat the bike up and wedged the head and antlers—now stuffed into a 30-gallon black plastic leaf bag—behind the handlebars. They idled out onto the trail blacked out.

"Too much risk," thought Gunter, "in taking the same route out." Instead, he turned onto a newly plowed firebreak. The bike bumped and twisted as they rode across the broken ground, fresh-cut roots tinged off the wheel spokes, and heavy-leaved branches scraped their faces. When they reached 310, Gunter shut the motorcycle off and laid it down in a field of chest-high broom sedge that grew along the road right-of-way.

"What are you doing?" asked Wright.

"You'll see."

Thirty minutes later, both men heard the roar of a log truck bearing down on them. Gunter sat the bike up. "Get on," he said, "and hold on tight."

"What? What the hell are you going to do?"

"Just shut up and do like I tell ya. Wrap your arms around me tight and don't let go."

The blowback from the tractor-trailer rig buffeted the men as it whipped past them at sixty. Gunter shot out of the tall grass, spinning up dirt and chunks of loose asphalt, hitting the highway lights-out.

"Turn on the gawd damn lights!" screamed Wright.

"I don't need any lights, you idiot! I'm trying to keep us from getting caught," hollered Gunter.

Gunter brought the bike up to eighty-five, holding it there until they'd closed within a few feet of the truck's solid-steel bumper. Then he throttled down to match the truck's speed, the bike's whine smothered by the rumble of the powerful diesel engine. "Perfect," thought Gunter.

Two miles down 310, Gunter cleverly cut the bike's engine, coasting down to thirty as he entered his driveway. The momentum carried them all the way into the front yard. The motorcycle came to a stop next to Wright's truck. Gunter knocked the kickstand down, and both men climbed off.

Bruce was still hidden under the trailer.

"Tommy, can you hear me?" whispered Bruce, talking into the ancient handheld radio. (Back in 1982, these radios were notoriously unreliable.)

No response.

"Tommy, you there?" Bruce frantically rapped the leather-bound chunk of metal with his knuckles, trying to bring some life back to it.

Finally, he heard, "What did you—" Bruce's frustration mounted with every second. This was the critical moment. He needed to talk with Tommy to get the senior officer's advice as events unfolded.

The unskirted trailer gave Bruce a partial view out into the front yard. By now though, the moon had sunk deep into the western horizon, casting long, broad shadows across the front yard.

Gunter and Wright spoke in hushed, low voices. The conversation sounded professional to Bruce, like soldiers talking about a military operation. "Deer . . . gun . . . meet again" drifted to him, but he couldn't tell for sure what was going on. He still couldn't see well, as both men stood in an area unlit by the moon. Of course, he'd heard the rifle shot earlier, but it was no guarantee they'd brought out a deer. Questions began to roll around in his head: What would happen if they hadn't killed a deer, and he ran out from under the mobile home now? The game would be up, and he, the rookie warden, would have ruined the whole detail.

The two poachers finished their conversation. Gunter walked up the steps and into his trailer, letting the screen door snap shut. Wright dropped the rucksack into the bed of his truck, where it landed with a solid thud, climbed into the cab, and drove out to 310—eastbound.

He accelerated quickly, the *wha, wha, wha, wha* of thick-lugged tires cutting through the night.

Bruce crawled out from underneath the trailer, ran across the yard and out to the highway, calling Tommy on the handheld.

"I got you now," said Tommy. "What happened?"

"I'm not sure, but a rucksack went into the back of Wright's truck and he hauled butt. It seemed to have some weight in it."

"Hold on."

By now Tommy had run back to his patrol truck, where he could talk on the more powerful radio. The stronger broadcast easily transmitted the two miles to where Wilbur and I waited. Having picked up only bits and pieces of earlier transmissions via the handhelds, we couldn't tell what had happened.

At that moment, Wright's truck passed us doing eighty, tires ringing and the radio blasting. Wilbur started the truck up. I jumped in and grabbed the mic: "Do you want us to stop him?"

"Stop him! Stop him! Stop him! I think he's got the meat."

"Ten-four."

Wilbur hit the gas, launching the Ramcharger out of the brush, fishtailing onto 310.

A Dodge Ramcharger, powered by a V-8, 360-cubic-inch displacement engine will top out at ninety-plus miles per hour. Wilbur had it up to top speed in no time, hurtling after Wright's truck that was now a mile and a half ahead of us, but blocked from our view by a curve in the road. We were running without lights. If Wright saw us closing on him, we'd never catch him.

The strategy was to get within a short distance of the suspect before turning our lights on. Seeing a set of high-beams and flashing blue lights suddenly fill up a rearview mirror diminishes the spirit of most poachers. And it discourages the tossing of evidence or thoughts of fleeing.

But there was one minor problem that neither of us had considered: We'd left the truck's windows down. The inside of the front windshield was covered with dew. The layer of thin moisture wasn't a problem for Wilbur to see through until we rounded the curve. There, three-quarters of a mile down the road, was another vehicle approaching us.

When the headlight beams struck our windshield, it turned a frosty white.

Wilbur was driving blind.

Our truck flew off the road and landed in a water-filled ditch spinning out of control. Round and round and round we went, gyroscoping down the ditch, while huge gouts of mud and grass and spray flew across the hood and past the windshield. On every revolution, massive pine trees whipped by my passenger window in a blur only six feet away. I flung my arms up in front of my face and braced for impact. "This is it," I told myself.

Incredibly, we ended back up on the highway, still headed in the right direction. Clods of thick mud thumped against the undercarriage, slung loose by the spinning wheels. Wilbur looked over at me and calmly asked, "Do you think we should turn our lights on now?"

"Hell, yes!"

"I have to admit that one fencepost did come a little close," said Wilbur, as he flicked on the lights.

"To heck with a flimsy fence post, what about those pine trees?"

He didn't answer, but I did see him crack a smile.

"What happened to the oncoming vehicle?"[1] I asked.

"Must have turned into the driveway of that mobile home just ahead, on the left."

It was time to refocus. I gestured to a pair of dim red specks in the far distance: "Isn't that Wright's truck way down the road?"

"Yes, that's going to be him. Look, he just turned left on State Road 19 heading toward Palatka. I hope we can catch up to him." We careened through the intersection and headed north toward Palatka. Wilbur had the gas pedal mashed to the floor. We rounded a curve and saw the Chevy's taillights ahead of us. Then we lost sight of them to another bend in the road. When we came round the curve, they were gone. Wilbur and I were looking down a long, empty straightaway. He'd vanished.

---

1. Back then, normal procedure was to pull over onto the road shoulder and let an oncoming vehicle pass.

"No way did he cover that much ground on this long stretch of high-way," I said.

"You're right. He 'made' us closing with him and spooked."

By this time, we'd traveled by Mondex, another undeveloped sub-division where the local scoundrels go to poach and do drugs. We'd already passed a dozen entrance roads leading into this mud-holed wasteland. By the time we went back and found Wright's tire sign, he'd be long gone.

"I guess we should go on ahead to the store," said Wilbur.

"Might as well, we've certainly got nothing to lose."

Part of the information we'd received was that the meat would end up at a mom-and-pop grocery store on the outskirts of Palatka, where supposedly it would be sold.

We drove to the store's parking lot. No black truck. We drove around back and parked. Five minutes later the Chevy wheeled up to the front door.

Wilbur and I ran out from behind the building.

I yanked the truck's door open and snatched Wright out from behind the steering wheel. Lying on the seat next to him was a stainless steel, Ruger Mini-14 semi-automatic rifle, loaded with a ten-round magazine filled with .223 caliber ammo. Wilbur kept an eye on our suspect while I checked out the back. In one corner of the bed was an olive-green rucksack—U.S. Army Alice pack. I pulled the flap up. Inside were three white plastic bags filled with fresh deer meat. The bluish-white muscle membranes glistened in the beam of my flash-light. There was not one hair stuck to the meat. I was impressed: to butcher a deer in the field without the benefit of rinsing water and not leave a hair required a sure and steady hand.

Wright "lawyered up," refusing to speak to us without an attorney present. We seized his truck, firearm, and the deer meat. He was ar-rested for night-hunting deer and possession of the meat during the closed season.

Because of legal technicalities, Gunter was later charged by a sum-mons issued through county court, rather than by citation or physical arrest.

Postscript

I interviewed Gunter for several days in October 2007 (see chapter 1). On the first day I came to his house—now a double-wide mobile home—I hadn't been there but a few minutes when he invited me onto his front porch to check out his deer antlers. The first thing he did was grab the rack of a modest eight-point buck that had been hanging loose on the wall. He proudly pushed them at me, saying, "This is the one you all never got."

"What do you mean?"

"Splinter"—his nickname for Bruce Hamlin because he was rail-thin—"never saw me bring this deer head in my home that night. I guess he couldn't see much lying underneath the trailer."

Gunter told me there was no doubt in his mind that Wright had "pimped him out" by telling his girlfriend they planned to hunt that night. He was sure that's how we came to be there. He kept checking my face when he explained his theory of how those events had unfolded, hoping I would slip up and reveal something other than what he had deduced.

Of course, I knew things Gunter didn't know. And what I had heard didn't exactly jibe with what Gunter thought had happened. But even now, after all these many years, I still like to make him sweat.

*   *   *

Author's note: To operate a patrol vehicle without lights at night can be an extremely dangerous undertaking. The word "dicey" only begins to do it justice. Back when the encounter with Gunter and his sidekick Wright took place, the GFC had no rules or procedures for driving without lights.

On October 26, 2001, two Florida game wardens, Roy R. Burnsed and Charles T. Randall—driving in separate patrol trucks—had a head-on collision with their lights out on a narrow levee in south Florida. Both officers were killed in this tragic accident.

For a time, patrolling without lights was stopped until the legislature amended Florida Statute 316.217 in 2004, which added that law enforcement officers can patrol without lights, provided they observe agency protocol and procedures. Interestingly, the Florida Police Chiefs Association and the Florida Sheriffs Association supported this legislation.

Currently, all Florida Fish and Wildlife Conservation Commission officers undergo rigorous night-driving training (the author was an instructor), where they attend lectures and practical driving exercises that educate them in these perils. The top speed allowed by agency policy is now fifteen miles per hour. And that's how it should be.

7

All for a Sack of Fish

February 1983

Tight and narrow, the den I'd hollowed out beneath the brush pile would have made a claustrophobic person cringe. Luckily for me, I didn't have a fear of enclosed places.

The mound of yard trash made the perfect observation post for my surveillance of the ramshackle patchwork of whitewashed buildings that I'll call Sammy's Fish House.[1] The decades-old structure was located in Georgetown and sat atop a cluster of crooked pilings that jutted out into the St. Johns River.

The reason I was hidden under the pile of woody debris was that an informant had called my home three days before. He reported that illegal game fish were being sneaked across the fish house premises once or twice a week.

Lookouts were often employed by commercial fishermen to wave them away from an intended landing site if a game warden had been spotted in the vicinity. This was standard operating procedure in the Georgetown area, whether it was a fish house, public boat ramp, or

---

1. A licensed wholesale business where commercially caught catfish could be bought and sold.

private dock. So I thought the brush pile a convenient and natural way to disguise my presence.

Day three of my stakeout had so far mirrored the two before: dull, boring, and tedious—until a thirty-some-year-old man walked out of a cinder-block building a few yards away. He was one of the catfish skinners. By the expression on his face and the cadence of his stride, I gathered he was on a mission of some importance.

I lay belly-down, breathing softly, while I looked out through the gaps of dried branches stacked around me. My eyes tracked each step of his white rubber boots as they scrunched in the soft, dry dirt. They became louder with every footfall.

Silence.

He'd stopped right in front me and planted his feet wide. He looked right and then left before he unzipped his pants and whipped out his member with the rapidity of a gunslinger clearing leather. A stream of bright yellow fluid gushed forth, landing on a stack of cabbage palm fronds that covered the entrance to my hide. Bright golden drops splattered in every direction. I pulled the hood of my rain jacket down tight around my head. "Not fun," I thought, feeling the light patter on the dark green plastic.

The stench of ammonia filled the air in my burrow beneath the head-high tangle of limbs and sticks and vines. I only had the space of a rolled-out sleeping bag to move around in. I couldn't scoot backward and I couldn't crab sideways; I could only go forward. And if I'd done that, the stakeout would be blown. So there I lay—in a urine trap of my own design.

"Brilliant," I told myself.

I pinched my nose and breathed through my mouth, praying for a gust of wind. The goal, of course, was to stay put until I'd caught someone. My instructors at the wildlife law enforcement academy had somehow failed to broach the subject of being pissed on. I would have to wing it.

Finally, he emptied himself of what must have been his morning coffee—several cups at least—and sauntered back to the skinning room with, I noted, a distinct pop to his step. "Well, isn't he a cheery bastard?" I thought.

It was now noon. I'd been here since 5:30 a.m. and wouldn't be able to leave until the fish house closed at 2:30 p.m. Since I couldn't go anywhere, I stared at the river, mesmerized by the shimmering waters on a bright, clear day while I mulled over the wisdom of choosing this particular brush pile to hide under.

*   *   *

When I first started as a rookie—five years before—my duties were explained to me in Spartan-like terms by one of my supervisors, Lt. Wayne King, who told me: "Your job is to catch every illegal commercial fisherman you can. The violations are rampant, the public is going nuts, and we need to put a stop to it. Do you understand?"

"Yes, sir," I replied.

So, being an enthusiastic young officer and a dedicated rule follower, I felt compelled to honor King's orders. I would try every way possible I could think of to catch these dastardly fish poachers.

On that day at Sammy's Fish House, I was watching for commercial fishermen who brought in illegally caught freshwater game fish— bluegills, shellcrackers, and speckled perch—from hoop nets.

Hoop nets are gigantic barrel-shaped fish traps designed to catch freshwater catfish. Up to five feet across and more than twelve feet long, they are fish-catching machines that can capture up to two hundred pounds of catfish in a week's time.

The traps are designed with an outer sheath of webbing wrapped tightly around four fiberglass hoops. Each end is closed off, with one end having two cone-shaped funnels pointing inward. Fish swim into a wide first funnel, then push forward through the second funnel, which spreads apart as they pass through, and then closes up behind them, sealing off any avenue of escape. When in a fishing mode, they are anchored to the river bottom—stretched tight between two nylon lines attached to anchors made of steel rebar or concrete block. They are restricted to certain sections of the St. Johns River and require the fisherman to have a freshwater commercial fishing license to operate them. Any game fish caught in the nets must be returned to the water immediately.

Author (*right*) and Warden Guy "Gator" Banks (see chapter 10) seize a small hoop net illegally set by commercial fish poachers in Little Rice Creek, 1980. Hoop nets can be legally fished only in certain parts of the St. Johns River.

Over the years I'd experimented with different strategies to catch these outlaw commercial fishermen. The most productive way I'd come up with was to wait for them somewhere along the shoreline, if I could figure out where they planned to drop off their illegal catch.

It had proven to be pure folly and an utter waste of time and energy to try to catch them on the water in my patrol boat. They had eyes like a hawk and would toss the contraband fish overboard—in weighted burlap sacks—at the first sight of a game warden on the horizon.

*   *   *

The whine of a big outboard reverberated across the water. The boat was motoring north from Lake George down the channel toward Georgetown and the fish house. I could see a flash of dark green every now and then as it passed behind the dock pilings of private homes to the east. Finally, the low lines and hooked-nosed bow of an eighteen-foot fiberglass Old Timer, powered by a big Mercury outboard came into view. It matched the description of the boat my caller had told me about.

When it came abreast of the fish house, the driver spun the wheel hard, whipping it in a tight turn that lined the boat up true with the dock. Then he yanked the throttle back, the stern sank down, while the bow angled high in the air. This was an intentional maneuver designed to block the view of anyone conducting a surveillance of the driver and his passenger from shore. They were waiting for a signal from a man who'd just walked out to the end of the dock. If he took his ball cap off, they'd throw the fish over the transom, taking advantage of the blind spot created by the raised hull.

The lookout kept his hat on, and I breathed a sigh of relief.

The boat settled into the water as it idled up to the dock. The passenger reached underneath the rough-board planks and grabbed a loose line. Then he used it to tie a slip knot around the top of a burlap sack. He picked the sack up and slung it up under the dock, where it landed between the pilings with a splash.

The catfish skinner walked out to meet the two men. Together they hoisted four black plastic fish boxes—weighing a hundred pounds each and brimming with catfish—up onto the dock. The skinner latched onto them with an iron J-hook hand tool and dragged each box through the open door of a cooler room used to chill the fish.

The passenger was in his twenties, had coarse, blond hair, and wore thick-framed sunglasses. He held his head back high and arrogant-like. The driver, an old man, sat slump-shouldered in the boat. He had a round, weather-beaten face and big hands, creased and calloused from years of sewing nets. I knew both men through prior fishing inspections on the river.

The fishermen climbed onto the dock and crossed to a dirt path that ran by the brush pile to a parking lot. They stopped just a few feet from me. "Where is she at?" the older one asked.

"I don't know," the young one replied. "But I'm going to be pissed if she doesn't show up soon. She's supposed to be waitin' on us."

A Chevy Impala roared into the dirt parking area, casting dust up around the wheel wells, turned around, and backed up to the men. A young woman sat behind the steering wheel. "Open the damn trunk," the young one snarled.

A metallic clunk and the lid popped open. The young man ran back to the Old Timer, retrieved the sack of fish from under the dock, and trotted back up the dirt path. I shoved the palm fronds aside and low-crawled—army style—out from under the brush pile. The old man heard the rustling and jumped back grabbing his chest, "Good Lord," he said, "you just about gave me a heart attack."

"We need to have a chat," I said.

I walked over to the guy holding the sack and took it from him. Then I laid it on the ground in front of me.

"You know, Bob," the old man said, shakily, "I was counting on those fish. The church fish fry is coming up this Sunday and I promised the congregation we'd have fried bream."

"Hold that thought for just a minute," I said, while I held up one finger.

I knelt down and undid the brown twine securing the sack. Bream flopped back and forth covered in beige-colored meal that stank with a sickly sweet odor. In the bottom of the sack was an eight-pound—cast-iron—window sash weight. I picked up a few of the fish, turning them from side to side to examine their mouths, and then dropped them back into the sack one at a time.

"Were you running hoop nets this morning?" I asked.

"Sure was," said the old man. "But we stopped on the way back and caught some bream with cane poles."

"Ah huh, and where are the cane poles?" I asked.

"Well, a friend loaned them to us and we gave them back to him before we came in," the heavy one said.

"Do you know how lame that sounds?"

"Well, Bob, it's true."

"Ah huh, and does the person you borrowed the poles from have a name?"

"Well, Bob, it's kind of funny you should ask that, because I seem to have forgotten it."

"Never mind—I'm charging you both with possession of freshwater game fish showing signs of having been caught by an unlawful method and possession of untagged game fish on the premises of a commercial fish house."

"What do you mean?" asked the younger one.

"What I mean is this: Based on my experience these fish came out of a hoop net. They're coated in soybean cake, which you use to bait your nets with. And here's the real kicker: None of these fish I examined have any hook marks in their mouths."

"Well, Bob," said the older one. "You do what you got to do."

I knelt beside the hole under the brush pile and pulled out my backpack (a black North Face cordura daypack). I left the raincoat behind.

I issued citations and cut them loose after I'd made an appointment for them to meet with the county judge. Then I slipped on my backpack, slung the thirty-pound sack of fish over my shoulders, and headed on down the fish house driveway. My patrol truck was hidden in the woods a half mile away.

When I'd begun this detail I'd hoped to catch these guys with more than just a sack of fish. The magic number was more than 150 pounds of game fish. Once that threshold was met, the penalty went from a second- to a first-degree misdemeanor with automatic seizure of the vessel.

Still, I'd managed to salvage something for my efforts. I would hate to have been pissed on for nothing.

8

The Cackling Man

A Saturday in April

I've often marveled at why people do the things that they do. Take, for example, the thirty-some-year-old guy I was looking at one Saturday morning through the lens of a 20-power spotting scope. He was shirtless, wearing blue jeans and a pair of cracked flip-flops. His tanned belly pressed tight against the protective chain-link fence at the south wall of the Rodman Dam spillway. He'd thrown his head back, mouth agape, emitting a cackle of hoots and hollers as he put on a show for the crowd.

Two hundred assorted fishermen stood shoulder to shoulder along the spillway walls. None of them looked happy.

The Cackling Man held a stout rod and reel in one hand and a four-pound largemouth bass in the other. He waved the fish back and forth, tail flopping, while bright-yellow roe streamed out from a gash in the belly. Then, with an exaggerated flourish, he tossed the fish high into the air, watching it cartwheel over and over until it fell into the churning waters twenty feet below. He raised his hands, palms up, like a pro football player trying to excite the crowd. But they remained silent, eyes down, mouths pinched into grimaces of angry disgust. The lack of applause didn't seem to bother him, though. That's because he was a thick-headed jerk.

This was the fifth bass he'd caught in the last hour. All of the fish were snatched in the gut with a shiny, nickel-plated 1/0 treble hook. I knew this because the powerful optics created the illusion of him standing right in front of me.

The spotting scope had a short tripod that could be spread open to sit on a table. I had no table to rest it on. So I kept the legs closed and gripped them with my right hand while steadying it against a tree trunk. With my left hand I made minor adjustments to the focus dial as I scanned the crowd, bringing each person into perfect clarity.

I stood in knee-deep water wearing hip waders and a camouflaged jacket, secreted under the dense shadows cast by a copse of red maple trees. Ringing the outside of this miniature wetlands patch were clumps of blackberry bushes. I had no fear of being discovered because these natural plant barriers provided little incentive for anyone walking by to explore into their prickly vines.

The Cackling Man was a trophy hunter. He wanted to catch a fish over ten pounds. All of the fish he'd caught so far that morning would have weighed under five. But I was patient. I'd spent many Saturday mornings waiting in this very spot, perfecting my technique for catching illegal snatch fishermen through trial and error. Stealth and timing, I'd learned, were the key ingredients for making a good case.

Snatch fishing is never allowed at Rodman Dam. The intent of the prohibition is to encourage fishermen to use an attractant like live bait or artificial lures to catch fish rather than randomly snagging the fish somewhere in the body with a razor-sharp hook and dragging it in. The fish should be given a choice: Do I bite the bait, or don't I?

The question for the fisherman should always be: How can I trick the fish into striking? That's why it's called fishing and not catching.

*　　*　　*

The target of my interest laid his rod and reel down and picked up a steel file. He crouched over and carefully sharpened each of the three barbs on his treble hook. It dulled regularly as a result of being scraped against the concrete wall.

Task completed, he stood up. He leaned over the fence, opened the bail on his spinning reel, and let the line spool free as the weighted hook dropped into the frothy currents. He closed the bail and worked the line up against the cement wall, where the bass bumped their heads as they swam into the flow. He swung the tip of his rod up high and then slowly lowered it, cycling up and down with the steady tempo of a pendulum clock.

A cigarette dangled from the corner of his mouth. If I tried to walk over to him—across one hundred yards of granite boulders—he would casually touch the cigarette's hot ashes to the plastic monofilament line. The line would part, allowing the hook to cleverly disappear into the roiling waters below. He knew the game wardens needed to get their hands on the fish or the hook to make a case against him.

Thirty minutes passed. Suddenly the tip of his rod doubled over. "I got another one," he bellowed.

The fish darted out into the middle of the release waters, pulled downstream under clumps of white frothy foam. The rod tip was jerking, the line stretched taunt. From my position, the line looked like the single strand of a milky-white spider web shining brightly in the clear morning sun.

I couldn't hear the reel's drag over the roar of gushing water pouring through the dam gates, but I imagined the screech of the gears as the fish ripped line from the reel, with the forceful currents helping to push it along. It looked like he'd hooked a good one.

The Cackling Man couldn't stay where he was. The congestion of lines being cast and retrieved by dozens of fishermen on either side of him made it too unwieldy to land a big fish. Instead, he had to move downstream to a grassy area at the base of the spillway where there were fewer anglers.

Holding the rod high above his head, he yelled out: "Fish on. I got a monster! Coming around behind ya! Coming around behind ya!"

Just as he walked behind an old black woman, the fish made an unexpected lunge, yanking the rod down to smack the lady squarely on top of a straw hat that covered her head. With a striking exhibition of elderly dexterity, she spun around and cuffed him with her hat. She sat the hat back firmly atop her head and shook one crooked finger at him. I couldn't hear her voice, but I could hear his, "Whoops! So sorry, ma'am. So sorry. Big fish! Big fish!"

Nonplussed, the Cackling Man careened through the dense crowd, ricocheting his way down the spillway wall. Much to the chagrin of the other fishermen, who bobbed and weaved, swatting away the swinging fiberglass pole whenever it darted their way.

Finally he reached lower ground and walked across the grass and out onto an erosion barrier of rip rap to fight the fish. Balancing precariously on a large rock, he managed to keep his rod tip up, the admonition of every good fishing guide. To drop the tip ensures instant disappointment as the strain transfers from the rod guides to the line, thus ensuring a break.

The fish rose to the surface, struggling against a hook impaled in its tail. The head swung to one side. I could see by its bucket-sized mouth that it was a wall hanger.

The Cackling Man reeled it into shore. He secured it with a thumb lock to the jaw and lifted his trophy out of the water. He performed a slow—not so graceful—pirouette, proudly displaying his magnificent catch for all to see.

No one was smiling.

The fish looked to be well over ten pounds. I prayed he'd keep it. The odds of him getting a larger one were slim.

The Cackling Man made his way back up the rocky embankment, showing the fish off as he went. But there seemed to be a new urgency in his movements now. The bleached white creases between the burnished ropes of belly fat opened and closed with greater frequency. Midway up the embankment, he paused to look around. Then he moved out in the high-speed shuffle of an overweight penguin. His paddlelike feet seemed perfectly tooled to pull his bulk up the incline toward the asphalt parking lot at the top of the dam.

I hung my spotting scope in a Y limb of the tree, shouldered my backpack, and pushed through the brambles and out into the open. I mentally crossed my fingers. If the Cackling Man looked back over his left shoulder, he'd see me. All he'd have to do then was run back to the wall and drop the fish.

He slowed to a lumbering gait as he approached the parking lot. He was beginning to tire. When he was fifty yards away from a white

A lead-head jig (*lower left corner of cooler lid*) was used to illegally snatch these largemouth bass in the belly at Rodman Dam, 1980s.

Nissan pickup truck, I took off at a dead run, leaping from one boulder to the next.

The crowd was silent. I could sense their anticipation. No one warned him I was coming. Not even a peep.

Leaner and more comfortable with a foot scramble than my rotund prey, I managed the uphill, 150-yard climb with little difficulty. I made a midcourse correction as I closed with him, and angled over to his backtrail so he wouldn't spot me out of the corner of his eyes. He walked up to the tailgate of the truck and dropped the fish and his rod and reel into the bed.

He leaned heavy elbows against the tailgate. His sides heaved in and out like a giant accordion. I walked up quietly behind him and tapped him on the shoulder. "State Wildlife Officer. How are you doing today?" I asked.

He waved me off with both hands, in a kind of frantic sign language I interpreted to mean, "For the love of God, can't you see I'm dying here?" I politely waited, allowing him a few moments to catch his breath.

He finally came around, huffing out, "I'd be doing a hell of a lot better if you weren't here."

"I thought you might say something like that."

"What the hell do you want anyway?"

I pointed to the fish lying in the bed of his truck: "I'm fixing to charge you with snatching that largemouth bass."

"Now, that's just total bullshit!"

I normally don't lecture my clients, but I made an exception for him. "You are, without a doubt, one of the rudest, most inconsiderate, insensitive persons I've ever run into at this dam. Your actions today have been solely self-centered. You take exceptional enjoyment in ignoring every rule of common decency involved with good sportsmanship and fair play. I'm going to charge you with illegally snatching largemouth bass, possession of freshwater game fish showing signs of having been taken by an unlawful method [hole in the tail], and I'm going to charge you with willful and wanton waste of wildlife for intentionally injuring those other bass that you threw back to die a slow but sure death. And if you want to continue running that mouth, I will put you in jail. Now, do you have any more questions for me?"

He let out an enormous sigh, shook his head, and said, "No."

I unslung my backpack and laid it on the tailgate of his pickup. I undid the top flap, pulled out my citation book, and began to fill out the paperwork. At the bottom of the citation were several blank lines to be filled in if evidence were seized. I wrote in one largemouth bass, a rod and reel, and a treble hook.

When the Cackling Man saw the evidence listed, he said: "What? You can't take my fish. It's a once-in-a-lifetime trophy. I don't care about the rod and reel, but you got to let me keep my fish."

"Not a chance. The fish goes with me. I'll be giving it to the boys' ranch as soon as I leave here."

"Well, ain't that some shit. Those little juvenile delinquents get to eat my fish."

"Life's a bitch. Get over it." I said sharply. "And they're not juvenile delinquents—they're simply disadvantaged kids. Now, do you remember what I just told you about running your mouth?"

"Yes."

"Very good, then." I handed him my pen and told him to press hard. I tore out the yellow copy and handed it to him.

He crumpled it up and stuffed it in his pocket. Then he wiggled his massive bottom up onto the tailgate and sat down. With no counterbalance, the front end of the truck lifted up perceptibly. He crossed his arms and tucked his chin, watching me like a petulant child who'd been chastised for bad playground behavior.

And that's the way I left him.

The fish had a good heft to it when I picked it up. (It would later weigh in at thirteen pounds.)

I carefully picked my way down the rock-strewn slope to avoid taking a tumble. I was heading for a footpath at the base of the spillway that would take me back to my patrol boat, hidden a half mile away in the Ocklawaha River swamp.

Over the roar of the dam's waters I heard people yelling. I glanced up to a sea of faces looking at me; some were shouting, others waving and clapping. All were smiling. They seemed pleased that I'd caught the Cackling Man. Never one to pass on the moment, I whipped off my ball cap and swept it down low in front of me.

It would be the only time in my career I'd get to take a bow.

9

Reconnaissance

1981, Lake George

It was 3:00 a.m. on a muggy September night as I waded through an eel grass meadow near the shoreline of Lake George. In a sequence of short, tentative half steps, I blindly probed the hard sand bottom, one wader-booted foot at a time. Everything would go along fine until my toe bumped into something hard. Then I'd freeze while my chest tightened into a solid knot, and I'd mutter a silent prayer, "Please don't move." When it didn't, I'd let out a sigh, relieved that it was just another submerged log.

A strong sense of the primordial invaded every pore of my body. The dark of the moon, the dank odor of aquatic vegetation, and the knowledge that enormous alligators were swimming around with impunity completed an otherworldly scene reminiscent of *Jurassic Park*. At the age of twenty-seven, I stubbornly held onto my youthful sense of invincibility, immune to the fact that with bad luck, I could be devoured by a dinosaur.

I pushed on through the knee-deep shallows toward the mouth of a canal that extended landward for a hundred yards. The back of the canal touched the loading platform of an old commercial fish house. The concrete-block and tin-roofed building opened on the canal side, making it an ideal site for a clandestine drop-off of illegal game fish.

To get there by car or truck required a long drive down a dead-end dirt road buffeted by a dense hardwood swamp on both sides. There was no way for me to get a look at the fish house in the daytime, hence my nighttime survey of the premises.

The fish house was owned by a man I will call Mike Blount. He had jet-black hair combed back in a wavy slick and sleepy eyes that bore an uncanny resemblance to the King of Rock 'n' Roll. The likeness had not gone unnoticed by his peers, who pinned him with the nickname Elvis, a moniker that seemed to please him.

It was his coarse, stubby fingers, though, that bore out the truth to his real trade. He was a commercial hoop net fisherman who legally fished for catfish, but who would also run some nets without a locator float, making them hard to find. The hidden nets would have a second funnel modified to catch speckled perch, a freshwater game fish illegal to take by any commercial fishing device.

In the past, I'd hidden in brush along the shoreline and watched Blount through a 20-power spotting scope as he stuffed croker sacks—coarse-woven burlap bags—with the silvery panfish. He'd fill them until the sides nearly burst and then choke the top of each sack off with a precut strip of rubber from an old tire inner tube. Each sack would weigh about a hundred pounds, not counting the chunks of concrete block in the bottom. The added dead weight guaranteed a quick trip down through the tannin-stained waters of the lake should a game warden appear on the horizon.

Lake George is simply too big to effectively sneak up on a commercial fisherman working illegal fish traps in the daytime. At 46,000 acres and forty miles in circumference, it is the second-largest freshwater lake in Florida (only Lake Okeechobee is bigger).

*   *   *

Starlight cast a faint sheen over the canal waters, allowing me to see dim shapes as I groped my way ahead. The dark outline of arrow-shaped pickerel weeds grew in mass along the canal banks. Dark clumps of floating water hyacinths bunched up against my waders. I began to worry about what might lie in wait, motionless under the mats of aquatic vegetation ahead. If a big gator lurked at the end of the canal, I'd be blocking his only path of escape.

But now I could see the dim outline of the square block building in front of me. Just a few more feet and I'd be close enough to see the layout.

Some may wonder why I didn't try to slip up to the fish house on foot. The answer comes in two parts: dogs and legal technicalities.

I narrowly escaped being bitten by two pit bulls on another late-night reconnaissance—at a different location—a few months earlier and did not wish to repeat the experience. Instead, I decided to cast my lot with the gators on a water approach. It afforded me complete silence, facing into a light easterly breeze, which put me downwind from the sniffing noses of alert canines.

The legal issues get sticky, but to make a long answer short, by law I couldn't enter the fish house premises without probable cause (knowledge that contraband such as illegal fish were stored there). But if I kept to the canal, I was fine.

I cupped the lens of my flashlight with one hand and flicked on the switch, so only a weak glow peeked out. Standing in the water next to the loading dock, I swept the diffused beam back and forth inside the building. The light glinted off a metal-sided refrigerated truck body at the back of the building. To the right were two plain wooden doors that opened to the outside. To my left was a storage room with another door. And to my far right was a second room with an open entranceway, where tools and outboard motor parts lay scattered about the floor. Moored against the concrete bulkhead of the loading dock was an eighteen-foot fiberglass Old Timer, powered by a 200 Mercury. The rig had the same basic design as my patrol boat, except this one was painted flat black and mine was olive green.

There was really only one place for me to hide when I came back. I'd have to sit in a swamp on the north side of the fish house. The south side of the canal was an open grassy area with no trees or shrubs or brush to hide me.

I quietly slipped out of the canal and found my patrol boat drifting at anchor where I'd left it a quarter mile away. I threw one foot over the gunwale followed by the other. Then I pulled up the anchor and used an eight-foot oar to pole out to deeper water before cranking the engine and heading home.

*   *   *

I first met Blount after a two-mile open-water boat chase across the south end of Crescent Lake one night. The pursuit had been invigorating, but uneventful. Blount finally stopped after I came alongside his boat and shined my headlamp beam directly into his eyes.

His partner sat quietly in the bow. Both men wore white rubber boots, blue jeans, and T-shirts smeared wet from the damp. The bulkheads held eight hundred pounds of squirming catfish. I suspected they'd been illegally taken with an electric shocking device. Of course, all of the evidence had been thrown overboard. There was nothing left for me to charge them with. No law existed at that time for fleeing or attempting to elude a law enforcement officer on the water.

At this point in my career, with only eight months on the job, I was very "green." Our conversation went something like this: "Bob, how are you doing this morning?" asked Blount, in an amiable tone I found infuriating.

"Don't ever run from me again!" I shouted.

This was only my second boat chase. The first one had happened two hours earlier with another boat that ended with the same result. Totally frustrated, I thought through the problem of not having a fleeing-or-attempting-to-elude law for vessels on the books, but couldn't come up with a satisfactory solution. "How," I wondered, "could the legislature have allowed this to happen?"

"Look here, Bob," said Blount. "There's no use getting upset. You must be kind of hungry after being up all night. How about a chicken-salad sandwich? I've even got some hot coffee in my thermos to go along with it. What do you say?"

"Hell, no! I don't want your sandwich, and I don't drink coffee!"

"Now, Bob," he said in a soft, soothing manner, as if he was lecturing a small child who had misbehaved. "When old Bob Logan [my predecessor] used to stop us, we'd sit here and have a bite to eat, 'chew the fat' and relax for awhile. If it worked out the next night he caught us with the equipment, that was OK. I guess what I'm trying to say is, sometimes things work out in your favor and sometimes they work out in ours. No use getting excited about it. All we're trying to do is make a living."

I thought my head was going to explode. Two boat chases in the same night. No evidence recovered. And now I was being lectured by Blount on how the good guy/bad guy relationship should work.

"Just don't run from me again," I stammered. With that, I cranked my engine and sped off into the night.

In the days that followed, I had time to reflect on my run-in with Blount. I came to realize two things from the encounter: he was one cool customer, and I had a lot to learn about poacher diplomacy.

*   *   *

Tuesday, one week later. By four that morning I was wrestling my patrol boat into a tiny creek swamp north of Blount's fish house. I had to push, shove, and drag it through a maze of fallen trees, dead heads, and free-floating logs. Bubbles of muck gas rose to the surface every time the hull rubbed against a log stuck in the shallow creek bottom.

I figured I'd gone far enough once I made it fifty yards up the narrow tributary. Thick shoreline brush would shield it from any daytime boaters who might happen by. For the moment, there was nothing else to do, so I leaned back in the driver's seat, threw my feet up onto the steering console, and took a short nap.

Two hours later, shafts of angled sunlight broke through the trees. I zipped on a tiger-striped camouflage jumpsuit, pulled on a pair of rubber boots, threw on my backpack, and headed into the swamp. I turned around to check the boat one last time. The bow line was tied securely to a cypress knee, and the boat was completely covered by an olive-green military parachute. Satisfied, I struck out for the fish house.

I sloshed through a quarter mile of murky water to a pair of cypress trees. Like Siamese twins, they had grown together at the base. The trees separated about four feet above the swamp floor, which made for a nifty saddle to hold my gear. I wedged my backpack into the gap and took out my spotting scope. I used both hands to steady it against the tree.

Forty yards ahead of me lay the fish house. I had a profile view of the loading platform's bulkhead. My sight picture through the scope was spotty, though, broken up in places by the low-hanging branches of a sweet gum tree.

I heard a thump and glanced at my watch—7:00 a.m. Another thump. It was Blount and his brother, clumping around the boat in white rubber boots, sorting out their fishing gear. Blount wore a T-shirt under a yellow bib-overall rain suit slicker. His brother wore the same outfit, except his slicker was orange.

Blount cranked the engine and let it warm up. Plumes of thick blue smoke puffed out from the exhaust ports. He pulled away from the dock, pointed the bow toward the lake, and opened up the throttle. The two men disappeared down the canal, leaving a vee-wake in their trail. I tracked the boat's engine by sound as it headed due west. Two minutes later it shut off. They'd stopped about a mile offshore.

An hour later, the boat headed back. Blount ran into the canal on a full plane, settling down into the water with just enough room to maneuver up to the loading platform safely.

His brother reached down below the gunwale, picked up a bulging burlap sack in a two-fisted grip, and heaved it up onto the concrete platform, where it landed with a squishy thud. He grabbed another sack and threw it up next to the first one.

I adjusted the scope's focus dial to zero in on the sacks. I figured I had about a five-second window to see them clearly before they went out of view. I let out half a breath and held it, as if I was taking up the slack on a trigger. The brother leaped out of the boat, grabbed up one sack, and disappeared with it behind a concrete-block wall. In a few moments, he returned for the last sack and went out of sight again. In that brief span of time, I saw what I needed to see: the sharp edges of broken cinder blocks pushing down against the bottom of the bags. Both sacks held illegal game fish.

The brother returned to the boat and sat down next to Blount. They zoomed out of the canal, throwing a wide, frothy wake up on the banks. I had no idea where the fish were hidden, but I decided to slip into the fish house for a quick peek.

It had been three years since my first encounter with Blount.

During that period, I'd devoted many weeks to trying to catch him, with no success. Persistence, I kept telling myself, would eventually prevail over any lack of skill on my part. I hoped my time had finally come. I had to see those fish.

An open door on the north side of the fish house beckoned me, and I walked through it. A balance-beam platform scale stood against the far wall near the tool room. Next to it sat a stack of empty fiberglass fish boxes. No bags were visible. I tested the knob on the storage-room door. Locked. A trail of water drops led from the door over to the loading platform.

Suddenly, I heard their boat coming. Blount had it peeled back. I couldn't risk a trip back to the swamp without being seen. So I slipped into the tool room and stood with my back pressed tightly against the wall just inside the entranceway. The odor of stale motor oil and grease permeated the tight space.

They idled up to the bulkhead. I heard a heavy thud, solid, like block on block, but muffled, and then scraping noises. The storage room door clicked open and quickly slammed shut. Rubber boots scuffed across rough concrete. I tracked the footsteps with my ears, but he didn't get into the boat. He took a detour instead and went over to the door I had walked in through moments before and locked it. Then he went over to the double doors at the front of the building and locked them, rattling the knob for a double-check before getting back in the boat. The boat left again.

When they were out of hearing, I tried the storage room doorknob. Still locked. I walked back to the tool room to wait. I was switched on now, so close to catching Blount I could taste it. I figured nothing could possibly go wrong.

Then I heard a diesel tractor in the far distance. "Not a problem," I told myself. "The guy's probably just working in a cabbage field nearby."

Chug, chug, chug. The engine noise got louder and louder and louder until the tractor was rattling away right outside the fish house doors. The engine shut off. "Good ol' Murphy's law," I thought. "If anything can go wrong it will."

I plastered myself flat against the inner wall of the tool room. If

Four hundred pounds of speckled perch—one of three commercial-quantities cases (more than 150 pounds) the author made at Blount's old fish house, 1980s.

anyone poked their head in, they'd have to crane their neck all the way to the right to see me. Just the thought of being found out irritated the hell out of me. I wanted to catch Blount and his brother clean, with the fish literally in their hands.

The front doors heaved as the tractor driver twisted the doorknob and pulled. He tried again, then went around to the north door and did the same. Dead silence. The tractor left. I finally exhaled.

The boat returned for a third time. The storage-room door opened and bags were dragged out. Fish tumbled into the fish boxes, slapping the sides as they jumped and flipped. A metal clang rang out as a box was set on the balance-beam scale. That was my cue and what I'd been waiting to hear.

I walked out of the tool room and came face to face with Blount. He looked back at me with little interest. "Hey, Bob, didn't expect to see you this morning." He didn't even blink.

There were a total of three fish boxes filled with speckled perch. A full box weighs around 100 pounds. The combined weight easily exceeded the minimum threshold of 150 pounds required by Florida statute for a commercial quantities case. The elevated charge was a first-degree misdemeanor that carried a maximum penalty of one thousand dollars and one year in jail, with a provision for seizure of the boat and motor.

"Mike, you and your brother are under arrest," I said. "If you want to try something we might as well get it over with now." I wasn't sure what to expect, but I always like to get these things out in the open in case the guy has got it in his mind to break bad.

"Bob, I'm not going to give you any trouble," said Blount.

I looked over at his brother. His face was ashen. He shakily lit a cigarette and placed it in his mouth backward, lit end first. I saw the flesh part between his lips. "Aw, shit!" he exclaimed, stomping around the cement floor while flailing his arms. Finally, he let out a bellow, followed by, "Gawd damn, that hurts!"

"I'll bet," I said.

I looked back at Blount; he shrugged his shoulders.

When I said they were under arrest, I didn't place the two men in physical custody by handcuffing them because, well, I kind of needed their help in arresting them. Our issued handheld radios never worked, so I didn't bother to carry one. Even if I went back to my boat, I still wouldn't be able to radio out to dispatch because the swamp was a dead zone.

My last contact with dispatch had been before I left home at 3:00 a.m. I had called in by landline to explain my work plans for a special detail. I never called in on the radio when I intended to work a stake-out. Back then just about every commercial fisherman in Putnam County owned a police scanner that they or their wives monitored 24/7. Some fishermen even set up a voice-activated tape recorder next to the scanner so they could review the previous night's transmissions after they woke up the next morning.

"I don't suppose you'd let me use your telephone to call for some help?" I asked Blount.

"Not a problem," said Blount. "We can walk up to the house and you can make the call from there."

Blount was clever and calculating. When weighed from his point of view, his answer accomplished what he wanted most: to get me off of his property. If he had a problem with the arrest, he'd take it up in the courtroom and not with his fists. The last place he wanted to end up was in felony court.

Within an hour, a couple of wardens showed up to help me.

Blount and his brother were charged with the illegal fishing violation and their boat and motor seized.

They were convicted in county court. Blount, however, appealed his case to the Fifth District Court of Appeal, claiming my entry into the fish house had been unlawful. The appeals court upheld the lower court's decision. Florida Statute 372.76 states, in part, "conservation officers shall have the authority when they have reasonable and probable cause . . . to enter any fishhouse . . . seize any fish or fish nets held therein in violation of law."

During my tour as a water patrol officer on the St. Johns River, I would make two more commercial quantity cases—three hundred pounds (Blount was not involved in this violation) and four hundred pounds respectively—at the old fish house. The sentences meted out by the county court simply weren't enough of a deterrent to persuade Blount or any of his like-minded associates to stop poaching the easily marketed perch.

*   *   *

Author's note: The author understands that Blount has gone straight and has stopped the commercial poaching of speckled perch. The author has no knowledge of any wildlife crimes occurring at the old fish house for more than twenty years.

10

Warden Guy "Gator" Banks

During my thirty years in wildlife law enforcement, I never met anyone quite like Warden Guy "Gator" Banks. Gator, as he is known to
everyone, presented me with a good bit of entertainment as a fellow
officer and more than a few challenges as his supervisor. He was a free
spirit who played by his own set of rules and didn't color between the
lines. Self-assured, he possessed the enviable talent of being able to
talk or fight his way out of most scrapes.

Gator also had an oratory gift for homespun one-liners. His ability
to sum up life's problems in a colorful way led to his cult-like following
with a certain faction of Putnam County's good citizens. Others, however, weren't quite as enamored with his folksy, often plainspoken
manner.

Regardless of how they felt, one thing was for sure. Anyone who
picked up a gun, cast a rod, or hauled a commercial fishing net knew
who Gator Banks was.

*   *   *

Gator came to the St. Johns River patrol crew in 1978, roughly a year
after I arrived. We first met one bright summer morning at a cottage
my wife and I rented at Acosta Creek, a boat marina located on a gently sloping hill north of Welaka, on the St. Johns River. I heard him
drive up and walked outside to greet him.

Warden Guy "Gator" Banks (*left*) and the author at the fuel docks of the old Sunset Landing Restaurant, Welaka, St. Johns River, 1979. By permission of Chris Christian.

He stepped out of his patrol sedan, closed the door, and with both hands carefully adjusted the wide-brimmed Stetson uniform hat. He walked up to me with a cowboy-like swagger and extended one hand, "Hi, I'm Gator Banks." The introduction reminded me of John Wayne striding through the twin doors of a movie-set saloon at high noon. Indeed, at an even six foot, square-jawed, lean, and tautly muscled, he had the self-confidence of a man who knew where he was going and what he was about to do.

It wasn't long, though, before curiosity caught up with me and I asked the inevitable question, the question I would later learn everyone asked him at some point: "How did you end up being called Gator?" Gator, being a natural raconteur, told me the story for a fact.

His father, Fred Banks, was a professional gator hunter back in the 1950s. He caught alligators alive and sold them to tourist attractions up and down the east coast of Florida, which was legal back then.

On the night of December 7, 1951, the night Gator was to be born, Fred was flat broke. He needed cash and he needed it fast. Doctor bills would have to be paid very soon for the delivery of the new baby.

Only one solution awaited Fred: load up the twelve-foot cypress-wood boat into the back of his 1948 Chevy pickup truck and go catch a gator. Fred's wife, Helen, had been in labor for at least a day and a half, so he was in a tricky spot. He needed the money, but he also had to watch Helen. "His logic," Gator explained to me, "was to put her in the boat with him while he hunted. Then he could take care of her if she had any complications."

That night was an unusually warm one for late fall, even in Florida. They caught a hefty eleven-footer down on the St. Johns River, near Picolata, in St. Johns County. Fred trussed the gator up alive and loaded it into the back of his pickup. "It was right about then," as the story was told to Gator by his dad, "that your mama's water broke."

Fred raced Helen to the East Coast Hospital in St. Augustine, where the Police Department is now located. He ran into the emergency room and came back with the doctor and a nurse. "My mother was lying on the front seat of the truck covered in blood," said Gator, "so they popped me out right there.

"The doctor glanced at the cargo in the back of the truck and told Daddy that maybe he should name me Gator. And that's what I've been called ever since."

* * *

We worked the same patrol area on the river for many years until I became his sergeant in 1986. It was as ticklish a job as any supervisor could have, because Gator was something of a nonconformist and

Warden Guy "Gator" Banks checks out the skinned carcass of an alligator dumped by poachers, 1991.

would occasionally break with agency protocol. I thought it had a lot to do with his having left home at the age of fourteen.

Self-sufficiency can come early in life when the tire-storage room of a filling station suddenly becomes your new residence. Gator pumped gas at night and went to school during the day, determined to earn his high school diploma. And he did.

In spite of the motivation behind some of Gator's choices, he had now come under the intense scrutiny of upper management. One escapade in particular became the catalyst for it all and has since become legend within the inner circles of old-time Florida game wardens. (I was an officer at the time.)

It began one day when Gator was on river patrol. He had become bored and decided he would like to kill some wild hogs (which are considered a nuisance in Florida). Having received an invitation from a landowner to kill as many as he would like the day before, it seemed like a good idea to start the killing immediately. Why wait, Gator reasoned, when there's nothing happening on the river right now anyway?

So Gator left the water and headed for the woods—in his marked patrol unit, a forest-green 1975 Plymouth Fury III sedan. In what would later turn out to be a fortuitous decision (one that likely saved his career), Gator, to his credit, told dispatch that he was off-duty.

Gator had a simple plan to kill the hogs. Wait by a hole in the fence where they crossed every evening and shoot as many as he could. Achieving this goal required a firearm that could deliver a steady stream of hot lead downrange. A Ruger Mini-14 semi-automatic rifle loaded with two banana clips taped back to back, each holding ten rounds of .223 caliber ammo seemed like it would do the trick. He carried a third magazine for a spare.

Gator had been putting freshly killed game—marsh hens, coots, ducks, squirrels, rabbits, hogs, and deer—on the family dinner table since he was a young boy. "We pretty much lived off our ability to hunt," recalled Gator. "If we bought processed food, I never knew it. We either caught it or killed it."

Gator sat on the ground about seventy-five yards from the opening in the fence. Close to sundown, the first hog poked its head through and gingerly stepped out into a clearing. Gator squeezed off one shot and down went the hog. Another stepped through, *Crack*, and then another, *Crack*, and yet another, *Crack*. Then the hogs—close to 150 of them—came crashing through the ragged wire opening in a confused frenzy. A steady stream of shiny brass shell casings arced through the air as the pigs tumbled and squealed.

When the smoke cleared, fifteen to eighteen hogs—Gator's memory is foggy here—lay on the blood-drenched earth. Gator had a problem. He had 1,500 pounds of fresh pork and nowhere to put it.

"How," wondered Gator, eyeballing his patrol sedan, "am I going to get these hogs to the butcher shop?" He gave it a little more thought, then walked over to the car and tore out the back seat. Problem solved.

Only one small hiccup marred what should have been a perfect ending to the story.

While traveling out of the woods that day (one of two trips), Gator stopped to chat with three deer hunters. One of them remembered Gator very well. The last time they met, Gator had been a Palatka police officer, and the hunter had been riding handcuffed in the backseat of his patrol car—under arrest for disorderly intoxication. He swore to Gator then he would find a way to get back at him.

The ensuing internal affairs investigation was long and vigorous. The man added fictitious details to the story, saying Gator had also killed a doe deer. That was a criminal violation and, if proven to be true, would mean his immediate dismissal.

In the end, Gator ducked a bullet, figuratively speaking, and was able to keep his job. No deer had been killed, but a pile of hogs had, which Gator freely and honestly admitted. His punishment was swift and sure. He was exiled, banished to serve three months of winter night patrol—in December, January, and February—on Crescent Lake. The orders were explicit. He could not leave the water until his eight-hour shift officially ended.

Gator remained undaunted and not the least worried about the outcome of his misadventure, because he had a plan. Not much happened on Crescent Lake when the temperature dipped below freezing. So to comfortably survive the frigid nights, he loaded an extra six-gallon gas can, a portable television, a chair, a thermos of hot coffee, and plenty of snacks into his patrol boat before each shift began. Then he headed straight to Bear Island, at the southern end of the thirteen-mile-long lake. He tied his boat up to a rickety wooden dock and hauled the gas can up to a dry, sandy clearing. He gathered up cabbage palm fronds and dead limbs and then stacked them into a head-high pile, poured out the gas, lit a match, and poof, instant bonfire, and enough warmth to last until daylight. Then he set the TV on a stump, cranked up the late-night shows, and proceeded to make the best of it.

At the end of his sentence, Gator was well rested and raring to go. But Bear Island would never be the same. Scalped clean of all its cabbage palms for fuel, the sun shone brighter there than it ever had before.

* * *

When I was promoted to lieutenant in 1989, Gator transferred off the water and came to work for me on the land, or "hill," as we like to call it.

A couple of years later, I got a call from the Putnam County Sheriff's Department dispatch late one afternoon. They said Gator was in the hospital emergency room. He'd been in a fight.

By now Gator had taken up weight lifting as a hobby. He'd bulked up considerably. He had the look of a longshoreman who manhandles fifty-five-gallon drums for a living. I figured the extra muscle put him well over two hundred pounds.

Gator also had a background in the martial arts and had been in several backwoods brawls and poker-game fights. He never went looking for a fight, but if one found him he wouldn't shy away from it either. On the few occasions he had to use his fists, he usually prevailed, a result of a no-holds-barred mentality learned from his father.

The first time he saw his daddy defend himself was at a turkey shoot—Gator would have been nine or ten at the time. In the early 1960s, they regularly attended these contests at bars and fish camps all over St. Johns County (located between Putnam County and the Atlantic Ocean). The rules were simple: Each shooter paid a dollar entry fee, which allowed them to fire one shot from a 12-gauge shotgun firing No. 8 pellets at a 10" × 10" white card target with an X drawn in the center. Closest pellet to the center of the X won the contest. Back then a turkey shoot meant big-money side bets, with the winner taking home a live turkey or the cash equivalent, about five to six dollars.

One Saturday they ended up at Palmo Fish Camp, about five miles south of State Road 16, on the St. Johns River. "We already had all of the turkeys we could eat," said Gator, "so Daddy took the cash instead. He won eleven of the twelve turkeys that day. Then some of the contestants accused him of shooting a trick gun or having fixed shells."

In shooting contests, an old adage floats around that goes something like this, "Beware of the man with one gun, because he knows how to use it." And so it was with Fred and the only gun he ever owned, a 12-gauge, Model 12 Winchester pump shotgun with a full choke. It patterned best when the bead was aimed at the left bottom corner of the target, about five to six inches from the center.

Warden Guy "Gator" Banks holds a Model 12 Winchester 12-gauge pump shotgun, just like the one his daddy used to win turkey shoots when he was a kid, 2011.

"That was the trick," Gator told me, "in knowing where to aim the gun. And we never fixed our shells by pouring corn syrup onto the pellets to make them stick together and shoot a tighter pattern. Daddy always shot factory loads. Anyway, Daddy pointed to the table where the gun lay and said, 'There's the gun and there's the shells, go ahead and shoot it.'

"Of course, some folks can't be satisfied, particularly if they've been sipping moonshine. A couple of them jumped on my daddy, and that was a horrible mistake. He was a carpenter back then and believed there was no problem in the world that a hammer couldn't solve. I learned right then that there's no such thing as a fair fight."

*   *   *

Earlier in the day that Gator got into a fight, he'd been off-duty, driving his personal truck south on Stokes Landing Road toward his home in Palatka. Two kids, probably no more than six or seven, were riding their bicycles in the middle of the two-lane blacktop, when a shiny blue Ford Ranger pickup truck crossed over the double yellow lines and whooshed past Gator doing close to a hundred in a forty mile-per-hour speed zone. The kids dove into a ditch. "I stopped to check on them," said Gator. "I thought one of them might have gotten clipped. When I saw that neither one was hurt, I decided to follow the truck. This guy was out of control. He needed to be stopped before somebody got hurt."

The Ranger pickup turned into a residence at the end of a dead-end road, and Gator drove in behind it. "I got out of my truck and held up my badge," said Gator. "He steered right for me."

Gator sidestepped the pickup's front bumper just as it grazed his left leg. He ran his left arm and shoulder into the half-opened driver's window and locked his fingers around the driver's throat in a death grip (a procedure not taught in any law enforcement academy). "Now he's dragging me backward across the front lawn," recalled Gator. "I thought if I grabbed hold of his throat he would stop. All he did was crank up the window and give it more gas."

Gator kept the heel of his hand jammed into driver's throat, while his fingers clawed at the bottoms of his eye sockets. By now Gator's feet churned furiously in reverse. Every time the truck hit a dip, his body whipped into the cab's side like a rolled-up towel being snapped in gym class.

Finally, the pickup ran into a tree in the backyard and came to an abrupt halt. "I tried to bust the window out with my right fist," said Gator. "When that didn't work, I forced my left shoulder through the window and was able to get it down enough to jerk my left arm out. I snatched the door open and threw him out of the truck, and that's when the fight started.

"This guy was twenty-six years old, about five ten, and in top-notch shape, as wiry as a palmetto. I couldn't lift my left arm. It was completely limp. So I hit him with a right, and he went down. He spun back off the ground like a damn coil spring and hit me square in the chest with a spinning back kick. It knocked the breath right out of me. The kid was hopped up on drugs and had some crazy power.

"I ran my right arm and biceps under his throat, cocked my elbow back, and tried to snap his neck. I pulled him around so hard his feet came literally off the ground above my head. I heard his neck crack and dropped him to the ground. When I reached down to check his throat for a pulse, he hit me between the eyes with a closed fist full of dirt and broke my glasses. I was cut and bleeding. Blinded, except for a little bit I could see out of my right eye."

The driver broke and ran for the house, and Gator retreated to his truck, grabbed an old bag telephone (original cell phone), and called the sheriff's office for backup. "He came out of the house carrying a .410-gauge bolt-action shotgun and stood on the porch, screaming for me to go away," said Gator. "I told him, 'I'm not going anywhere. One of us is going to die right here, or both of us, because I ain't leavin' until you put that gun down and give it up.' The only gun I had was a .380 six-shot pistol I had pulled out from the side-door pocket of my truck. He carried the shotgun cross-armed and never pointed it at me. I had made up my mind if he brought the gun down on me, I would shoot him."

A few minutes later a Putnam County sheriff's deputy arrived on the scene carrying a Heckler and Koch MP5 submachine gun. He chased the bad guy around the corner of the house and was able to arrest him without further incident.

*   *   *

When I arrived at the hospital, Gator was standing up with his left arm in a sling. He was covered in filth, his blue jeans torn and tattered, the broken glasses stuffed in the pocket of a once-white T-shirt.

"Son of a bitch hurt my shoulder bad," he told me. "Damn near ripped it from the socket."

"Well," I said, "I'm happy to see you one piece. It could have gone a lot worse for you. How bad is the suspect hurt?"

"I don't know. They transported him here because they thought I'd broken his neck. But just before you came, the doctor told me an X-ray showed it wasn't broken."

"What a shame."

I motioned to a table in a break room. "Why don't you come in here and sit down for a while?"

"Why?"

I waved a folder full of forms at him. "We have to fill out the workman's comp paperwork."

Postscript

Gator was released with bumps and bruises and a badly wrenched shoulder, which would require a complete joint replacement later in his life. Even after the surgery, he is still unable to raise his left arm above shoulder level.

As it turns out, the bad guy had been out on bond, having been arrested only two weeks before the altercation with Gator for firing four or five bullets through a plate-glass window of a motel in St. Augustine. Eventually, he was sent to prison.

After a *thorough* review, management awarded Gator the Superior Accomplishment Award for Heroism & Valor.

Well deserved, I might add.

11

Night Chase on the St. Johns River

Of the many poachers I've chased, none caused me more frustration than Roger Gunter, who had the rare talent to sense when a game warden was hot on his trail. Some might call it good luck, others an intuitive ability to feel the moment.

I wasn't sure how he did it, only that in the summer of 1988, Warden Gator Banks and I had had enough. In June, we'd struck out on five all-night river stakeouts. Now it was the first week of July and still no sign of him—until dispatch called me at home one evening. A confidential informant reported that Gunter would be electric-fishing that night. I called Gator, and we scrambled to go. Maybe, we told ourselves, this would be our lucky break.

July 10, 1988

A moonless night provides the best cover. And that cover afforded a blanket of concealment for Gator and me as we sat quietly in our patrol boats, drifting with our lights out in the gentle currents of the St. Johns River. Five miles to our south, the glow of Palatka's streetlights on the horizon created a black void between it and where we waited near the mouth of Rice Creek. A mile or so to our west, the pumps and machinery were audibly grinding away at the Georgia-Pacific Paper Mill.

We'd been on stakeout since midnight, and it was an hour before predawn when we first spotted the flicker from a boater's headlamp several miles to our south. It wasn't much to study—just a few faint blips on the horizon. But it drew our attention as we focused our binoculars on the vessel.

The boat headed our way, but not before it made a brief stop at each channel marker, where the current slackened on the downstream side. These calmer waters were natural fish-holding areas, and poachers knew it.

Like a firefly trapped in a bottle, the boat operator's headlamp bobbed and weaved as he scurried from one end of the boat to the other, frantically scooping up catfish with a long-handled dip net. A distant *thump, thump, thump* echoed out as he beat the net against the bulkheads, knocking loose the catfish whose spines had become entangled in the webbing.

These sights and sounds were familiar to Gator and me. They were the signature of a "monkey-fisherman"—someone who used an electric shocking device to illegally catch catfish.

After a couple of minutes, the light blinked out. The whine of a powerful outboard engine reverberated across the water as the boat planed off. It ran "black," or without lights, to the next navigation aid. Gator and I set our binoculars down and began to get ready. It was Roger Gunter, the man we'd been waiting for.

The Other Boat

Slick with catfish slime, the fiberglass deck of the other boat made for unsure footing. Gunter ignored the slippery peril beneath his bare feet. Dashing from one end of his eighteen-foot Old Timer to the other, he scooped up splashing fish before they swam beyond the reach of his fourteen-foot aluminum dip net. But he never forgot about the open center-hold[1] in his haste, where one slip would mean

---

1. The center-hold is formed by two fiberglass dividers, permanent fixtures set crossways in the boat and about six feet apart. The purpose of the dividers is to contain the fish in the middle of the vessel and to keep them from spilling into the bow, or driver's area.

instant and blinding pain from the ice pick–like spines of hundreds of writhing catfish.

The muscles in his arms and back ached from hefting the awkward metal net. He liked a metal handle over a wooden one because it sank. The dip net had to be on the river bottom in seconds if the game warden showed up. For added insurance, he'd drilled holes every eight inches along the handle so air would escape from inside the hollow metal tube.

The strain of this night and the previous night had begun to wear on him. This would be his second all-nighter without sleep. Trying to juggle his job at the paper mill along with electric-fishing had always been a challenge.

Finished with netting all the stunned fish in the immediate vicinity of his boat, Gunter took a break to look and listen. He sat quietly while he scanned the horizon in a 360 all the way around his boat. Then he closed his eyes and concentrated on the night sounds. Sorting through the background noise of motorcycles and tractor-trailer rigs crossing Palatka's Memorial Bridge far to the south, he strained to hear the gentle thrum of a game warden's outboard engine creeping up on him.

He opened his eyes and asked himself, "What's out of place?" He took in the twinkling lights of waterfront homes, the blinking reds and greens of channel markers, and the streaming reds from distant car taillights whipping across the Memorial Bridge. Everything seemed to fit. It was time to go.

Gunter cranked the 225 Yamaha and let it idle. He flipped open the lid to a small cooler and pulled out a bottle of Budweiser. Twisting off the cap, he took a long, slow sip, savoring the bitter nectar for just a moment before snuggling the bottle between his legs. He eased the throttle forward and felt the cool breeze brush his skin as he rushed off into the night.

Life was good for Gunter with five hundred pounds of catfish in the boat's hold and just a few channel markers to go. By daylight he'd have the fish sold for a tidy sum, a healthy supplement to his income from the mill.

The other boat zoomed out of the pitch-black gloom. Gator and I tracked its racing silhouette as it briefly blocked out house lights along the far shore like falling dominos. Then it powered down, settling into the water with a soft *kersplash* near a blinking red channel marker only a hundred yards away. The headlamp popped on. Gunter began to scoop catfish knocked momentarily senseless by the electric shock as they zigzagged and rolled, boiling the water into a froth.

Gator untied a line that had lashed our boats together and pushed away. I grabbed hold of a nylon string hanging down from my headlamp—a hardhat with an aircraft landing light mounted to it—and twisted it with my fingers to take up the slack. I bit down on it to keep the light firmly attached to my head. I set out a couple of marker buoys by my feet. Made from empty plastic soap bottles, twine, and lead weights, the homemade floats, once deployed, provided a reference point when we came back later to search for evidence thrown into the water. Lastly, I attached the kill switch lanyard to my life vest.

I was ready.

Gator and I had previously decided who would take the lead on Gunter. It had not been a difficult decision. The shallow-draft, seventeen-foot fiberglass Blazer bass boat I was driving sat only eighteen inches out of the water. Powered by a 150 Mercury, it handled hairpin turns like a race car in the Monte Carlo Grand Prix. Gator's boat, however, was a high-sided, eighteen-foot fiberglass Answercraft, powered by a 175 Mercury. I likened it to a Volkswagen bus lumbering down the highway, albeit a pretty quick one.

I would go first.

The other boat's light shut down. Its engine revved up as the prop caught hold of solid water.

I shifted into forward gear. Like a skeet shooter aiming ahead of his target, I pointed my boat where I thought the other boat would cross in front of me.

The bow of Gunter's boat rose up, peeling back a pearly white wake in the starlight. I shoved the foot throttle to the deck, the hull hesi-

The author's three-year-old son, Jason, sits behind the wheel of his seventeen-foot Blazer patrol boat, 1987.

tated while the propeller gathered water and then shot off like a dart. It felt like riding a surfboard with an engine strapped to it.

I toggled my headlamp on. The 110,000-candlepower beam cut through the inky black, casting a circle of blinding white light around a black, eighteen-foot Old Timer plowing through the water thirty yards ahead. The driver snapped his face away from the light as I barreled in toward his starboard side. His stringy, reddish-blond hair stood up in a gust of wind as his right hand slammed the throttle wide open.

We were off.

My world had suddenly been reduced to the screaming whine of outboard engines, siren wails, flashing blue lights, and the steady sweep of my headlamp beam. My radio speaker couldn't project over the racket. I couldn't talk to dispatch—or even Gator, for that matter.

I felt the adrenalin dump. The involuntary shaking and tightness of vision was a problem for me in the first minutes of a pursuit. The only way I knew to overcome it was to keep breathing. Concentrating on making my diaphragm move in and out seemed to help.

My hull slapped the water as I skipped over Gunter's starboard wake before making a hard right that brought me in tight behind his transom. "This is as real as it gets," I told myself, eyeballing the narrow gap of only a yard or so between my bow and the backside of his engine cowling.

The cone from my headlight beam shone straight ahead. But the only thing I could see was the other boat's propeller spray as it crystallized in the bright light, blinding me in a silver-white sheen of oily water droplets. Those droplets blasted right up my nose. The burnt residue dribbled down the back of my throat, causing me to hack up nasty petrol-coated phlegm, a pungent reminder that this wasn't a video game.

Years ago a boat-racing mechanic had advised me to stay out of the "dirty water," or prop wash, where the chase boat's speed could be decreased by a mile and a half an hour. I nudged my steering wheel to the right until I was riding in the calmer water outside of Gunter's wake.

Gunter led me north downriver toward Jacksonville, the largest city on Florida's northeast coast. It was an hour away at the speed we were traveling—about sixty miles per hour.

Gunter started to make large, sweeping turns from shoreline to shoreline and a mile or more apart. I wasn't sure why he was driving in this S-shaped pattern. It seemed like a tactic designed to draw me into the turbulent water of the engine's prop wash. If I fell into his trap, the gap between us would gradually widen to the point where I would lose sight of his transom and then the race would be over.

Gunter Flees

Gunter jerked his face away from the light while he slammed the hand throttle forward and mashed the up-trim button. The bow of his boat lifted up, but not as fast he would have liked. He did a quick calculation and figured the extra weight from the fish would cost him five to ten miles per hour top end. But he'd been here before and knew that game wardens used a variety of boats. Most of them couldn't stay with his, and that's what he was hoping for now, even with the extra weight handicap.

Gunter snuck a quick glance over his shoulder and saw the green and red navigation lights of a boat falling back. But the other boat, the one with the spotlight, was tucked in right behind his transom. It looked like neither of them would have a speed advantage. Whoever won this race would probably be the one who had the most gas. He'd already burned most of his in a run to Crescent Lake and back, a round trip of sixty miles. And now he was running dangerously low on fuel.

Gunter scooted down in his seat and gripped the steering wheel with both knees. He gathered up the wires from the monkey machine that lay in a tangled heap by his feet. He wound them tightly around the device, made up of a short wooden board—about eighteen inches long—that an antique telephone magneto and electric motor were strapped to. Should he be forced to throw the device, one loose wire might accidentally wrap around the propeller and bring his boat to a dead stop.

Gunter glanced up just in time to see the rapidly approaching shoreline. He snatched the wheel hard—in time to avert a crash by steering back toward the river channel. He repeated the maneuver several times before the monkey machine and wires were wrapped into a neat package.

Job done. Gunter sat up straight. He snatched up the beer and guzzled down the rest before tossing the empty bottle into the river. Then he scanned the shoreline, tracking subtle changes in the terrain as it contrasted against the gray-black, star-speckled sky. The river curved to the left a couple of miles ahead, where it made the hard turn to the north near Palmetto Bluff. He would have to shave the west shoreline close in order to miss the pound net—a gigantic commercial fishing trap made of stout cypress poles and thick webbing—a couple miles past the bend.

The Game Wardens Continue the Pursuit

My headlight beam was sucked up into the night every time I shined it to either side of Gunter's transom. With no backdrop, nothing reflected back at me, as the shoreline was too far away to illuminate. It was like looking into a black hole with no reference points to orient myself by. Ironically, Gunter, who was running without lights, had the advantage of being able to pick out key landmarks along the shoreline and use them to gauge where we were at.

Ten miles into the pursuit, neither one of us had gained or lost any ground. I sensed Gator was somewhere behind me, probably following the back-glow of my headlight. But I had no way to estimate how far or how close he might have been to me.

It was time to change tactics.

I shut off my lights and siren and eased in behind Gunter's outboard. I was snugged in tight, hoping to hide in his prop spray. It was a ruse to trick him into thinking I'd broken off the pursuit. "If he thinks the threat is gone," I told myself, "maybe he'll back his speed down a smidgen." Then I could come alongside and take care of business.

The trick didn't work, but it did give me an opportunity to look out into the horizon and check for landmarks. I could see we'd come around the bend at Palmetto Bluff. The pound net was somewhere up ahead, extending out from the west bank. I thought I was far enough out into the river to avoid it when Gunter wheeled hard left into the shore.

I flipped my light on him and saw he was running outside of a patch of cattails in shallow water. "Not a problem," I thought, "I've got him pinned between the bank and my boat."

I swung my light back in front of my bow. My heart skipped a couple of beats. Out of the gloom emerged the pound net—dead ahead, only two seconds out.

A pound net is a formidable device: two hundred feet of thick webbing and vertical cypress poles that project out in a straight, perpendicular line from the shoreline into a box or pound. The pound is constructed of thick cypress poles staked out in fifteen-foot-deep water, overlaid with horizontal cross members constructed in a 20' × 20'

Pound nets can be an extreme hazard during a boat chase.

square, a huge bag of webbing hangs from the cross members, dropping straight to the bottom. It acts like a giant fish corral and can catch
up to two thousand pounds of catfish in a week's time.

I took a mental snapshot of the picture before me and realized I'd
miss the pound, the most dangerous part of the net to collide with.
But I still had to cut through the "lead," or line of webbing extending
out from the shore, and split it between two cypress poles. I nudged
my bow a tad to port and passed between them in a blur. At 6,000
revolutions per minute, my boat prop cut through the net like a hot
knife through butter.

I shifted my beam back to where Gunter had been moments before.
He'd vanished. In those couple of lost seconds, we'd spread far enough
apart that I'd lost sight of him.

I turned into the shoreline and picked up the bubble trail from
Gunter's outboard and followed it for a mile out into the middle of
the river before losing it all together.

It was over.

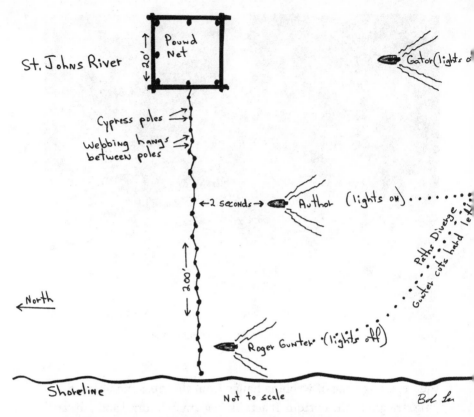

The Gunter boat chase, as the three boats approached the pound net. Sketch by author.

I throttled back and let the hull settle into the water. I was in a deep funk. This had been a contest, much like a chess match, and I didn't like losing.

"Hey, boss," said Gator, as his voice crackled over my radio speaker. "You better come back here and help me out."

I looked back toward the pound net and saw a headlamp beam bouncing around inside it. I grabbed the mic: "Are you all right?"

"Yeah, I'm fine. I've just got a little problem with the boat. Did you see enough to make the case?"

We talked for a few more seconds before I hung up the mic and headed over to him. I came alongside the pound net and grabbed a wooden cross-beam to steady my boat. And there was Gator, leaning back comfortably in the driver's seat, his feet propped up on his boat's gunwale, drinking a cup of hot coffee from his thermos bottle.

His patrol boat was impaled dead center into the pound, or box part, of the net. Broken cypress poles and pieces of bark littered the deck, along with a broken windshield.

"Looks like you had an exciting night," I said. "How did you keep from getting your head torn off?"

"Ducked," said Gator. "I actually saw it a few moments before impact and had started to back the throttle down before I hit it."

"Good for you."

"By the way, I thought you knew where you were going," said Gator, quietly eyeing me over the rim of his coffee cup. "After all, you are the boss." Like a good wingman in a fighter-jet squadron, Gator had been trailing me lights-out, running blind, when he hit the net.

"Um," I said. "Well—"

"Let me help you out with that. Roger got the best of you, didn't he?"

"Ah . . . yes," I said, with a big sigh.

"Now, see, doesn't that feel better?"

"Not really."

Gunter Continues to Run

The light behind Gunter disappeared. He looked over both shoulders and wondered, "Where in the hell did he go to? That sneaky bastard's up to something."

Gunter looked ahead for some clue of where the pound net was. He had to make sure he missed it, and then he'd worry about how to shake the warden.

He wheeled hard left toward shore at the same time he looked back over his right shoulder and saw a dark streak heading toward the net. "There that son of a bitch goes," he thought. "He's done screwed up now."

Gunter cut across a shallow flat of eel grass until he met a strand of cattails, where he turned to run a parallel track alongside of them. He'd just congratulated himself on missing the net, when he felt a good jolt. His bow had sheared through one of the poles, sending a forearm-sized piece of cypress spinning lengthwise down the boat. It smacked him on top of the head before careening off into the night.

Gunter let out one long, lonely howl that was swallowed up by the wind. He swiped his hand across the top of head but didn't feel any blood.

Still conscious, he looked back in a wobbly gaze and saw that the warden had turned into the shore, sweeping his headlight back and forth searching for him. Gunter turned hard right and kept turning right as he crossed the two-mile-wide river, turning back to the south along the opposite shoreline. Ultimately, the teardrop-shaped maneuver would cause him to loop back into his original path several miles to the south.

As Gunter approached Federal Point—an elbow of land sticking out into the river—he checked behind him one more time. Satisfied, he faced forward again, only to see a long apparition appear out of the dark. "Son of a bitch!" he yelled.

Directly ahead was a wooden dock, 300 feet in length. He scanned left to right and saw an opening to his right, where there should have been support pilings. He shot through it, hunching down for the impact to come. Perhaps it was divine intervention, or maybe good luck, but Gunter had driven through the only section of the dock under construction. The missing posts would be replaced the next day.

Gunter powered down and eased into a patch of cattails just beyond the dock and shut his engine off. He twisted long stems up into a clump so he could wrap the wires of his monkey machine around them to keep it hidden and out of the water. He dropped his dip net alongside the machine so it rested atop dense mats of vegetation between the reeds. He put his engine in reverse and backed out into the river.

He was motoring south toward Rice Creek when the outboard coughed twice and sputtered to a stop. "God damn," he thought. "This just isn't right. I've beat these bastards, and now I run out of gas. They'll be heading back this way any minute."

Gunter jumped out of his seat and spread his legs wide. He frantically rocked the boat back and forth, trying to jiggle the last few drops of precious gas out of the fuel tank and into the engine. He dropped down into the driver's seat and tried the key. The starter spun a couple of times before the engine caught.

Fish Creek was off to his right. It was the closest place to hide. He idled up it, carefully picking his way through the log-strewn waters until he came to a shallow slough, where he eased his boat in behind a clump of cypress trees. He shut off the engine and leaned back in his seat to rest for a moment. The morning light began to creep through the river swamp. It was pleasant and quiet, just like the swamps along Rice Creek where he'd been raised.

Gunter could barely hear a garbled voice coming from the police scanner that hung from a knob on the steering console. He turned up the volume.

" . . . did you see enough to make the case?" Gator's drawling voice crackled.

"I know it was his boat," I responded, "but I never saw his face. And you know Roger. He'll lawyer up if we try to interview him. I have to be able to put him behind the steering wheel of that boat to make an arrest. And I can't do it. We've lost him again."

Gunter cracked a tight-lipped smile, "This is just too much fun," he addressed the awakening creatures of the day and tipped a beer in celebration.

12

Thanksgiving Turkey

On a Wednesday afternoon, the day before Thanksgiving, I was about midway through my daily jog on a scenic out-and-back course that wound through an 8,500-acre tree farm in south Putnam County. The air was chilly and the sky clear—perfect conditions for a six-mile cross-country run.

I had no expectations on this day other than to finish. Usually my runs were bereft of any excitement except for the occasional toe-trip on an exposed root, followed by a hard thump, and me spitting out a mouthful of dirt and leaves. Then there were those rare occasions when I did a quick side-step to dodge a coiled rattlesnake that lay directly in my path. Those were terrifying encounters that left me shaky and wobbly-kneed for sure, but those instances, thankfully, were few. So I loped along with a wary eye on the ground ahead, content to enjoy the glorious pine-scented air.

The terrain was a quilted patchwork of cutover tracts, planted pines, shallow ponds, and a creek that carved a narrow gouge through gently rolling sandhills. On the eastern side of the property lay a dense loblolly bay swamp. Bears liked the secretive, nearly impenetrable understory of twisted wait-a-minute vines and devil's walking stick. Numerous deer and wild turkey fed across the park-like landscape with little fear of humans, the result of a strict "no hunting" policy by the landowners.

My turnaround point for today's run stood no more than the length of a football field in front of me. Making it to the metal cattle gate meant I'd hit the three-mile mark. The mental boost, the positive psychological shift in knowing there was less rather than more to go always felt good. I looked forward to it.

The distance to the gate lessened with each stride as I plodded ahead, struggling through soft, sugary sand that offered scant traction. My size 12, extrawide running shoes performed like snowshoes under these conditions. They sank four to five inches with each flat-footed step before I could shove off from the firmer ground below.

To travel through these woods alone, totally focused on plowing through the loose soil put me in a Zen-like state, where I could soak in the calm and the peace and the quiet.

Boom!

The shotgun blast rang out crisp and clear in the dry autumn air. It had come from Old Welaka Road, an unpaved county road that ran in front of the gate. I sprinted ahead. I wanted to get a glimpse of the shooter before he fled.

I leaped up onto the middle rung of the gate, standing tall with my feet arched and my calves stretched. Now I could see above the roadside brush and east, down the road in the direction of the gunshot. A midsized white Toyota pickup truck sped over a hilltop, streaming a trail of dust in its wake.

I vaulted over the gate and hit the ground running. My feet adjusted to the packed dirt and switched over naturally to a heel-to-toe stride. Being sensitive like most runners are to the ground beneath them, I felt like I'd been freed from a tether.

I needed to locate the exact spot the shooter fired the gun from. The pickup's tire tracks would be the first clue to examine. Since the Toyota was the last vehicle to travel along the road, its tire sign would lie on top of all the other tire tracks.

I zeroed in on a spot a quarter mile ahead on the south side of the road, where the truck had pulled over.[1]

Road hunters often flee immediately after shooting an animal and return some time later to pick it up. Usually they put the gun up and may even switch vehicles. This gives them plausible deniability if they're stopped by a game warden: "Officer, you can look through my truck all day long. I got nothing to hide."

The more important question for me was, How long before the shooter returned? It could be minutes, or it could be hours. I decided not to dawdle around. He could show back up at any moment to recover the downed animal, whatever it was. And when he did come back, I expected him to be switched on, all nervous and twitchy-like, with his head on a swivel.

I covered the quarter mile in less than ninety seconds. Now I was standing where the truck had stopped. I sniffed the air eagerly. The faint odor of burnt gunpowder hung like an invisible cloud around me. I did a quick 360 sweep. There, not thirty yards away, lay a dead hen turkey in the brown, frostbitten Bahiagrass. Its gray-blue head and neck were twisted all askance, the result of its final death throes.

I looked around for somewhere to hide. "Where," I wondered, "were the jettisoned junk refrigerators and washing machines when I needed one?" The back roads of Putnam County were infamous for the copious amounts of litter dumped there, and now there was none to be found. Disappointed, I continued to search for a suitable place to hide one skinny white man dressed in a pair of brief jogging shorts and running shoes.

The bird lay behind a barbed wire fence and inside the tree farm, surrounded by sparsely planted two-foot-high pine trees. The young trees were topped with lamp shade–sized crowns of thick green pine needles—not nearly big enough to provide me with cover. But seventy-five yards beyond the bird and up a shallow slope grew a lone

---

1. Human nature follows a set of learned behaviors. All drivers have been programmed to pull off to the side if they plan to stop. Therefore, even on a remote, rural road, a poacher will often unconsciously turn the steering wheel and edge toward the road shoulder before coming to a stop.

cabbage palm. The Florida state tree would have to do. This one was a healthy specimen. Nearly forty feet high, with a thick crown of sagging, dark-green fronds atop a trunk scaled with old leaf-stem bases all the way to the ground. These leaf-stem bases—very brittle and jagged when dead—poked out up to a foot from the main trunk. They made it impossible to snuggle up against the trunk without being gouged. To make it work, I would first have to snap them off from the ground up to about my height. Then I could tuck in tight behind the trunk, maybe even turning sideways to remain hidden from the shooter when he returned for his prize.

I walked up to the nearest fence post, put both hands on top of it, and pushed down, raising my upper body up—picture a pommel horse gymnast—and over the top strand of barbed wire. The legs, of course, must follow. The trick was to put a bare amount of weight onto the middle strands with each foot as I climbed over. I never fell using this method, or damaged a fence.

The digital readout on my watch said 4:30 p.m. It would be dark in two hours. I hoped the shooter planned to come back in the daylight. What I was about to do broke every rule in the then Game and Fresh Water Fish Commission policy and procedure manual about how to apprehend a suspect. While I waited behind the cabbage palm, I added them up: I had no gun, no handcuffs, no flashlight, no radio, no badge, and no one knew what I planned to do, or for that matter where I was.

My decision to *go* would be based on how many people showed up and if guns were displayed. If it looked like I could pull it off, I'd go for it. Otherwise, I'd observe and then come back later in uniform and find the culprit(s).

Seldom does a good game case appear on a silver platter. The temptation to catch this guy was enormous. I was still conflicted, though. "I really shouldn't be doing this," I told myself.

It got colder with every minute that ticked by. The light sheen of sweat I'd worked up during the run had begun to feel like ice water. The air temperature was hovering in the upper-forties and I wasn't even wearing a T-shirt. Shivering, I jumped up and down behind the palm tree, hugging my chest and trying to stay warm.

After thirty minutes, the faint whine of a four-cylinder engine wavered faint then loud, then faint again, as it traveled up and down the low hills coming my way. The Toyota truck broke over the top of the closest knoll and drove past where the turkey lay.

I flattened myself against the cabbage palm and peeked around one side. The midsized truck traveled a quarter mile before it made a three-point turn and came straight back, rolling to a stop alongside the fence. The bird now lay between me and the lone man who sat behind the steering wheel of the truck.

He was jittery, I could tell. I'd seen that owl look before. His neck twisted back and forth while he panned the horizon. Then he shot a nervous glance into the rearview mirror before he dropped his gaze to look through the front windshield and beyond. He alternated between the two sight planes so he could keep tabs on traffic that might approach from the rear or ahead. Finally, the driver's door swung open. He walked around to the tailgate and affected a nonchalant poise, both elbows resting on the tailgate—the prequel, I was sure, for his next move.

Intuitively, I could feel him gather his nerve up to go for it. He was gaunt, about my height, with brown, close-cropped hair, wearing blue jeans and a camouflaged hunting jacket. The obvious lack of body fat told me he had the potential to offer some good sport in a foot race.

He suddenly dashed for the fence, scrambled over the top, and ran full-tilt for the bird, chest forward, arms pumping furiously.

The best time to step out on a suspect is not when they're facing you. If conditions allowed for it, I liked to come up from behind. I waited for a few more seconds. Timing, after all, is everything.

He picked up the turkey and whirled around for the return trip. I dashed out from behind the palm and barreled downhill. The accelerated pull of gravity on the declining slope gave me great speed, and I caught up with him before he reached the fence. He never heard me. His feet were slapping the ground so hard they drowned out the noise of me pounding up behind him. I tapped him lightly on the left shoulder. When he turned his head to look, I leaned down and snatched the turkey out of his right hand and said, "You're caught."

He spun back to his right. The color drained from his face. His mouth and lips were quivering, like a fish out of water, but no words came out. I took this to be a favorable sign.

"Do you know who I am?" I asked.

"Yes . . . you're Bob Lee . . . the game warden," he said shakily.

"Excellent! Then you know why I'm here."

"Listen," he blurted out. "I know I've done a bad thing, but I didn't have no money for a Thanksgiving turkey and I promised my ol' lady I'd get her one. And now I'm caught; ain't this some shit? My ol' lady is going to be so pissed. I guess you're going to take me to jail now."

"Actually, no, I don't plan on it as long as you cooperate with me. I'll issue you a citation and send you on your way. I'm actually a pretty decent guy once you get to know me." (You've got to lay it on thick when you don't have a gun.)

"Oh, that would be great."

"Technically though, you've really screwed up, because you shot this turkey inside private property that's fenced. I could charge you with felony trespass. But I'm not. I know the owners well, and I think they'll go along with me if I just charge you with taking a hen turkey during the closed season and illegally hunting from a county road. Do you have any firearms in your truck?"

"No. I put my shotgun up at the house before I come back for the turkey."

"OK, I need for you to drive me up to the outboard repair shop in Welaka. I'll have someone bring me my citation book, and then I'll kick you loose after I've issued you the citation."

He drove me up to the shop, where I called my wife.

She brought me my citation book and identification. I showed him my badge just to make sure I went by the book—finally. As I began to fill out the citation, he started "working me."

"I hate to ask you this," he said, "but do you think you could get the fine reduced? Me and the ol' lady are in a real tight for money. I have my own lawn business, and things haven't been going well lately. I don't supposed you'd let me keep the turkey too. Thanksgiving is tomorrow."

He seemed like a decent sort. I'd heard he was an OK guy, someone who was just trying to get along as best he could. In a town with a population of only 546, you can pretty well keep tabs on who's doing what.

"Here's what I'll do for you," I said. "I can't lower the fine, but I'll talk to the clerk's office and have a note sent to the judge. I'll suggest lowering it to under a hundred bucks. I have to keep the turkey because it's contraband. I'll receipt it to a needy family here in Welaka when we're done. And one more thing, I'm going to let you keep the shotgun and your truck. By law I could seize both."

"Holy cow," he said. "I didn't know that. I really appreciate you doing this."

"Yeah, consider it an early Thanksgiving day treat from me. But I expect you to do me a favor now. Nothing comes for free."

"What's that?"

"If you ever hear of anyone doing anything illegal, I want you to call me." I handed him a tan-colored business card with my office and home phone number printed on it. "We have something called a Wildlife Alert Reward Program that pays good money. In fact, an illegal turkey case like this would pay out $750."

"Heck, yeah! I'll be giving you a call for sure. That's more money then I make in a week."

I handed him a yellow citation copy and sent him on his way.

My wife and I drove over to an elderly black woman's home in Welaka and gave the bird to her. She didn't have a turkey for Thanksgiving either and was right proud to get the hen we brought her. She looked frail and spindly, so I offered to clean it for her. But said she had done it before and could handle it all by herself. She grabbed the bird by both legs and hefted it up and down a few times to get a feel for the weight. Her lips parted into a bare-gum smile. "Yes, sah," she said. "I do believe this bird will cook up right fine. Thank ya."

My wife dropped me off at the metal gate on Old Welaka Road. I still had three more miles to run.

About a month later at two in the morning, the telephone rang on my bed stand. It was the lawn-care guy with a tip. Someone had just shot a deer.

13

Ocklawaha River Boat Chase

It was a beautiful spring day, and I was on water patrol in a pristine stretch of the Ocklawaha River below Rodman Dam. The Creek, as the locals like to call it, is fed primarily by Silver Springs, far upstream and east of the city of Ocala. The river and all of its meandering side creeks flow through a vast swamp that has changed little since the 1900s, when paddle-wheelers first ferried well-to-do northerners on alligator sightseeing tours. This setting, with the moss-draped trees, delicate wild orchids, and birds of fine plumage often reminded me of a jungle backdrop for a Tarzan film. In fact, escaped monkeys from the Silver Springs Zoo are occasionally seen swinging through the trees by fishermen.

My patrol vessel, a seventeen-foot fiberglass Blazer bass boat with sleek, low gunnels, powered by a 150 Mercury, could easily glide in and out of the smaller creeks. With only a slight nudge to the steering wheel, it dodged semi-sunken trees, slipped across shallow-water logs, and ducked beneath the trunks of half-fallen cypress. It performed as well at high speed as it did at low, and that was the beauty of it. In the past, I'd had faster patrol boats assigned to me. But what this one lacked in top-end speed it made up for in maneuverability. Taking a string of hairpin turns in this boat was a lot like going for a roller-coaster ride. All the driver had to do was hang on and not get slung out.

I'd just motored around a bend in the Ocklawaha when I saw a young couple fishing out of an aluminum johnboat beneath the Hwy. 19 bridge. I pulled alongside to see how their day was going and ask if they'd caught any fish—my normal preamble before popping the big question, which was, "By the way, I'd like to see both of your fishing licenses."

The wife looked at the husband, and he looked at her before he turned back to me saying, "Look, officer, I'm so sorry, but we don't have any."

"I tell you what; I'm going to offer you my two-for-one special."

"What do you mean?" asked the husband, arching his eyebrows in puzzlement.

"It's my special marriage discount. Any money for a fine would come out of the same pocket, whether it's one citation or two. So there's really no point in issuing two citations, when I can write just one and make the same impression. Wouldn't you agree?"

"Officer, that sounds like a great deal," beamed the husband.

I popped open my citation book and began to write, bearing down hard on multiple copies with a black ballpoint pen. And that's when I heard a boat engine puttering back in the swamp. I cocked my head to one side to get a better course on it. It came from a side creek that flowed into the Ocklawaha about fifty yards upstream.

Moments later a black, sinister-looking, flat-bottomed wooden boat with a sharply raised vee-bow idled out into the river. At thirteen feet in length, it was clearly overpowered with the 80 HP Mercury bolted to its transom. Manufactured by a local boatbuilder named Myron Warr, the unique hull design came in different lengths, with even larger outboards, and was a favorite among those of an outlaw bent. The upturn in the forward keel provided a tremendous "hole shot"—the ability to leap out of the water and get on plane fast, like a dragster punching through the quarter mile, thus providing a precious few seconds lead on the game warden in a chase, a window of opportunity when evidence could be thrown over the side undetected.

A slender, brown-haired man in his mid-thirties, wearing cutoff blue jeans and no shirt, drove the boat. A woman of about the same age with bleached blonde hair and broad shoulders, wearing a camouflage sleeveless T-shirt and not very flattering short-shorts, sat forward of him in the middle bench seat. They hadn't seen me, but seemed to be on a mission, their eyes fixed to a spot on the water's surface right in front of them. The man threw a metal trap drag with line trailing behind it—much like a grappling hook—into a high arc before it plopped into the water. He pulled the line in hand over hand, dragging up a plastic-coated, heavy-duty wire cable from the bottom. The cable had a series of single drop lines tied to it, each one attached to an individual blue crab trap. I knew the owner of those traps, and it wasn't the guy pulling them now.

It's a third-degree felony to rob someone else's crab traps. If the man actually emptied out one of the traps, he'd be taking a trip to jail. The fact that his drag was now hooked to the cable gave me ample reason to be suspicious.

The woman spotted me as he brought the cable into the boat. She reached over and gave her partner a beefy shove on one shoulder, then pointed excitedly in my direction. When he looked up, his forehead creased into an expression that lawmen recognize the world over: "Rabbit."

He dropped the cable, jumped into the driver's seat, and punched the throttle. I hit the gas, while shouting to the husband and wife over my shoulder, "No citation today . . . get a license next time."

And we were off.

The Ocklawaha River is a treacherous body of water. It has miles and miles of blind curves, submerged logs, and gnarly, half-sunken trees. It's a natural obstacle course that has to be read carefully and constantly or else the boat driver will crash. Fortunately, I'd had the benefit of running this creek hundreds of times—both day and night. Those experiences, coupled with numerous boat chases and a few minor wrecks, had taught me to respect this body of water because it can hurt you.

We headed west—upriver. The outlaw's boat flew through the straightaways and lay flat into the G-wrenching switchback turns like a nitro-fueled go-kart. The driver had some talent—not surprising when you consider that most guys like him started driving boats at about the same age they learned to tie shoes.

I stayed behind him and wondered what was he thinking? It was broad daylight, middle of the day, and we were going upstream, where it would eventually take us to Rodman Dam. And that would be the end of it, unless he wanted to beach the boat and strike off on foot, which was a real possibility.

I had no problem staying with the boat that I guessed was running somewhere in the upper forties—much too fast for the double-back turns, one stacked on top of the other. I hung back, staying far enough behind so that if they crashed, I wouldn't get tied up in the wreck.

The woman sat facing backward—hair whipping into her face—so she could watch me over her partner's shoulder. I pointed at her, and then made the universal sign to shut the engine off with a flat hand slice across my throat. She stared back at me with blank eyes. No acknowledgment of any kind that I was even there. She ignored me, along with my flashing blue light and siren, seemingly oblivious to her partner's ill-thought-out decision to flee.

We'd traveled about a mile and a half when the man turned around to look at me. When our eyes locked, I saw pure desperation. I knew then he was about to do something stupid. Instead of taking the next curve, he continued straight toward a wall of old-growth cypress trees. It looked like a suicide mission to me. Then the boat disappeared.

He'd found a trickle of a creek to run up, a creek so small its width was only double that of my boat. To complicate matters, this was during a three-month drought. Every stub, stump, and snarly tree would be exposed in the meager waters of this tiny, overgrown tributary.

Even my patrol craft had limitations. Driving it through the hazards of a waterway that would gradually squeeze down to a pencil-sized stream could not end well. (You can only jam a wine cork back in the bottle so far before it becomes stuck.)

I reconsidered; perhaps he wasn't stupid at all and had lured me into a trap instead. One thing was for sure: he enjoyed the advantage now with his lightweight, narrow-beamed boat.

I throttled back as I entered the creek, made a right turn following his prop wash, and caught a brief glimpse of the black transom before it whipped around a lefthand bend fifty yards ahead. Somehow he'd managed to cross over a partially sunken swamp maple with only a foot of water covering its lower trunk. I came into the ninety-degree curve at about twenty-five miles per hour, crossing where he had crossed. I stiff-armed the steering wheel.

Wham!

The engine's lower unit crashed into the submerged tree trunk, knocking me forward briefly. Then the foot rode up and over the unforgiving hunk of wood, bouncing me and the stern up into the air. The steering wheel shook violently now, rattling the bones in my wrists, elbows, and shoulders. Instead of the nice smooth ride I'd enjoyed moments before, it now felt like I was driving a heavy-duty cement truck. I figured I'd bent a prop shaft or busted a propeller blade. But I still had steerage—barely—so continued on.

We entered a natural water tunnel created by the overlapping canopies of dense bank foliage. Tree branches slapped my face and shoulders, filling the boat up with leaf litter, broken limbs, and hundreds of spiders desperate to find a new home. And that was me.

Through gaps in the greenery, I saw a white object fly out of the other boat and splash in the water. I made a mental note and barreled ahead.

The next curve came fast, with a huge obstruction in the way: Three massive cypress trees, their rootballs, along with part of the bank had collapsed into the water at a righthand bend. The partially submerged trunks leaned over at a shallow angle, blocking most of the creek except for the lower portions covered by a six-foot-wide patch of water closest to the outside of the curve.

The other driver spun the steering wheel hard before entering the turn. His boat flipped up on one side and rode right around those trees, showering spray onto the bank.

"He's good," I told myself. "He's really good."

It would have been impossible for me to do what he did. My vessel had more beam and required more water both in depth and width to make it.

Two seconds left to make up my mind. Do I go for it or not?

Yes!

But instead of taking his route, I choose to aim for the base of the fallen trees just above the waterline. My plan was to ride up onto them, with my boat out of the water and my starboard gunwale leaning hard into the wood—but with just enough of my propeller below the water to maintain forward motion and ring those trees in a half-circle pattern until I dropped off into clean water on the other side.

One second left.

The bow kicked up as I hit the clump of cypress trees at about fifteen miles per hour, sliding up onto them, higher and higher and higher, until I came to an easy stop. The boat engine was screaming, the propeller free-spinning in the air. I turned the key off and leaned back in my seat, quietly taking stock of the situation. I was sitting high and dry atop the trees, five feet above the creek, canted precariously at a 30-degree angle.

Not what I'd planned.

I brushed a couple of dozen spiders off my pant legs, arms, and face, and knocked several more off the bill of my ball cap. I carefully climbed out of the boat. Then I leaned into one of the tree trunks for balance as I monkey-crawled up it to where I could see up the creek, in the direction my suspect had fled.

And there he was—trapped. A bank-to-bank logjam of epic proportions, massive trees, one blown down on top of the other blocked his only avenue of escape.

He wasn't going anywhere. At least not by boat.

I scrambled higher, until I was about fifteen feet up and could clearly see the driver and he could see me. He was about seventy-five yards away. Now for the tricky part. I knew he would try to hoof it out through the swamp if I didn't do something pretty quick.

This would be a whole new experience for me. The first time I ever tried to arrest someone while perched in a tree. I put both hands around my mouth to form a megaphone and hollered, "Can you hear me?

"Yes," he yelled back.

"I am a State Wildlife Officer. You are under arrest. Do not leave that boat. Do not crank your engine. Do you understand?

"Yes."

And just for insurance, I grasped both hands together in a two-handed pistol grip—minus the gun—and pointed it at him. "I will shoot you deader than hell if you leave that boat. Do you understand?"

"All right, all right, I got it. Just don't shoot me."

"Excellent," I muttered to myself. "I'm finally making some progress with this guy."

I sat down on a forked branch to study him for a moment. And that's when I saw the splash. He'd thrown something else overboard. He just wasn't getting the message.

"Listen to me, you son of a bitch," I yelled. "Stop throwing stuff overboard and sit still. I'm coming to you."

I shimmied down one of the tree limbs until I hung about four feet above the swamp floor and let go. Splat. I sank up to my waist in dark, stinking mud. Bubbles of swamp gas oozed up, while the odor of decayed vegetation engulfed me. "Great, just great," I thought. "And now my leather gun belt and gun is soaked in this nasty slop. What a job it's going to be to clean it."

Wallowing my way forward, I carved a path through the mud, careful to avoid the poison ivy. It was everywhere, sprouting out of the swamp in thousands of bright-green vines.

I slogged ahead until I came to a group of cypress trees, where I could step up onto the roots and out of the muck. I jumped from the base of one tree to the next, kind of like when I played hopscotch as a kid. Soon I was standing on the creek bank talking with my two new clients.

"What did you throw in the water just a few minutes ago? I asked.

"A couple of gigs," answered the man.

I was close enough now that I could see a diving mask in his boat. "Put that mask on and jump in the water and get those gigs for me." The creek opened up here to form a pool of deeper water.

"I can't see the bottom."

"I don't care. You threw them overboard, you go get them. And I mean right now!"

He donned the mask and jumped in, diving straight down into a ten-foot-deep hole. He came back up with two eight-foot-long metal pole gigs (a spear with multiple tines or points; these had three each), threw them in the boat, and crawled back in. "Now, I want you to paddle your boat over to me. Do not start your engine."

When they were within arm's reach, I leaned out, grabbed the bow, and slid it up on the bank. Both of them handed me their driver's licenses. I didn't recognize their names, but at least I knew who they were. I'll call her Cheryl and him Rick.

Once I'd looked through the boat and saw there were no firearms on board, I switched gears and started my Officer Friendly chat: "I want to apologize for speaking so rudely to you before. It's all part of the game. After all, it is my job to make sure that you don't get away."

"Oh, that's OK," said Rick.

I read both of them their Miranda warnings and continued on with our talk.

"Listen, Rick, I've got to know. Why did you run from me?"

No response. He sat there quietly holding his head. His predicament had finally sunk in.

"Let's try this." I said. "What did you throw overboard after we entered this creek?"

"A bass."

"So you threw a largemouth bass over. Did you gig it?"

"Yes."

"Outstanding! See, we're making headway. But I don't think we had this hellish pursuit just because you illegally stuck a bass. Why did you really run? Are you wanted?"

"No, no, I'm not wanted."

I had no way of checking. The Ocklawaha River was a dead zone for radio traffic. Dispatch didn't even know I'd been in a chase.

Rick and Cheryl sat side by side in the bow of their boat, while I started the engine and idled us back down the creek to my patrol boat, still perched in the trees. I drove around the three cypress trees, pulled to one side, and tied off.

It felt odd to look up in order to see my patrol boat. I visually checked underneath the hull, inspecting it for cracks and holes. It looked fine, except for the propeller. It was now a three-blade instead of a four. But other than that, it looked seaworthy. The problem now was getting it back into the water. I would have to use my prisoner for help. I'd learned a long time ago that flexibility and improvisation were two very important elements of game warden survival.

"Listen," I said to Rick, "how about climbing up this tree with me and let's see if we can push my boat back into the water?"

"You want me to help you, and you're going to put me in jail?"

"Look at my boat, Rick, and tell me how it got there."

He sat there with his hands clasped in his lap, staring into the water.

"Well, let me help out with the answer. You led me in here, and it's because of you that my boat's sitting up in these trees." I gestured up at my boat. "So you can sit there and sulk or man up to the situation and help me get my boat out. The quicker we do this, the quicker I can get you to jail so that you can bond out and go home."

"So I'll be able to go home tonight?"

"Yes, if you can come up with the bond money."

"Come on, baby," said Cheryl, as she leaned her head against his shoulder, "just help him out so we can get out of here. I just want to go home."

Rick climbed up with me. We got on the high side of the boat and gave it a good shove. It wouldn't budge. It was caught on a small knot sticking out from one of the tree trunks. We tried it again, only this time really bearing down on it. The boat broke loose and slid on down the trees landing with an easy *kersplash* in the creek.

I put Rick in my boat, placed a life vest on him, and then handcuffed him.

I turned to Cheryl. The unkempt hair and sweat stained T-shirt told me I was about to ask a rhetorical question. "Do you know how to drive a boat?"

"Oh, yeah, I can drive a boat."

"Good, I want you to drive your boat. We're going to convoy to the boat ramp together. Drive at a slow speed and stay in front of me." We only had two miles to go before we were at the Hwy. 19 boat ramp and I was looking forward to getting both of them onto dry land.

When we came to the spot where Rick had tossed the bass, I reached down into the two-foot-deep water and picked it up off the bottom. The seven-pound fish had three evenly spaced holes—through and through—that matched the spaces between three tines on one of the gigs.

As we motored along, I kept thinking about Rick and what made him spook when he first saw me. Was there something else going on here that I didn't know about? It wasn't until I got to the boat ramp and examined the outboard engine's serial numbers that I found the answer.

The motor was stolen.

*　　*　　*

This story illustrates the difficulties that game wardens on solo patrol often encounter in remote areas. Situations are suddenly thrust upon them where they have to make split-second decisions. Solutions to problems don't always play out as expected. The outcome is always in question, and if it goes badly, then only the warden can figure a way out.

Postscript

Interestingly, of the many boat chases I had during my thirteen-year tour on the St. Johns River and its tributaries, this was the only time I got to arrest someone for fleeing or attempting to elude a law enforcement officer on the water. In earlier boat pursuits, no law had existed, which left me and many other wardens facing the frustrating dilemma of only being able to charge the suspect with a wildlife violation or else let them go.

In 1980, the Florida legislature passed a law making it unlawful to flee or attempt to elude a law enforcement officer on the water, with the penalty of a first-degree misdemeanor. By 1987, it had been amended to its current form, where the penalty became a third-degree felony—punishable by a five-thousand-dollar fine and up to five years in prison—with the added provision that the boat and motor be forfeited upon conviction.

14

The Choo-Choo-Poo-Poo Case

On the second Wednesday of February 1990, I stood before the podium of the Palatka Kiwanis Club, shuffling with anticipation. I was dressed in a crisply pressed Class A uniform: long-sleeved shirt with a military tuck that would have made a drill sergeant proud; a tie that lay precisely down the front of my shirt, held in place by a hand-polished clasp; and black leather boots, spit-shined to a mirror finish. I was a runner back then and knew I cut a clean, confident figure as I looked out into the expectant faces of the noontime crowd.

Thus I began my presentation, "Ladies and gentlemen, you are looking at the only person who has ever stepped in a pile of human feces and had something good come out of it." It may not have been the catchiest opener, but I had their attention as a fit of chuckles rolled through the group. And for the next twenty minutes I told them how, by complete happenstance, I'd stumbled into the biggest case of my career.

* * *

My scatological adventure actually began on November 28, 1988. On that day I was making the "rounds"—talking with people I knew up and down the St. Johns River about any poaching activity they may have seen. Face-to-face time, I had found out, could be a lot more productive than merely asking someone to give me a phone call.

Many of these folks had come to expect, even look forward to, my surprise visits. So it wasn't unusual that just before noon, I was driving up to a dingy-white shack at the southern abutment of the Buffalo Bluff railroad bridge, a mile south of Palatka. The building served as the living quarters/office for whichever bridge tender happened to be on duty at the time. Their primary job was to raise and lower the drawbridge for big boat traffic on the St. Johns River.

As my truck rolled to a stop, a narrow wooden door swung open from inside the rickety structure. Out stepped a short man, wearing plain gray work pants and a scuffed, blue denim long-sleeved shirt. Bill Goff, fifty-five, was a seasoned railroad veteran who had heard the tires of my Dodge Ramcharger crunching on the loose railbed gravel and had come outside to investigate. He didn't get many visitors.

"Hey, Bill," I said. "What's been going on?"

"Not much, just fixing to walk the bridge to do a safety inspection. You want to come?"

"Sure."

Safety inspections consisted of clearing tracks of fallen train debris and checking for proper rail alignment. It would be a good chance to stretch my legs.

Railroad bridge tenders often lead a hermit-like existence. Cooped up in tiny buildings, they wait to be hailed over marine band radio or by the toot of a boat horn to signal a bridge needing to be raised. I often thought the insular lifestyle made it difficult for many of them to jump into a conversation full bore. I'd learned that Bill needed to talk around a bit before getting to the point. So I stuffed my hands into my pockets, letting the conversation circle around train schedules and track maintenance as we walked along.

Because of the cracks between the railroad ties, I had a tendency to look down in front of my feet, measuring each step so they'd fall on one tie and then the next. Bill, I was sure, could walk the bridge blindfolded without tripping. He dodged the airy gaps between the heavily creosoted wooden timbers with the nimbleness of a mountain goat.

Upon reaching the north bank, we turned around for the return trek back to my truck. I glanced up for a moment, looking across the bridge to the southern shore. My eyes followed the twin ribbons of shiny steel track passing through the river swamp and beyond, to a distant, fixed point on the horizon. The mixture of man-made symmetry juxtaposed with nature held my attention for a moment, as I wondered what the shoreline must have looked like before the railroad had been built.

During that brief reverie, my boot slipped with a soft squish. Instinctively, I picked up the sole for a quick inspection. Sticking to the bottom were pieces of damp tissue paper spackled with familiar-looking brown spots.

I turned to Bill and asked, "Is this what I think it is?"

"Yep," he chuckled, "you done stepped in shit. I would have thought that as many times as you've been down here, you would have known to avoid these little land mines."

"Where did this come from?" I asked, ignoring the dig. Bill was a "Joe Friday" kind of guy, direct and to the point.

"This glob here," he said, pointing to the tracks in front of us, "just came from the southbound Amtrak passenger train that passed through just before you got here. You can see how the tissue paper is still wet and plastered in little pieces against the north side of the railroad tie, which shows it came from a southbound train. They've only been doing this for the last one hundred years. Most of the passenger cars still haven't been fitted with holding tanks, except for those up in the Northeast corridor."

Bill, I realized then, could read the vagaries of train excrement like an 1800s fur trapper could read beaver sign. I wasn't sure this skill had any real-life value other to keep one's shoe clean, but at that moment he'd impressed me.

We walked along in silence for a minute or two as I mulled over this disgusting revelation. I was turning over in my mind the possible significance of this since the then Game and Fresh Water Fish Commission (GFC) had recently become the lead agency for investigation of environmental crimes in Florida.

Never one to pass on a heaven-sent gift, I asked Bill, "Would you be willing to testify in court?"

"Yep, it's been going on long enough."

I spent the next couple of days reviewing this news with my regional supervisors, who in turn sent it up to headquarters in Tallahassee. And it was of no surprise to me when I found out that the brass weren't about to ignore this low-hanging fruit. The case had the potential to be a real show-stopper, and they knew it. I received the go-ahead to spend all the time and resources necessary to conduct an investigation into the illegal dumping of human waste by Amtrak into the waters of the St. Johns River.

Dennis Bayer, an assistant state attorney for Florida's Seventh Judicial Circuit, was assigned to work with me on the case. Eager and fresh out of law school, the twenty-seven-year-old self-proclaimed environmental activist, armed with an undergraduate degree in marine biology, was the only lawyer within the four-county circuit uniquely suited to prosecute environmental crimes.

He'd grown up as a navy brat, bouncing all over the globe with his dad from one far-flung duty station to the next. In Hawaii he'd experienced the azure waters of paradise, fishing, swimming, and diving and generally living a life most kids could only dream about. That wonderful experience, though, stood in stark contrast with his next home in Japan. There, in 1970, he witnessed true pollution for the first time: Day after day, trash and garbage washed in and out with the tides, while horribly disfigured fish fought to survive in waters poisoned by mercury. He thought to himself then, "This isn't right."

When I first met Dennis, he impressed me as someone who would come across well to a jury, particularly women. He had a full head of straight brown hair, a robust tan, and stood an even six feet, with the lanky, relaxed frame of a surfer. In fact, he'd help take the University of Florida Surfing Team to the nationals in 1984. But what set him apart from most of the surfers I'd met was that his diction didn't carry the affectations of surfer-speak. Instead, his speech conveyed a sense of dignity, delivered in a measured tone more suited to the courtroom than the beach.

We became quick friends, and as it turned out, we needed to be: neither one of us realized at the time that we would spend the next year working nearly full-time on the Amtrak case.

In our initial strategy sessions, we worked out a simple plan for the investigation and prosecution of Amtrak. The foundation of our case would be based on two Florida laws: (1) Under Florida's Litter Law, it's a third-degree felony to commercially dump litter, including raw sewage, onto public lands or waters. The penalty carries a fine of up to five thousand dollars and five years in prison. (2) The Sanitary Nuisance Law also addresses the problem of a corporation dumping raw sewage into public waters with the added caveat that the "health or lives of individuals, may be threatened or impaired" and "directly or indirectly, disease may be caused." The penalty is a first-degree misdemeanor carrying a fine of up to one thousand dollars and up to a year in jail.

One day, not long after Dennis came on board, we met at the state's attorney's office in Palatka to discuss the evidence I would need to collect for a successful prosecution. I sat down with pad and pen ready while he leaned back in a cushioned swivel chair, loosened his tie, and began to tick off the points from a mental checklist: "Get pictures of Amtrak dumping waste; get witness statements; get statements from victims who had fished under the bridge and got hosed by the train; and, oh, here's the fun part for you, Bob, you'll need to collect samples of human feces for lab work."

"Whoa, now!" I exclaimed. "You've got to be kidding me. I know crap when I see it, and so does everyone else."

"Listen, Bob, Amtrak is a quasi-governmental agency that will receive nearly $600 million in subsidized funding from the United States government this year alone. I promise you they will hire an army of lawyers to defend this case. On the prosecution side, it will be mostly you and me putting the case together. John Tanner [state attorney for the Seventh Judicial Circuit] will run the political gauntlet for us. We have to anticipate every roadblock they may throw at us. Now here's what you'll need to do to collect those samples . . ."

So began many weeks of Amtrak stakeouts, from which I learned the whims of human nature would decide my success or failure. An unwitting passenger had to flush at the precise moment his or her rail car passed over the bridge.

One morning, I finally witnessed a gush of frothy white spray emit from a red pipe mounted to a rail car's undercarriage. I was reminded of my dad—a World War II B-24 copilot—who often sprinkled his war stories with the phrase "bombs away."

When the train had passed out of sight, I walked out onto the tracks and kneeled down at the Spot. I held a wooden tongue depressor in one latex-gloved hand and a clear glass jar in the other, poised to capture my first specimen. Gravity dictated that I catch the foul concoction soon before it slid off the railroad ties and fell into the swirling, tea-stained waters of the river below. And so, with a quick scrape, I collected my first sample and headed off to the lab, wondering all the while if this wasn't the low point of my career. I concluded from this experience and several more like it that there was no glory in the collection of human excrement, regardless of how noble the cause.

The weeks turned into months, and one final task remained on Dennis's list without a checkmark next to it. I knew from having worked thousands of hours on game and fish stakeouts that those who can suffer the tedium of waiting the longest will often win the prize.

On the afternoon of May 18, 1989, I watched, hidden in the bushes near the southern abutment of the Buffalo Bluff Bridge, while two elderly couples fished underneath it in a sixteen-foot runabout. Now I would never wish misfortune on anyone, but I did have a job to do, and if the hands of fate guided a light plume of slimy spray their way, then so be it.

To the south, I could hear the distant whistle of a northbound passenger train chugging my way. The growl of powerful diesel engines soon gave way to the *clickety-clack, clickety-clack* of steel wheels hitting jointed tracks. Suddenly, the Amtrak train blew by in a thunderous roar, while the ground thrummed like a metronome with the beat of each passing car. I shakily stood my ground, watching each undercarriage whip by in a flash. When one car had crossed over the bridge my eyes swiveled back to the next, locking onto each one with the tenacity of a skeet shooter tracking a clay bird.

One car near the middle gave me my lucky break.

"Yes, yes, yes," I told myself, "there it is." Seven months of waiting and I was finally rewarded when a watery blast of liquefied human waste showered the fishing boat.

Mary Trammell—one of the star witnesses in the Amtrak case—can be seen sitting in the bow of this runabout just minutes after being sprayed with the liquefied human waste of an Amtrak passenger train, 1989.

Oh, what a glorious day.

I excitedly ran up the embankment, my feet slipping and sliding with the crunch of loose gravel, and down the bridge to a point immediately above where the boat was tied off to a concrete pylon below. Looking down at the foursome, I introduced myself and asked the crucial question, "Did anyone get wet when the train crossed?"

"Well, yes," answered a mannerly white-haired lady, who introduced herself as Mary Trammell. She glanced at her clothing, looking from one side and then to the other and pointed with one well-groomed fingernail to some stains on her pants. "These red-and-brown-looking specks showed up on me after the train passed."

"Excellent."

This was a major coup. For without a victim, the actions of Amtrak fell into the theoretical, where the defense would have tried to remove the human element from the state's case. No victim, no crime.

By now the state attorney's office, along with the GFC, had issued press releases detailing the basis for the investigation. These were the first criminal charges ever filed against the National Rail Passenger Service, aka Amtrak, and the media went apoplectic.

Newspapers, national magazines, radio, and television stations clamored to put their own spin on the David and Goliath story of rural Putnam County, then population 64,259, pitted against the U.S. government, lightly veiled as Amtrak.

Warden Hank Starling became my go-to man for ferrying the press up to the railroad bridge by water. He was an old salt and a bit crusty, a former submariner who was given to distilling the spoken word into efficient, military-like acronyms delivered in a deep baritone and with the utmost gravitas over his patrol radio. To achieve the desired tonal quality—at least in Starling's mind—he would squeeze the mic button in a vise-like grip and drop his voice an entire octave. His flair for theatrics notwithstanding, he was as good a man as I have ever met.

"The Big Rig," as Starling affectionately called his patrol boat, was a pea-green twenty-one-foot Answercraft, a fiberglass vee-hull that flared into the shape of an oversized bathtub. Completely seaworthy and reliable, it became the vessel of choice for media transport. Once or twice a week, we'd carry an energetic crew of budding television personalities up to the bridge. I'd lead them on a short hike up the gravelly northern embankment to get a picture of me pointing at a steaming pile of fresh human dung.

Again, thoughts of whether or not I had reached a new low in my career crossed my mind more than once as I watched myself on the nightly news, gesturing with all the enthusiasm I could muster at a new pile.

I knew my celebrity was complete when a friend traveling in one of the western states gave me a call to tell me Paul Harvey had mentioned me on his radio show. Apparently my fifteen minutes of fame were to be used on parsing out the finer points of raw sewage.

Other states had also opened up with salvos against the rail service. Health officials in Oregon, Washington, Utah, California, and Nevada had used civil lawsuits to attempt to force Amtrak to stop dumping kitchen and bathroom wastes. Their efforts had met with limited success.

Although the strongest direct action had been initiated in Oregon, where the state legislature in 1987 passed what was termed the "Choo-Choo-Poo-Poo" bill. The legislation was prompted by railroad workers who had been splashed on more than one occasion while working on a rail bridge in Oregon. They were incensed that the rail service continued with the antiquated practice of expelling its waste as it had 150 years ago.

Or, as Howard Kleinberg, a reporter for the *St. Petersburg Times* put it, "Waste systems are little different from when Lincoln rode the train from Illinois to Washington, D.C., to assume the presidency in 1861."

These and other points of contention caused the tide of public opinion to steadily build against Amtrak. Increasingly, they were forced to explain themselves to the media. One of the questions continually pressed upon them was, "Why weren't kitchen and bathroom wastes disposed of in the same manner as on buses and planes?"

To answer this question, Amtrak representatives zeroed in on the maximum length of time the three major modes of public transportation could be required to hold human wastes: Holding tanks on buses up to eight hours; on airplanes up to fourteen; whereas on trains, holding tanks had to be capable of containing wastes up to seventy-two hours before they were emptied. The technology, they argued, had to be significantly advanced for practical use on the rail service's longer routes before passenger cars could be retrofitted.

Cost was another reason for the lack of functional rail car holding tanks. Initial figures bandied about by Amtrak officials in the press ranged from $73 to $300 million. Finally, one train representative settled on the sum of $147 million as the price tag for fixing the problem. Congress, of course, would have to allocate the money.

In a conciliatory gesture—one likely designed to placate the jury—Congress allocated $500,000 toward research for advanced human-waste retention systems one week before the rail service was set for trial.

* * *

On the morning of November 28, 1989, the Putnam County Courthouse was abuzz. Reporters, news crews, photographers, and court groupies milled around the hallway outside Circuit Judge Robert Perry's third-floor courtroom waiting for day one of the trial to begin.

Perry was a no-nonsense judge—polite, smart, and articulate. A childhood victim of polio, the wheelchair-bound, white-haired jurist had an oratory style reminiscent of turn-of-the-century politicians who gave impromptu stump speeches. While Perry may have been strict, he wasn't immune to the nostalgia of trains, as he revealed during an earlier hearing in October, when he noted: "I'm a railroad junkie. I've lived within sight or sound of the railroads in this area of the state all my life.

"The first job I had out of law school was representing the then Atlantic Coast Line Railroad, and I was one of the attorneys for them. . . . I've ridden in passenger trains for the Coast Line since I was a small child. I travel all over the world, in Europe, and South America, even Australia, to ride the trains."

His passions for the railways did not, however, keep him from denying the defense's motion to dismiss, based on the argument that federal laws preempted state laws.

Meanwhile, tucked away inside a cramped meeting room on the ground floor below, Bayer and I sat shoulder to shoulder on one side of a plain table under soft fluorescent lights. Our interest was keenly focused on the man sitting across from us, who looked to be in his late thirties, wore a light-gray suit, and had dark, thinning hair.

He had come highly recommended as an expert and an authority on rail car design, specifically the mechanizations of how train waste disposal systems worked. He would provide the foundation for my testimony the following day.

Before his arrival in Palatka, our train expert had done extensive evaluations on the toilet systems of several different rail car models. The state attorney's office had tentatively agreed to pay him the princely sum of ten thousand dollars.

Dennis wanted to test him, though, before he put him on the witness stand. Today would not be a good day for surprises.

"Bob, please show him the photo," said Dennis.

I pulled an 8" × 10" glossy out of a manila envelope and handed it over. The train expert leaned forward on his elbows, carefully holding the print by the edges, while a look of puzzlement slowly spread across his face.

"Maybe he just doesn't see it," I thought. So I leaned across the table and pointed with one finger to a stream of water gushing from the elbow of a red pipe attached to the underside of an Amtrak passenger car, frozen in time by the camera near the center span of the Buffalo Bluff railroad bridge.

"What do you know about this?" I asked.

He brought the picture closer to his face. Finally, he shook his head and laid the photo down on the table. "I've never seen that before."

Bayer looked shocked. "What?" he asked "How can you not know? You're supposed to be the expert in rail car design."

"Well, yes, that's true, but not for this particular model."

Bayer inhaled sharply then slowly let it out while staring at our not-so-expert expert. Then he said, in the typically unflappable manner I had come to expect from him: "Well, it's good we found this out now and not this afternoon when you'll be testifying. I'll keep my questions to what your studies showed of the waste retention systems on the passenger cars you tested."

Our rail car expert looked unsure of himself now. He knew he had flunked his first test.[1] It didn't take a mind reader to know he was worried about a fee reduction.

A state attorney's investigator stood in the lobby waiting for Dennis, while one hand steadied three cardboard file boxes strapped to a wheeled carryall. Together they would maneuver the hundreds of pages of case reports and research materials up to the third floor by way of a tiny elevator. "Good luck," I told him.

My testimony wasn't scheduled until the following day, but I would still be sequestered, along with the other witnesses.

The jury was chosen by noon. The afternoon session would begin with the state's first witness, Mary Trammell.

---

1. The author reviewed transcripts of the witness's testimony and found them to be credible and on point. He was paid $4,424.22 for his services.

By permission of the *Ocala Star-Banner*.

"Do you fish very often?" asked Dennis.

"No, I don't fish as often as I'd like. I have a paralyzed son . . ." She and her husband, William, a former master sergeant with the U.S. Army, were the sole caretakers for their paraplegic adult son, who required around-the-clock care. Any opportunity for them to get away and fish was a special time.

Bayer moved smoothly through the preliminary questions, bringing her up to the day in question, May 18, 1989, just after the Amtrak train had passed over the bridge.

"Now, when you say 'sprayed' . . . what did you feel?" asked Bayer.

"Well, it was like water but it wasn't water. It was discolored like chocolate." Only Mrs. Trammell could put such an indelicate subject into the context of candy.

Bayer asked what she did after being sprayed.

"Well, you pull up anchor and you go home and take a shower. . . . I was pretty messed up. I had on a light-blue jumpsuit and it had the brown spots all over it."

On cross-examination by Ed Booth, the lead defense attorney, Mrs. Trammell never wavered from the description of the substance she had been slimed with.

In a follow-up interview with a reporter for the *New York Times*, Mrs. Trammell recalled her testimony, adding: "We don't go under the bridge to fish anymore. We wouldn't go back unless we had an Amtrak schedule first."

Day two. The morning began with a spirited debate between Booth and State Attorney John Tanner. Booth read to Judge Perry a quote from the *Florida Times-Union* newspaper published earlier that morning: "State Attorney John Tanner, who in the past has said his office wanted only an injunction stopping Amtrak from dumping the waste, said for the first time yesterday there was a possibility the State would seek a jail term."

Tanner's statement to the press had spooked five of the six Amtrak employees scheduled as witnesses into not testifying for fear of incarceration, which, of course—as Tanner correctly pointed out during his rebuttal—was always a possibility under the statute.

Booth recommended that the state's case be put on hold until the federal case seeking an injunction against the state could be heard. (Since 99 percent of Amtrak's stock was owned by the U.S. government, the defense would argue in federal court that federal law preempted state law in this matter.)

Judge Perry, after listening to the frothy rhetoric, summed up his decision in three terse sentences: "Tensions run high in a high-profile case. Nothing worth achieving comes easy. This trial, I think, needs to go forward."

Being the only investigator in the case, I was first up in the witness box. Booth engaged me with a string of seemingly benign questions until the end of my cross-examination. Then he craftily tossed out the last inquiry. Like a lob in tennis, it was incredibly slow in coming, but not so easy to return.

The first commercial littering charge was based solely on my eyeball account of what had happened. No sample had been taken. There was a strict six-hour maximum time limit to get a sample to the lab, which was an hour and a half away in Daytona Beach and closed for business at five o'clock. The dumping had taken place at four in the afternoon. It was understood that I didn't have the sample tested to determine human origin when Booth asked, "What is the basis for my determination?"

My response, "I feel like I know what it is when I see it."

An elderly man in the audience nodded, a woman seated in the back wearing a floral-print dress giggled, and similar reactions rippled through the courtroom, all in confirmation of what seemed to be an easy question to puzzle out. The old axiom "keep it simple, stupid" was never put to better use.

Day three of the trial was taken up with more witnesses for the state: railroad employees who had seen repeated dumping of wastes on the tracks, and the biologist who stated that the feces samples I had provided showed they came from a human rather than an animal.

By Thursday, the final day of the trial, only one witness's testimony had yet to be heard: William Claytor, for the defense.

I happened to be standing on the sidewalk outside the front entrance to the courthouse on Reid Street when a black Lincoln Continental drove up and parked. The rear door swung open, and a man dressed in a long, dark overcoat stepped out. He shut the door briskly and marched up the stone steps as a puff of wind flipped his coat open, accentuating an air of self-importance as the double glass doors closed behind him.

Claytor was Amtrak's president and chief executive officer, and a past secretary of the U.S. Navy and deputy secretary of state. He made a compelling figure and spoke with the clarity and understanding of a Washington insider as to the challenges the rail passenger provider had faced when the government first took over most public commute by trains in 1971. He explained the history of problems associated with waste disposal systems on trains and how they were valiantly trying to solve those problems now. "It was not Amtrak's intention," he said, "to cause any discomfort to the people of Florida. Believe me, the last thing we want is to have to disrupt rail service in Florida."

The closing statements for the prosecution were tag-teamed, with Bayer and Tanner delivering them together. Bayer summed up the fundamentals of the case, while Tanner gave a stirring speech on what it meant to be an American and how the common folk had become the victims of big government.

Booth emphasized that the state had not proven its case because they had not shown that the sewage went directly into the water, nor had they proven that it landed on Mary Trammell, since no test had been made of her jumpsuit.

Perry sent the jury to the deliberation room in the late afternoon. After the bailiff secured the heavy wooden door, Tanner leaned over to Bayer and said, "They'll be out a little before six."

"What makes you say that?" asked Bayer.

"Because they'll want to get home in time to watch themselves on television."

The clock ticked on while reporters sat quietly in the back, heads bowed over narrow notepads as they scratched away on the next day's copy. The only television cameraman (Judge Perry had conceded to having one camera in his court) took advantage of the lull to put in a fresh videotape; all of the footage was shared jointly with broadcast stations from central and northeast Florida. I sat in one of the middle rows, squeezed in next to people on either side.

I was ready for this to end. My thoughts drifted to general gun season just two weeks off. I was going through a mental checklist of what I would have to do to get ready for my new assignment. Just a few days before I'd been promoted to lieutenant and would be responsible for a new land-based patrol area encompassing three counties.

Forty-five minutes later, a soft knock came on the jury-room door—a verdict had been reached. Single-file they trooped back into the courtroom until all six men and women were seated.

The court clerk read the verdict: guilty on all three counts of commercial littering. (Not listed on the verdict scorecard was the one misdemeanor count of sanitary nuisance. The judge had earlier split that charge off and sent it down to county court.)

A single rap from Judge Perry's gavel sent reporters on a mad dash out through the double wooden doors, into the hallway, and down the stairwell to the second floor, where the only public pay telephone could be found.

* * *

January 19, 1990—the day Amtrak was scheduled to be sentenced in Judge Perry's courtroom. The defense never showed up, nor did representatives of the rail service. They didn't need to. They'd convinced the United States District Court, Middle District of Florida, out of Jacksonville, to enjoin the proceedings with a temporary injunction.

However, a brief five-minute hearing was held in the nearly empty courtroom. Court transcripts show Judge Perry was apparently miffed over a federal judge having the temerity to stop his sentencing of Amtrak. He closed out the hearing with this parting shot, "[F]ederal judges are all-knowing and omnipotent, but the weather will control the size of their funeral just like it will mine."

The final resolution of the Amtrak case came in October 1990, when the U.S. Congress passed legislation that effectively usurped the authority of any state to file civil or criminal charges against the rail service retroactive to 1976 and forward until 1996. Thus, it gave the rail service ample breathing room to retrofit their passenger cars with modernized holding tanks without fear of prosecution. The bill was signed into law by President George H. W. Bush in November 1990.

Court cases like these never seem to be finished, and a dangling thread still hung in the air. So it was on February, 15, 1991, that another hearing before Judge Perry was held, asking for dismissal of the state's case and the jury verdict. Ed Booth, speaking for the defense, gave a definitive presentation, detailing all that had happened in the ensuing fourteen months.

When it came Perry's turn to speak, the hard-headed country judge dug his heels in. Neither President Bush, nor Congress, nor Mr. Booth was going to shove him around. He fired back: "I am concerned that Congress has an irrevocable conflict of interest in this case and I wish there was some way they would recognize that, because somehow, somewhere, they, by their actions are depriving some of the citizens that send them to Congress of their day in court with due process. They are the owners of Amtrak and, as such, could not be thought to be an impartial body."

Motion denied.

Perry retired from the court in 1992. Circuit Judge Stephen Boyles, a previous state attorney for the Seventh Judicial Circuit, was left to decide the fate of the Amtrak jury verdict. During a little-advertised hearing on January 6, 1992, Boyles set aside the jury verdict of Amtrak and dismissed the information.

Congress ultimately allocated $85 million to retrofit 544 of Amtrak's passenger cars. What exactly that meant and how effective these new devices were, or if they had ever been installed, I didn't know. I had moved on to my new position as patrol supervisor of Putnam, St. Johns, and Flagler Counties.

Twenty-One Years Later

Whenever I'm detained by the blinking cross-arms at a railroad crossing, I still check for the telltale gushes of water from the undercarriage of passing Amtrak trains. Indeed, old habits do die hard.

It had been a good many years since I'd noticed any discharges. So it was with some optimism that I e-mailed Karina Romero, the manager of Media Relations for Amtrak in Washington, D.C. After a brief introduction in which I told her of my book and my past involvement with the rail service, I asked her what percentage of Amtrak trains now have pump-out type holding tanks?

Romero: One hundred percent of Amtrak's trains, including all of those that travel through Florida, have waste-retention tanks.
Me: Outstanding!

15

When Feathers Fly, Birds Die

Thin rivulets of murky water gurgled around the soles of my rubber boots and continued to course along the sandy runoff bed at the bottom of a twelve-foot-deep, overgrown drainage canal. The canal was dug in the shape of a horseshoe that bordered three sides of a twenty-acre commercial baitfish farm. The reason I happened to be in such an obscure spot was an anonymous telephone call I had received the night before.

The caller, a man of indeterminate middle age with a strained voice and a hesitant manner, reported there was an ongoing slaughter of wading birds at the farm and that I should explore the canal around the property. "You'll find all the evidence you could ever hope for," he assured me, and then abruptly hung up.

Overhead, dense tree canopies shielded direct sunlight from shining below the rim of the canal banks. But on this December midday in 1990, there was enough natural light to see the dull gray and blue of scattered feathers, the remains of a great blue heron. I stooped to pick up the breast bone, shook it loose from a clump of matted pine needles, and brought it to my face. The faint odor of rotted meat still clung to it. I rubbed one finger across the waxy surface and down the bony keel where the chest muscles attach and felt the straw-sized hole where a .22 caliber bullet had cleanly punched through. I tossed it aside, curious to see how many more birds had been killed. I walked a few more feet, ducked under a mass of hanging grape vines, and stepped out to the other side. At my feet, the stream washed over the limp carcass of a recently shot kingfisher; a couple of yards up the left bank, entwined in tall grass, were the delicate bones of a common egret; midway up the right slope lay yet another deceased bird, a shriveled cormorant with matted brown feathers and tight, mummified skin. For the next two hours, I hiked beneath the heavily vegetated tunnel while jotting down on a pocket notepad each deceased bird, the species, and its location.

Recon complete, I tallied close to three dozen carcasses. The disgusting revelation of what I'd found—a graveyard for the "who's who" of Florida's iconic wetlands birds—did not sit well with me. The wholesale slaughter of these gentle creatures—whose only purpose in life was to catch tasty minnows and fingerling fishes—needed to stop.

*   *   *

Five days later. The morning mist melted away as a winter sun broke clear and crisp in the east. Warden Bobby Stewart and I watched the fish farm from a hide deep in the shadows of a nearby swamp. Shafts of first light slipped between the moss-cloaked cypress trees and shimmered across quarter-acre-sized fish ponds. The wide, grassy roads between them had now turned a drab brown from the frosty nights.

Great blue herons of elegant plumage perched high on the branches of tall cypress trees, while other birds of the marshes and lakes—common egrets, snowy egrets, limpkins, little blue herons, and the occasional osprey and kingfisher—skittered or hovered in the air above. The feasting was about to begin for these hungry migratory nongame birds (protected species), whose annual pilgrimage south included a brief pit stop to gorge on commercially raised fish at what amounted to an avian fast-food takeout.

The landscape was well lit, when at 7:30 a.m., two men walked out the back door of a tin-roofed, cinder-block supply shed. They paused under the eaves, smoking cigarettes, and eyed the ponds. Occasionally one of them would gesture toward a bird at perch or aloft. One great blue heron seemed to be of particular interest. The bird sat very high and regal in the crown of a cypress, framed against the orange and blue and yellow layered hues of a beautiful sunrise. The distance between the men and the heron exceeded one hundred yards.

One man stubbed out his cigarette, picked up a .22 caliber rimfire semi-automatic rifle with iron sights, and took aim. *Crack, crack . . . crack, crack, crack . . . crack.* Bullets hit stout limbs with a *thwack*; others ricocheted into the sky with a high-speed buzz. The long-beaked bird twisted its head back and forth, surveying the terrain below. Finally, it somehow understood the folly of remaining a stationary target and leisurely took flight, outspread wings flapping slowly up and down.

"Did you get it?" I asked Stewart who knelt beside me.

"Perfect," he replied, while squinting through a video camera braced against the trunk of a three-foot-wide cypress.

Stewart, twenty-six, had been part of my crew for about two years. Unlike a lot of rookie game wardens, he'd come to the then Game and Fresh Water Fish Commission with real-world experience, having been a former military and civilian police officer. He was blond-haired, with a square jaw and blue eyes. He stood six foot one and weighed in at 205 pounds, every ounce solid muscle. To stay in shape he played softball, racquetball, and the occasional round of golf.

What I liked most about him, though, was how he handled a stakeout. He never complained or whined or fidgeted. Others would get antsy after only a thirty-minute wait. And he had the instincts of a hunter—the key attribute necessary to catch wildlife violators "flatfooted," or in the act.

* * *

The shooter carried his rifle over to a white golf cart and sat down in the passenger seat with his feet propped casually on the dash. The gun was cradled in his lap, barrel pointed toward us. The second man took the steering wheel and drove south on a perimeter road along the western leg of the U-shaped canal.

The route they'd chosen would bring them to within thirty yards of us, but on the opposite side of the canal. The shrill whine of the electric motor alternated pitch as the wheels hit bumps and dips and patches of tall grass, while the driver's foot jiggled up and down on the accelerator pedal.

By some bizarre coincidence, the cart jerked to a stop—right in front of us. The rifleman jumped out, looked in our direction, and mounted the gun.

"Better take cover," I whispered and spun around behind the giant cypress. Stewart tucked the video camera into his chest and fell back behind the tree trunk moments before—*Crack . . . crack, crack.*

Bullets blasted the bark off a tree branch sixty feet above our heads. The excited squawks of a snowy egret rang out as it flew away.

"Do we get battle pay for this?" asked Stewart, with a mischievous grin.

"Not a chance."

I peeked around the tree to eye our suspects through a pair of 7-power binoculars. The men were close enough now that I could make out their individual features. The rifleman had a brown beard, and the driver had long brown hair tied back into a ponytail. Since Bobby and I didn't know who they were, we gave them the monikers of "Brown Beard" and "Ponytail." Hence, each time they shot at a bird we recorded these names along with the date and time.

The two men turned their attention to the far end of the farm, fixated on a group of white ibises flying in an erratic pattern over a corner pond. With a whir of the electric cart, they bounced off in hot pursuit.

*　　*　　*

In the world of conservation law enforcement, "attempt to take" (attempt to kill) cases carry the same penalty—with a few exceptions—as "take" (to actually wound or kill) cases. The problem with the charge of "attempt to take" is that the defense often suggests an alternative reason to explain the defendant's actions. "They were merely trying to scare the birds. They would never have harmed one." Thus, to have a frozen bird carcass or two as evidence would be immensely helpful to our cause should we go to trial. In my experience, juries didn't like "attempt to take" cases. They want to *see* dead meat.

We worked the stakeout for eight days, between the end of December 1990 and the third week of January 1991. We documented several employees of the farm shooting at a variety of protected species: buzzards, ospreys, great blue herons, and a plethora of egrets.

Up until the date of January 21, 1991, we had only witnessed them kill two wood ducks with a shotgun. Now, on what would be the last day of our stakeout, a blond-haired man in his early thirties, dressed in pressed blue jeans and a button-down shirt, strode out from behind the equipment shed. Four yellow Labrador retrievers danced and pranced alongside him.

"I'll bet he's the owner," said Stewart. "Let's call him the 'Money Man.'"

"Sounds good to me."

The Money Man stood with his hands on his hips, surveying the ponds in the clear morning light. He went into the shed and returned a few moments later carrying a 12-gauge semi-automatic shotgun.

"I got a good feeling about him," said Stewart.

"So do I. That shotgun is a lot more forgiving than a twenty-two. He's got the look, too, like he really wants to whack one of these birds."

The Money Man sauntered out toward the center of his property, mounted the gun, swung on a high-flying egret, and pulled the trigger. He missed. Then he angled away from us toward the east side of the property. The yellow Labs were in dog heaven, scampering from pond to pond as they gleefully flushed up birds for their master.

The Money Man was nearly a quarter mile away. We only had an 8-power zoom lens on the video camera. I worried about the quality of the images captured if he actually killed a bird.

"What do you think about setting up the camera over where the Money Man's heading?" I asked.

"I can do it."

"Good, I'll stay here and watch him through the binoculars. Hopefully his aim will improve and we can put this one to bed."

Bobby picked up his gear, stepped over the canal rim, and skidded down the bank out of sight.

Twenty minutes later, he called me on the handheld radio. "I'm set," he whispered. "He's about thirty yards from me."

The dogs scared up a tricolored heron from one of the ponds to the south. It circled around once and headed straight for the Money Man.

This bird, judging by its lack of caution, must be a newcomer to Florida and, I hoped, a bit more gullible. It continued to plow ahead through the air. I had my fingers crossed.

"Bird heading your way," I said.

"I see him."

The heron casually winged its way north at an altitude of only twenty yards. The Money Man saw the bird and froze. As it passed overhead, he shouldered the gun and swung. The bird flinched at the sudden motion below. Too late.

Boom! Boom! Boom! The heron exploded in a cascade of feathers and fell to the earth. Money Man picked the bird up and tossed it over the canal bank like a piece of household garbage.

"I got it all on tape. The bird landed right at my feet," said Bobby.

"Good job. Let's wrap it up."

Thirty minutes later, Bobby and I drove through the fish farm entrance. The Money Man was still walking around the ponds, hunting for more birds. Bobby went to get him, while I rounded up the rest of the employees. We needed to have a powwow.

You never know what the reception will be when you drive onto someone's business and tell them they've committed a series of wildlife crimes documented on videotape. I was pleasantly surprised, then, when the Money Man took full responsibility for the bird killings. He even admitted to shooting one of the kingfishers I'd found in the canal back in December. Indeed, he was appropriately contrite. He was no dummy, though, and knew how to talk to the law.

"Listen," he said, "I thought I could shoot any bird that was eating my baitfish." He swept one arm across the ponds behind him to emphasize his plight and added, "I've got a lot of money tied up here."

"You seem like a decent enough sort," I told him, "but I find it very hard to believe you didn't know it was illegal to shoot wading birds, which are protected. The heron you shot this morning is listed as a species of special concern, one level below threatened, which is one level below endangered. Let me be clear, do not shoot any more of these birds. You already have enough problems."

"Hey," he said, raising both hands up in mock surrender. "You don't have to worry about that. I take full responsibility for what's happened, and I'm willing to pay my fines and the fines of my employees. But what I am supposed to do about the depredation of my fish?"

"I'm going to put you in contact with some folks from the U.S. Department of Agriculture. They'll review your situation and offer recommendations on how you can legally scare the birds off your property. I know with certain species, like buzzards, they have issued depredation harvest permits in the past. But that will never happen with wading birds."

Bobby wrote out the citations, five each to three employees and five to the Money Man, for a total of twenty. The charges were mostly for attempt to take, except for a kingfisher and the tricolored heron. Brown Beard had shot two wood ducks during the open season and was charged for not having a hunting license and a federal duck stamp.

One last detail remained. I grabbed the video camera, pushed the "on" button, and filmed Bobby as he stood with the ponds in the background. He held the tricolored heron up by its neck, the sleeves of his long-sleeved uniform shirt rolled up, with white long-john underwear sticking out from underneath. These were the last images on our tape of "The Fishpond Bird-Killing Case."

*　　*　　*

It did not go to trial. The Money Man made good on his word. He paid all of the fines, which came to just under one thousand dollars. Paltry? Yes, but I'd learned a long time ago not to fret over the outcome. I wasn't the person in charge of sentencing. That was up to the judge.

Three months later, Bobby and I paid the fish farm a visit. We wanted to see what adjustments, if any, the Money Man had made to his operation. The change was dramatic. Thousands of dollars' worth of heavy duty creosote poles had been set vertically all around the ponds and lined in between. The poles supported an intricate criss-cross patchwork of one-hundred-pound test monofilament fishing line. The Money Man told us it had done the job: the structure acted like an invisible trampoline, repelling winged intruders every time they dove in for a fish snack.

Problem solved. Case closed.

16

Summer Turkeys

On an ordinary day in August, I was waiting in the Taco Bell drive-thru in Palatka when I got a call from dispatch: "Call a complainant about some turkeys that have just been killed."

"Ten-four."

Dead turkeys in the middle of the summer meant an out-of-season case on the nation's premier game bird, the North American wild turkey, which is a major game violation.

I was all about it.

Regretfully, though, I would have to forgo my favorite combo—two Taco Supremes, a cinnamon twist, and a large Pepsi—to investigate this case. I hoped it would be worth the sacrifice, because if I didn't catch the culprits, I'd be miffed about having missed my favorite lunch.

I called the complainant, whom I knew.

"Lieutenant," he said, "you can't tell anyone that I've called you."

"I'll never say a word."

"You know a lot of people think you're an ass, but I think you're OK."

"Well, I appreciate that."

I paused for a moment, awash in the glow of his tepid compliment. In my line of work, I'd learned to be thankful for whatever kudos I could get, even a backhanded one.

Earlier that morning, the caller had reported seeing a flock of hen turkeys walk into an oak hammock beside the Old Starke Road, just down from Bud's Grocery Store in the community of Bardin. A few minutes later, an old blue pickup truck with two men in it pulled off the road and stopped where the turkeys had disappeared into the woods. Everything stayed quiet for a moment, and then several shots rang out that sounded to the caller like a .22 caliber rifle.

He hadn't seen the men shoot at any of the birds, but he suspected some had been killed. Like he told me, "These guys are crack shots. They don't miss. If you find any dead birds, they probably will have been shot in the head or neck."

I was skeptical about those last three words, "head or neck."

Turkeys are notoriously skittish and unpredictable, their vision legendary. A turkey's head swivels and bobs and weaves in a seemingly constant search for danger. Only when it's satisfied that no predator lurks nearby will it dip its beak to feed and then only for a second or two. To make a rifle head shot on a turkey would be a lot like trying to hit a bouncing ping-pong ball. We're talking some serious country sharpshooting, right up there with the legendary Annie Oakley.

I pulled out of the drive-thru lane and waved at the lady cashier who was handing out bags of tacos as I passed. Luckily, I hadn't placed an order yet.

Once I was outside of Palatka, I turned onto the Bardin Road, a busy two-lane blacktop that cuts north through the pine forests and cow pastures of west Putnam County. As I drove along, I rolled over the possibilities in my mind of how to make this work.

Without having been to the scene, I knew it would require a special effort—and perhaps a little luck—to pull this one off. The fellas that had shot at the turkeys were well known to me. In fact, one of them had been the ringleader of a ten-man deer-poaching ring that my men and I had caught the previous hunting season.

Catching a seasoned poacher once is difficult. But to go back and try for seconds is nearly impossible. Poachers have a learning curve too. And they always step it up a notch the second time around.

*　*　*

On any given day, a dozen or so dusty pickup trucks can be found parked at odd angles in front of Bud's Grocery Store. "Bud's," as the locals like to call it, is the pulse and heart of Bardin. It is the only general store in this tangled neighborhood of rural farmhouses, modest mobile homes, and worn-out single-wides fronting washboard dirt roads that rarely see a motor grader. The white cinder-block building with a red-brick facade needs no special adornments to attract its customers. The owners of the store don't put on airs nor do the people who frequent it. Simple is just fine, thank you. It's the country way.

The country way also includes lots and lots of talk. Rumors fly and gossip is spread by the good folks of this community—population 424—whenever they frequent Bud's. No one can drive by this local landmark without somebody else knowing about it—especially someone driving a green Ford Bronco with a blue light mounted on top. A game warden passing down the Bardin Road is tracked with the precision of a laser-guided missile. Phone lines hum and CB radios crackle at the first sight of green.

* * *

Several men standing outside of Bud's gave me "the look" as I drove by, their heads swiveling in unison as I passed. Checking my side mirror, I saw one of them pick up the receiver from an outside pay phone.

What was more troubling, though, were the deep grooves of muddy tire tracks crisscrossing the store's parking lot. It had just rained, and the wildlife crime scene I was heading to was right around the corner. Trying to find any evidence now would be tough.

Unfortunately, I couldn't devote more than a few minutes to searching the area. If the suspects had killed any birds, they could butcher them at any time. It's always easier to recover them in a whole condition. Otherwise, the dressed birds go into a freezer and the remains end up scattered halfway across the county. Time was of the essence.

I turned onto the Old Starke Rd. and traveled a half mile before I found where a truck had turned around next to a stand of live oak trees.

There was no blood to be found back in the woods. More interesting was the lack of turkey feathers. There were none that I could find, and this puzzled me. A fatally shot turkey will flop all around, knocking off feathers along the way. I'd never examined the kill site of a turkey that didn't have at least a few feathers scattered about.

But I may have looked in the wrong spot. The turkeys could have been shot anyplace along the road up to the truck's turnaround tracks. Usually, a kill site can be found by backtracking a suspect who's come out of the woods or following their foot tracks where they entered. Not today. All of the dirt and undergrowth and grasses were rain-splattered and impossible for me to read.

I leaned against the hood of my truck for a minute as I tried to figure out the angles. My options were limited. I hadn't recovered any blood, feathers, or cartridge casings. Except for the washed-out tire tracks, I hadn't seen anything during my cursory search to validate what the caller had told me. Still, I believed him. He was the type of person who wasn't prone to exaggeration. Plus he thought I was "OK." And that was good enough for me.

I got in my truck and headed back toward Bardin. I was driving straight to the home of my primary suspect, whom I will call David, the ringleader of the deer-poaching ring we'd caught the year before.

David lived in a well-tended double-wide mobile home atop a small sandhill about a mile away. A large screened-in porch fronted the trailer. Two sun-bleached wooden sheds stood to one side, where a deer-skinning rack made of pressure-treated four-by-fours jutted up between them.

To reach his home, I traveled down a bumpy track of dirt and grass that wound through a stand of turkey oaks and pines before ending in a sprawl of sand and weeds and leaves in his front yard. Sitting in this makeshift parking area was a faded blue Chevy pickup.

I parked the Bronco next to the truck and headed for the front door. A loud, clear voice boomed out from the porch, "Bob, how you doing?" exclaimed David. "I've been expecting you."

"I figured as much."

"Come on up here with my cousin and me. We're having some iced tea. You might as well join us."

I opened the side door to the screened-in porch and looked in. David and his cousin were seated at a Formica-topped table. Two big glasses of iced tea sat in front of them. His cousin's bare feet, cracked and calloused, poked out comfortably from underneath the table.

"Thanks," I said, "but I'm busy right now. How did you know I was coming?"

David was slouched back in a plastic chair, doing his best to hold back a grin. He seemed to be immensely pleased with himself. I got the feeling he planned to put on a show, a little redneck theater of his own design, where he would be the puppetmaster and I would be the puppet. I hate it when somebody knows I'm coming.

"Well, Bob," he said, "someone gave me a call. They said you were messing around down on the Old Starke Road. Now what would you be doing down there?" The cocksure twinkle in his eyes told me I would have to dig deep if I was to stand any chance of catching him and his cousin.

"I was looking for the turkeys that you and your cousin killed about an hour ago."

"Now, Bob, you've done hurt my feelings. After what happened last hunting season, you should know that I've gone straight. I don't do anything wrong anymore. I swear to God."

David leaned back even farther now, if that was possible, hands clasped contentedly over a wide tan belly that escaped from under his T-shirt. The top of his shorts were unbuttoned to give his stomach the freedom it deserved.

"You can swear till hell freezes," I said. "We both know that you and your cousin killed some birds. You guys don't miss."

"Well, thank you for the compliment, but this time you're wrong. But since I like you, Bob, I tell you what I'm going to do. You can search anywhere and anything on my property that you want, including the inside of my home, all around it, underneath it, and even inside my freezers. Now how does that sound?"

"I'll take you up on that."

"OK, Bob, where do you want to start?"

"Your truck."

I walked up to the truck and looked in the bed. It was clean. "Too clean," I thought.

"David, did you just wash this truck out?"

"Well, I might have given it a once over. It was due."

"Did you wash it here?"

"Nope."

"Uh, huh."

I heard a car engine and looked up to see a Putnam County sheriff's deputy drive into the yard. I'd given him a call on the way over. He was a friend of mine. I'd asked him to keep an eye on David and his cousin while I conducted the search. Just to make sure they played fair.

The skinning rack had a set of gambrel hooks for hanging deer. But that wasn't what I was looking for. I was looking for a small-diameter rope hanging down with a slip knot in it. Typically that's how a turkey is skinned, by putting the head and neck in the noose and letting it hang down so the hunter can dress it properly. There were no feathers on the ground either.

I did a full circuit around the yard, poking around at anything of interest, and then searched everywhere inside the home and under it. David paced me every step of the way in his signature footwear—unlaced tennis shoes. I ended up back where I'd started, in the front yard next to the Chevy truck. I was about to ask David if I could redo the search when I happened to glance down at my feet. Lying in the leaves was a single feather. As I bent over to pick it up, David took a step back and stumbled. He almost fell.

"Gotcha," I thought.

I slowly twirled the feather in my fingertips as I admired its subtle, yet beautiful iridescence in the midday light. It was a small feather, somewhat triangular with a brown bar across the top. It was the breast feather from a hen turkey. And it was dry.

"David," I said, while I held the feather up in front of his face. "What do you think this is?"

"Well . . . Bob," he said slowly, "I . . . don't . . . really . . . know." Mouth slightly agape, he was finally stumped for a snappy rejoinder. Then he rallied. A bit of spark had come back into his eyes, "Oh, I know, that feather came from a coot. It must have dropped off when it flew over."

"A coot. Come on now, you can do better than that. You and I both know that this feather came from one of the birds you and your cousin killed."

"Bob, I just can't help you," he said, with a shrug. "But if you want to keep on looking around, go right ahead."

He didn't have to worry about that. I didn't plan to leave until I'd found those darn birds. Where they had been hidden, though, was the question and a real stumper for me.

I'd already been there an hour and searched every possible place on his property and around the mobile home. So I stood there for a moment, looking out toward a distant tree line that defined where David's property stopped to the south. That was really the only place left to look.

But there weren't a lot of woods to search. The next mobile home was a couple of hundred yards away, its shiny metal roof barely visible through a break in the trees. Still, I thought it was worth a try.

I left my deputy friend sitting on the porch with the cousins while I walked to the property line. I came to a white sand road that ran through a cluster of live oaks. Anyone crossing the road should have left obvious and well-defined tracks, or so I thought. I kept to the edge, checking along it for any foot sign. It had just rained, so how hard could it be? But there was no indication that anyone had crossed. And that's when I noticed a clump of palmettos the size of a large house on the other side of the road.

Palmetto thickets are a poacher magnet. They love to hide illegal game inside these dense bushes. And most game wardens know it. Even so, the endless number of hiding places can frustrate the best of searchers. The trick is to stay with it until every square foot has been pounded out.

I had all afternoon.

I walked across the road and into the waist-high fronds and carefully pushed through them, ever-mindful that a coiled rattlesnake could be hiding somewhere up ahead. I took my time and slowly cut back and forth.

Fifteen minutes later, I finally caught a break. In a patch of sand between the runners of the plants was a barefoot track. It was made after the rain. A thin layer of damp sand had stuck to the person's foot as he pulled away, exposing the powder-dry sand beneath.

A .22 caliber rimfire rifle was used to shoot these four hen turkeys through the head by a Putnam County poacher, 1995.

The tracks led deeper into the plants, and eventually stopped at a small open area the size of a tractor-trailer tire. And there lay the prize.

I counted one, then two, then three, and one more for a total of four hen turkeys. They had been left in a pile on top of some dead palmetto thatch. Their bodies were all askance, their dusty-blue heads and necks twisted at awkward angles.

All of the birds had a similar wound that was caked with drying blood. It was a small circular hole that a soda straw could have slid through. The coup de grace had been delivered by a single .22 caliber bullet to the head.

I was impressed.

The barefoot tracks led out of the palmettos and back in the direction of David's home. I followed them, curious to know how this guy had gotten across the sandy road. The footprints came up to the road and seemed to vanish into a scattering of oak leaves. That was until I got down on my hands and knees for a closer look. Then I could just see a silver dollar–sized scuff mark here and another one there, where the ball of his foot had touched down lightly in the sand between the leaves. The man leaving these tracks—my bet was David's cousin—had quickly soft-stepped across the road on the balls of his feet.

I casually walked up to the front porch where David and his cousin were still waiting in the shade. I dropped the birds onto the door step for proper theatrics and proudly announced, "It's over with David."

"By golly, Bob, I really didn't think you could pull this one off. But let's get this straight. I've always been square with you when you finally had me right. What do you need for me to do?"

"I need for you to fill out a written statement detailing everything about the killing of these birds."

"Not a problem, just give me a pen and paper. How about that iced tea now?"

"Sure, why not?" I pulled up a chair.

17

The Daniel Boone Syndrome

During my thirty-year career, I've dealt with many game poachers. And what I've discovered is that many of them have one thing in common: a secret desire to feel like those rugged mountain men from America's early frontier days. This malady I've labeled the Daniel Boone Syndrome.

There's nothing wrong with having the affliction. In fact, many legitimate hunters have it as well. I, too, am thoroughly infected, having reached a stage in my life where I've shunned the modern high-powered rifle for its antiquated cousin, a Hawkins 1800s percussion cap, .50 caliber black-powder rifle.

The condition manifests itself in many different forms. But when properly diagnosed, it can be used to gently pry a confession from an unsuspecting poacher, like a dentist wiggling out a numbed tooth. The game violator will never realize that he's admitted to his crime until it's too late.

*   *   *

On the opening day of archery season in September 1994, I struck out for an afternoon of foot patrol. My feet bounced with each step, kicking up brown dust puffs into the warm, dry air as I crossed a freshly plowed peat field on a west Putnam County cattle ranch. The swath of three-foot-deep, dark-brown, spongy humus was four miles long by a mile wide. Known collectively as Coral Farms, these fertile grounds were divided among a handful of corn growers, dairies, and cattle ranches.

The land I was hiking across was owned by Howard Griffin and his wife, Debra. Their 1,600-acre spread capped off the northern end of this superrich strip of long-decayed plant life.

In the far distance, to my south and west, were islands of hardwood hammock surrounded by green fields dotted with grazing cattle. I imagined the deer that must be lying in the cool shade of the hammock's tangled woody edges, waiting until twilight to feed.

I'd left my patrol truck hidden behind a patch of marshy brush that the farm tractors couldn't knock down without sinking out of sight. I was careful to hide it in this way because I didn't want anyone walking along the outside of the ranch's fence line to spot it.

My plan was to check a string of small out-parcels that ran along the property's northern boundary. Hunters would routinely seek permission to lease these five-, ten-, and twenty-acre tracts of land, hoping one of the big bucks from the Griffin Ranch would jump the fence. Deer in this area were widely known to have trophy-sized antlers from the enriched soil.

In 2001, a typical buck scoring 146⁶⁄₈ points on the Boone and Crockett scale was killed during modern gun season just a mile south of the Griffin property. It still stands as the highest-scoring typical rack ever recorded in Putnam County.

The types of people who hunted these mini-leases ran from the totally legitimate to the wildlife crooks who cheated. The cheating took place when they decided to leave their bow and arrow at home and pick up a modern gun instead.

Today I wasn't interested in checking legal hunters. I could talk to them anytime. No, today I wanted to catch a cheater. And I thought I had good area picked out for it.

I walked to a spot in the fence where the remnants of an abandoned logging road were still visible and climbed over. Lack of use had reduced it to a sandy path that wound through a dense oak hammock. Waist-high palmetto bushes crowded in from both sides, forcing me to walk between the bright-green fronds.

Each one of my steps left a track that a blind Boy Scout could follow. I would have preferred to walk to the side of the trail where I could hide my foot sign. Not today, though.

The side of the path was littered with dead fronds and stems and sticks. Had I chosen to walk there instead, the racket would have been a dead giveaway that something big was afoot in these woods. Silence was more important than worrying about whether or not someone discovered my foot sign.

Deer and turkey tracks mixed and overlaid each other in a confusing scatter ahead of me. Game traffic has a tendency to beat down human foot sign within a couple of days, leaving only a faint outline and depression for the tracker to see. No one had walked here for at least a week that I could tell.

Still, I scanned ahead and up into the trees, looking for the abrupt, sharp right angles of a metal hunting stand.

Generally there are two types of stands used in Florida. The first is a "climber," which is hiked up the tree by the hunter in a series of caterpillar-like movements until the desired height is reached, anywhere from fifteen to twenty-five feet. The second is a more permanent stand called a "leaner," which is an angled ladder with a sitting platform on top, attached to a straight-trunked tree by straps or chains.

Florida hunters typically hunt from trees to get above the scent and sight level of deer. A game warden had to keep his eyes glued into the far distance if he hoped to spot a hunter before the hunter saw him.

The path led out from underneath a sprawl of live oaks and intersected with a private dirt drive that led to a mobile home. I stepped into a stand of crooked wood to listen, straining to hear the sound of a car engine idling along. Nothing.

I walked back onto the trail and quickly crossed the road, careful to step from one patch of leaves to the next in order to hide my tracks. The trail entered a stand of scrub oak and continued up a shallow slope that ended on a sandy knoll, where a thin stand of mixed oaks and pine trees grew.

All around me were deer scrapes, where the bucks had pawed the ground underneath the low limbs of young live oaks and then marked their territory with musk and urination for the does that would visit later. It was a ritual carried out every fall during the rut, or mating, season for deer.

Any hunter with even the most basic knowledge of deer movement would realize this area would make good hunting grounds. I looked around and noted several more trails and paths that intersected on top of the rise. I was standing in the middle of deer heaven.

I stepped off to one side of the trail to study a climbing tree stand left hanging at the base of a pine tree. My eyes ran up and down the tree's trunk, noting fresh angled cuts dripping with amber-colored sap. At the base of the tree was a heap of loose pine bark. The hunter had used it recently.

The sand all around the stand was cut and pawed and scraped by deer and turkey. Tiny husks about the size of a pencil eraser lay scattered about—the remnants of whole corn kernels. The hunter was using bait, which was legal on private land in Florida.

If it had been me, though, I would have placed the stand twenty yards off to one side so it wasn't smack dab in the middle of the scrapes. Too much human scent spooked deer into becoming nocturnal and defeated the whole purpose of hunting them during the daylight.

It was six in the evening. By now the hunter should have shown up. On opening day of archery season, most bow hunters were perched in their stands by four in the afternoon.

I was considering what to do next when, out of the side of my eye, I saw a man. He was dressed in full camouflage, slowly trudging up the slope toward the top of the hill where I stood. On his left shoulder was a camouflaged five-gallon plastic bucket of some weight, by the look of his slumped shoulder. Over his right shoulder was slung a short-barreled rifle with a thin piece of string for a sling. He was looking down at the ground checking for tracks. He hadn't seen me yet. If I moved, he'd see me. We were that close. So I chose to wait and let him spot me. Then I'd start talking.

He picked his head up and our eyes met. He was in his late twenties, thin, about my height, five foot ten, with a smooth-shaven, pleasant-looking face.

"Hey," I said, "how are you doing today?" He froze in midstep as I walked toward him.

"Oh, ah . . . fine," he replied. He had the "in-between look," the look that said, "Do I stay or do I run?"

He stood still as a statue, though.

"Here, I'll take that gun from you," I said. "I'd like to check it out." I already had one hand wrapped around the camouflaged string sling and slid it off his shoulder. "Go ahead and put your bucket down. I'd like to talk to you for a minute."

He lowered the bucket—filled with whole corn—to the ground without saying a word. His eyes followed my right hand as I grasped the blued-steel bolt to his single-shot .22 caliber rimfire rifle and yanked it back. A .22 Short cartridge flipped out. I caught it with one hand before it fell to the ground. Rolling it over in my fingertips, I studied the stubby brass shell casing with the short, round lead bullet seated firmly in one end. No taller than a dime standing on its edge, it was hard for my long fingers to hold onto.

I had a big problem. The cartridge I was holding was more suitable for killing rabbits or squirrels at close range than a deer. The fact that it wasn't a .22 Long Rifle made a lot of difference. The .22 Long Rifle round is not legal to kill deer with, even during modern gun season. However, poachers frequently kill deer with this round, providing the shot is well placed. But a .22 Short—that was a diminutive cartridge by anyone's definition.

My initial read on this guy was that he planned to hunt deer with this gun, and that after he'd emptied the corn bucket onto the ground, he would climb the tree with the rifle he had carried and hunt until dark. What puzzled me was why he chose the .22 Short over a .22 Long rifle. I rolled it around in my mind for a few seconds and decided it must be the lower report given off by the smaller cartridge. It was less likely to arouse the suspicions of nearby residents.

He wasn't one of our regular clients who knew the law as well as we do, and what should or shouldn't be said to a game warden. Today I was dealing with a novice. So I decided on a line of questioning to match the caliber of poacher who stood in front of me.

An in-the-woods interview is a lot like improvisation night on a small-stage theater. You have to know your subject, have the ability to think quickly on your feet, and be able to keep talking if the person you're speaking to gives short, clipped answers. A good many confessions are lost because the interviewer simply runs out of things to say. Not a problem for me. I took a firm breath and calmly began.

"Give me just a minute," I said. "I need to read you something." I pulled out my Miranda rights card and read it to him. He said he didn't mind talking to me.

"What's the gun for?" I asked.

"To shoot snakes with," he said. "I just like to carry it around—"

I held up one hand, like a traffic cop stopping a steady stream of cars coming through a major intersection. "Hold on for just a second."

I didn't want him to get too deeply into a lie. Once a complete lie is told, the suspect loses face by having to admit to the lie later. A confession comes easier if that hurdle can be avoided.

"I want to explain something to you," I said. "If you would please wait until I'm finished, I'd appreciate it."

"But—"

I held up my hand again, "Just stay with me for a minute, that's all I ask. Humor me. Please."

I gave him a look of brotherly concern. We weren't related, of course, but I wanted him to know that I understood what he was going through and that I was here to help.

"Look at me," I said. Pointing to my face with one stiff forefinger and then to the top of my head. "You see all of these wrinkles and this bald spot?"

He smiled.

Then I pointed to the brass name plate under my shirt pocket that said 1977. "That's the date I started working as a game warden. All of those years mean I've been around a long time. I've caught hundreds of poachers. What I'm doing here this afternoon with you is no different than what I'll do next week, and the week after that with someone else. This isn't my first rodeo, and it won't be my last.

"I've checked a lot of hunters in my career. Good ones and bad ones. I can tell by looking at you that you know what you're doing. Of all the areas to hunt, you've chosen the one spot with a dozen deer scrapes stuffed into a spot the size of a small house. You've perfectly positioned your deer stand for the right kill lanes. And you're decked out in camouflage right on down the camouflage sling of your rifle. I believe you're one hell of a woodsman. And I'll tell you what else I think." I lowered my voice to almost a whisper. I wanted him to strain to hear my next words. "I don't believe you're the kind of hunter that would shoot a doe deer. No, sir. I believe you're the kind of hunter that would only kill a good buck." He stood a little taller now, shoulders back.

It was time.

Very quickly I asked, "Would you have killed a big racked buck if it had walked out on you today?"

Without any hesitation, he said, "Yeah, I would have killed a good buck if I'd seen one."

"How come you're using .22 Shorts?"

"They were the only bullets I had in the house."

"One last question. Do you even own a bow and arrow?

"No, sir."

"Thank you for being honest."

In that brief moment he'd forgotten that it doesn't matter if it's a buck or a doe. One is just as illegal as the other to hunt with a modern firearm in archery season. By admitting to the buck, he took the high road as an expert woodsman who would only kill a deer worthy of his talents. The last question was the lock. It's harder for him to come back later and say he was only carrying the gun for snakes and intended to return with a bow and arrow to hunt deer.

I took off my backpack and laid it on the ground, unzipped the top compartment, and pulled out a folder with blank written statement forms. I handed one to him along with a pen. He filled it out as to what he planned to do that afternoon. When he'd completed it, I talked to him about the right and wrong way to hunt. I issued him a citation to appear before the county court judge and sent him on his way. The rifle I kept as evidence.

I detected a little bounce in his step as he walked away. He was happy as hell, a modern-day Daniel Boone.

It's not every hunter that's complimented by a game warden.

18

Close Call

The bright, clear days of spring are the purest of the year, yielding pleasant daytime temperatures that are remarkably free of bugs and humidity. This is the time of year—beginning two weeks before the opening of spring turkey season—when game wardens hike up to five miles each day in search of illegal turkey bait. It's a lot like a big boy's version of an Easter egg hunt: the turkey poacher hides his bait well off the beaten path, and the game wardens come along behind a day or two later and try to find it.

The most popular bait is cracked corn, better known in game-warden lingo as "yellow helper." But there are many more seeds that turkeys find just as enticing and are a lot harder for us to detect.

These attractants form the basis for most unlawful turkey cases in the spring. Anyone who hunts turkeys—only gobblers (male birds) and bearded hens can be taken—within one hundred yards of a bait site is in violation of the law. The reasoning for the law comes down to a matter of fair chase. The hunter should be skilled enough to call a gobbler without the help of tasty bird snacks left on the forest floor.

Those who understand turkey behavior—and a lot of hunters do—know that most turkeys will visit a bait site within an hour after flying down from their morning roost. All the illegal turkey hunter has to do is sit in his blind and wait, and occasionally give a hen *yelp* or *purr* or *cluck* to hasten the lovesick gobbler's demise.

The game warden's job is to stealthily hide in a bush nearby and wait for the hunter to call. Once this key element of the crime is witnessed, the miscreant can be cited. Case closed.

I've always found the whole experience to be great fun, except for one morning when things didn't quite work out like I'd expected. To be honest, I'm lucky to have survived.

Saturday, March 17

It was 4:45 a.m. on the opening day of spring turkey season. I wore knee-high rubber boots as I slogged through a water-filled drainage ditch along Bellamy Road, in north Putnam County. My ball cap was tucked low, shielding my eyes from the glare of a bright full moon that gave the surrounding greenery an ivory glow. Private hunting lands composed of pine forests surrounded me for miles, crisscrossed by rough logging roads and twisting hardwood creeks that offered scant relief in the otherwise, flat, featureless terrain.

Over the years I'd learned to be exceptionally cautious, some might call me phobic. That's why I was in a ditch and not walking in the graded dirt along the road shoulder, where my foot tracks could easily be detected. As a poacher once admonished me—after critiquing my efforts to catch one of his rivals—"You get sloppy, and you'll get caught. A good poacher always checks for game-warden sign before entering the woods."

I climbed out of the ditch and around a metal culvert to the entrance of a white sand road. It stretched south into a hunt club where there was a bait site a half mile away. (I'd discovered it a few days earlier while scouting the area.) A thick wire cable—installed to prevent access—lay in the dirt unhooked. It should have been strung taut between two railroad tie posts that marked the club's entrance.

I stood at the edge of the road, on matted pine needles, and studied the damp sand in the ambient lunar light. Fresh tire tracks cut through the dew and led straight into the club.

This wasn't supposed to happen. I'd gotten up at the incredibly painful hour of 3:00 a.m. so I could beat the hunter into the woods. I checked the direction of the sign again, this time studying the wave pattern in the tracks, where the rear tires had spun up dirt as the truck pulled away from the entrance. The angle of the pattern confirmed that the truck had gone "in" and not "out."

"This guy," I told myself, "wanted to make darn sure he claimed his spot before another hunter got to it first."

Now I had a problem. I paused for a moment to think it through. There was no way I could get close to the hunter to observe him, an impossible task with the surrounding landscape awash in lunar light. I figured he'd be resting in his vehicle, waiting for the predawn, when he'd leave his truck to go set up.

Much of the terrain was planted pines with a dense undergrowth of saw palmettos and gallberries. It was not feasible to circle around through the woods and come up on his flank—not without sounding like an overgrown bear crashing through the brush. My only choice was to walk in another ditch, one that paralleled the hunt-club road, where the shadows cast by a stand of fifteen-foot pine trees would offer some concealment. Then I'd try to sneak in as close as I could without being seen.

I set out at a fast pace. I wanted to be hidden before the hunter left his truck because I didn't know which way he would head. Sometimes an obvious bait site, like the one I was heading toward—whole corn scattered in a clearing—was simply a ploy. And the real bait site—the one he intended to hunt—could be hidden deep in the woods.

When I was within 150 yards of where I thought the truck would be parked, I pulled an 8 × 30 monocular from my back pocket and looked down the road. Nothing. I quietly eased down another twenty-five yards, stopped, and glassed again. There I caught a glint of the moon reflecting off the chrome from the side-door mirror of a pickup truck. The bait site was past the truck and around a curve.

This was as close as I could get to the hunter without risk of being discovered. He could be sound asleep, or wide awake, staring out the truck's windshield into the lightly lit terrain. I had no way of knowing.

I stepped into the low cover alongside the ditch and pushed ahead for fifteen yards until I came to small opening in a patch of chest-high gallberries. These slender, woody-stemmed bushes grow thickly together, often intertwining to form a vision-proof barrier. The thickness, though, was a handicap and made it a less than ideal location for a backcountry stakeout.

The best places to hide have little breaks in the brush, like the gun ports in old forts, where you could peek out, but no one could peek in. I removed a raincoat from my backpack, spread it flat on the ground, and sat down on it cross-legged to wait. An hour passed, then *bam*.

It was muffled, but I could still make out the sound of a truck door being shut. The gray hue of first light began to brighten the horizon— turkey time was here. *Caw, caw, caw,* pause, *caw, caw, caw.* It was a crow call made by the hunter.

A gobbler called back.

The male bird was still on the roost. At this time in the morning and at this time of year, a gobbler will respond to a variety of manu-factured birdcalls, including the owl and peacock. These calls are only used to locate a bird. Gobblers will not come to a birdcall unless it replicates a hen turkey.

The hunter doesn't want the bird to move in his direction until he's set up in a blind. And that location is often determined by the bird's proximity to the hunter.

I was waiting on the west side of the road, and the bird was about seventy-five yards across the road to the east—closer to my location than it was to the hunter.

Over the years I'd gotten pretty good at gauging the distances from me to a turkey, between the turkey and the hunter, and how close the hunter was to me. These distances can be estimated by studying the tone of various calls and understanding how far sound will travel in any given patch of woods. Thirty minutes passed, and the eastern skyline glowed with a tinge of orange.

Yelp, yelp, yelp, pause, *yelp, yelp, yelp, yelp, yelp, gobble, gobble.* The bird was off the roost and moving, but not toward the hunter, who had just yelped to the bird with a wooden box call that imitated a hen.

Turkey-hunting strategies are complex, so I won't go into them here except to say this is a tricky business for the hunter who chooses to creep closer to the bird rather than wait for the bird to come to him.

The bird shifted back and forth, practically teasing the hunter by cautiously probing the imaginary fifty-yard perimeter around him. Getting a gobbler to cross that invisible line was the tough part. Once the hunter coaxed him across, the bird would probably come into shotgun range, a distance of about forty yards.

But turkeys can be fickle, and this bird started moving away from the hunter, toward my location. If it stayed on that course, it would step onto the road fifty yards south of me.

Thump, thump, thump . . . the hunter ran north, up the road, slowed to a trot, and then finally stopped—right in front of me. He slipped into the brush on the opposite side of the road. His breaths came fast and hard. He wasn't used to running, and I could hear the rasping of chalked wood as his box call shifted in his pocket. He quietly spread the bushes apart while he set up a hasty ground blind.

My plans had changed. I decided not to check the hunter as he was too far from the bait. There was no sense, I reasoned, in exposing myself simply to ask for a hunting license that I was reasonably sure he had. I wanted him to kill the bird so I could move on to other areas that needed to be checked. Sometimes you just have to fold your cards and hope for a better day.

The hunter was out of my sight, hidden about twenty yards from me, but I didn't feel like I was in any danger. The last time I'd heard the bird gobble it was about to step onto the road. I figured the hunter would shoot down the road as the turkey came to him, which according to my calculations should put me well out of his shooting lane.

What I didn't know, what I couldn't see, and what I would only find out later was where he had placed his hen decoy. Instead of putting it down the road, he had placed it right in front of him. So it was directly between us!

Yelp, yelp, yelp, yelp, yelp.

The bird didn't respond. This was typical: for those last few yards, they often approach in silence and with great caution. Once the hunter started to purr, I knew the gobbler was close. It's usually the final whisper of love before . . .

Booommmm!!!

My first thought: "Holy shit!"

The entire shot charge from a 12-gauge, three-inch magnum round of No. 4 birdshot had mowed down the brush six inches in front of my feet.

I jumped up before he let loose again. "State Wildlife Officer! Don't shoot! Don't shoot anymore!" I shouted, while frantically waving my hands high above the brush.

"What the hell are you doing in there?" he yelled. "I almost shot you!"

"Just listen to me for a moment," I said, while trying to get my breathing under control. "If you'd shot me, it would have been my fault."

"I would sure hope so!"

I walked out onto the road to have a look at the bird. The body was still flopping, but the head wasn't. It's the only turkey kill I've seen before or since where the head was completely severed by the shot charge.

I checked his hunting license, which was valid. I wasn't happy about being found out; on the other hand, I was very happy not to have been shot. I handed the license back.

I turned to leave when a narrow shaft of sunlight slipped through the trees and lit up one side of the road in a pale glow. Something caught my eye within the lightened area of sand. I stepped up for a closer look. It was a hazel color and a tad bit larger than a pin head. There were dozens of them sprinkled all up and down one side of the road. They were millet seeds, and they'd been put there intentionally.

They hadn't been there when I walked along the road several days before, but they were there now. I turned back to the hunter and said, "By the way, I'm going to need your license back, and I need to look at that shotgun of yours." He handed me his license and shotgun and let out a long sigh. He knew what was coming.

I unloaded the gun and pocketed the shells until we completed our business. I always carried a citation book in my backpack.

As I made the two-mile hike back to my truck, with the gobbler strapped to my pack, *sans* head, I thought about another Florida game warden who hadn't fared as well as I had.[1] He was accidentally killed by a turkey hunter.

The moral to the story—as I always cautioned my officers before opening day of spring turkey season—is, "Sit behind the biggest damn tree you can find."

---

1. On December 24, 1950, Warden James R. Fields was accidentally shot and killed by a turkey hunter. The ensuing investigation revealed the suspect was hunting turkey for his Christmas dinner and mistook Fields for game.

19

Night Run

One O'Clock Saturday Morning, December 1992

I'd just wiggled my butt into the narrow confines of one of those quick-pack portable chairs when a light arced across the horizon. I brought my binoculars up and fingered the focus dial. The glowing shaft from a spotlight filled the circular lens. Framed against a ceiling of low-hanging clouds, it reminded me of a gigantic *Star Wars* light saber.

After a few moments I pulled the binoculars away. The night sky was a blank slate. The light gone.

There it was again. Only now it had moved a quarter mile to the north. I traced the translucent beam with my eyes and followed it down to where it disappeared behind a distant tree line and back up to where it touched the clouds. As my eyes roved between those points, I tried to work out where their position was in relation to me. It was kind of like sketching in the missing corner of a triangle.

I got it.

My best guess at a rough triangulation made me think the light was coming from a vehicle about two miles east of my position and inside a private ranch near the town of Pomona Park, in south Putnam County.

By this time in my career, I'd been on the job for fifteen years and was well acquainted with all of the large landholdings in my home county. This tract of land was no exception.

It was 3,500 acres of longleaf pines, palmettos, and cow pastures, a typical Florida cattle ranch and just above sea level. During the summer months, any rain at all would turn these pastures into puddle-ridden mosquito havens.

While I couldn't say it for sure, I had a good feeling that whoever was inside that vehicle had a gun and planned to kill a deer.

* * *

Hunting deer at night has been unlawful in Florida since 1828, when the first law was passed making it illegal to "fire hunt" west of the Suwannee River. The origin of fire hunting goes back to the Indians, who would stalk through the woods and swamps at night with a bow and arrow and a pine-sap torch, hoping to mesmerize a deer long enough to loose an arrow at it. Back then the Indians hunted to survive. Sportsmanship, or rather the lack of it, was never a consideration.

Like many game-law prohibitions, night hunting for deer is based on the principles of fair chase. There is no talent, skill, or any sport at all in hunting deer at night with a gun and light. It's too convenient and easy, and the end result, if left unchecked, could be an overharvest of the herd.

Modern-day penalties are stiff and can result in the forfeiture of vehicles and firearms, loss of hunting privileges, heavy fines, and jail time. Recent changes to the law make anyone convicted of this wildlife crime eligible to have their hunting and fishing privileges revoked in thirty-two other states.

* * *

I gathered my chair up and ran back to my patrol truck. It was hidden behind a brush pile thirty yards off a blacktop road. The road circled around a clear-water lake where the deer came out at night to munch on shrubs and other delicate plants growing in the yards of nearby residents. The word was out that this was the place to shoot a deer

Sneak lights are used when patrolling "black," or without lights.

at night, even at the risk of putting a rifle bullet through someone's living room window.

But the sudden appearance of the distant spotlight changed my plans. Stakeouts, by their nature, are mind-numbingly tedious. The opportunity to chase down a suspicious light would provide me with a welcome break.

It took about fifteen seconds to prepare my patrol truck—a 1992 Ford Bronco—for driving lights-out. I lowered the windows to hear the night sounds, and a possible gunshot. Then I shut off the head-lights, brake lights, and dash lights, covered the radio console lights with a towel, and turned on the sneak light.

The sneak light is a dim light tucked underneath the front bum-per—on the driver's side—that casts a narrow, moonlike glow out in front of the vehicle. It provides enough illumination to help the driver stay on the road and avoid obstacles like telephone poles, disabled ve-hicles, log-truck trailers, and someone taking a snooze in the middle of the roadway—it happens. It's also difficult for another person to see from any distance, hence its use when slipping up on bad guys.

I felt a smidgen of adrenalin kick in as I turned over the ignition and headed toward the ranch. There's nothing else quite like hunting down another human in the dark—by yourself.

The dull glow of a stop sign gradually emerged from the darkness. I turned left onto an old asphalt road pocked with cracks and shallow potholes.

I kept a steady watch in front of the driver's side to make sure the left front tire stayed on the road. The main gate to the ranch was about a half mile ahead on the left.

Outside my driver's window, slivers of white light flashed through a stand of old-growth pines. The light would waver, pause for a moment, and then sweep in broad strokes through the trees leaving a cascade of deep shadows behind. Whoever was working the light was still inside the ranch.

When I was a hundred yards from the main gate, I shut the sneak light off and eased onto the road shoulder and parked. The pines would shield the Bronco from being lit up by the light.

I got out and used both hands to slowly press the driver's door shut until I heard a dull click. I walked to the gate and peered through the gloom. While I couldn't see the terrain, I knew from previous patrols that a two-rut dirt and grass track led away from the gate and ran straight north for two miles through the heart of the property.

A truck was parked in a pasture facing away from me, its brake lights glowing bright red. It was about a half mile away, and someone was on foot, walking around with a flashlight.

Crack!

The small-bore rifle shot stirred a frenzy of activity around the vehicle. People milled around out in the open, cutting back and forth in front of the flashlight and the brake lights of the truck.

The main gate to the ranch has never been locked. In the past, it had always been secured with a small chain wrapped through the gate and hung on a nail. I reached for the chain and found a padlock.

I had a lock-pick set back in the truck. But that would take a couple of minutes, and I needed to hold a pen light in my teeth in order to

Typical string of keys carried by land-based game wardens to access a myriad of private and public properties.

pick a lock at night. I also had a rope ring with about two hundred keys on it for landowners in three different counties. I didn't have time—about thirty minutes—to try every one of them either. I needed to make something happen now, or these guys would disappear.

I jogged back to the truck and radioed dispatch. I gave them my location and told them I'd be chasing down a truck load of deer poachers on foot, without a radio.

Back then, issued handheld radios weighed a couple of pounds. They were about as much use for communication as talking into a chunk of lead. Better to leave it behind and lighten the load. The only item I carried in addition to my duty gun belt was an aluminum flashlight.

At this time in my life, I was a runner and averaged thirty-five to forty training miles a week. I'd previously competed in the Florida Police Olympics, where I'd run a personal best in the mile of 4:58, securing a third-place finish. It certainly wasn't an Olympic time, nor would it have raised an eyebrow at a high school track meet. But it was a personal record, and, as any recreational runner knows, that's what really counts.

I climbed over the gate and started jogging toward the truck, confident I'd have the suspects corralled in a few minutes. "Piece of cake," I told myself.

It wasn't long before my inner gyroscope went all cockeyed. I began to trip and lurch my way down the road as I tried to get used to running in the dark. It's a lot like acquiring sea legs.

Vertigo sets in quickly at night because the eye and mind can't compute a horizon that isn't there. Not being able to see the ground throws off the stride because the body doesn't know when to brace for the next foot strike. It was frustrating, especially on a night when the cloud cover blotted out all available starlight and made the horizon indiscernible. It felt like I was running through a cave with two red orbs—the pickup's brake lights—dangling out in front of me.

When I was a quarter mile from the truck, it started moving away. Thoughts of Murphy's law, "If anything can go wrong, it will," began to echo inside my head. Tonight would be a real pisser. I could feel it coming.

Someone standing in the truck's bed turned on a Q-Beam spotlight and began shining it across the pastures and occasionally behind the truck. Every time the beam swept toward me, I'd fall down into damp grass and onto the random cow flop with a soft splat. I'd wait until it passed over, then jump up and try to regain lost ground.

The truck sped up and I picked the pace up accordingly. I was still feeling good, though. It was a comfortable night, around fifty degrees with no wind.

The truck turned onto a beaten side trail that circled around the outside of a large pasture ringed with planted pines. By now I was praying they'd find something to shoot, anything, so I could close the gap and take care of business.

After about a mile and a half, the truck's course gradually started to loop back toward the main road. Only this route would take it to another gate away from where my truck was parked.

I had to change tactics. I wasn't gaining on them and I was still pounding it out, squishing my way through a gauntlet of cow patties. I'd been running at a sub-six-minute-mile pace, and my breaths were coming harder as the uniform, boots, and gun belt started to weigh me down.

The shortest distance across a circle is through the middle. I left the road and headed across the pasture at a dead run. My goal was to head them off.

Tinnggg!

A five-strand barbed wire fence can build up a lot of spring tension when a 170-pound object (me) smashes into it. I felt the barbs pierce my forearms and chest before I was catapulted backward through the air. I landed on the damp earth with an ignoble thud.

"What the hell!" I shouted and immediately regretted saying it. I hoped those bastards in the truck hadn't heard me. It felt like I'd been smacked in the chest by a major league ball player swinging a giant cactus for a bat.

Damned if it didn't hurt.

I gingerly climbed over the fence and continued on, this time with less enthusiasm and a lot more caution. I felt like an extra in a B-grade zombie movie as I stumbled ahead, hands out in front, blindly waving in the dark.

A few more strides and I tripped on a tree stump. I fell headfirst into a shallow drainage canal where I landed in a Slurpee-like mix of knee-deep mud and bovine excrement. My boot laces had come undone, allowing the odious mixture to seep inside. I crawled and staggered forward, gamely trying to get back up to speed. But my boots were leadened by the foul concoction, causing me to huff and puff even more as I plodded ahead.

Flashbacks to my dad, family vacation, and the "shortcuts" he dearly loved. Those hastily improvised routes around big-city traffic snarls often turned out to be the long way around. So it appeared that I, too, had been blessed with the same affliction.

The next two hundred yards brought me to two more fences, which I managed to see in time to avoid another prickly impalement. Why the landowner had put so many cross fences in one pasture I didn't know. But I decided three were enough. I took a leap of faith and began running all-out. I grimaced inwardly at the thought of hitting five taut strands of barbed wire again.

In what seemed like no time, I was across the pasture and closing on the truck. It had finally slowed down. The brake lights were on and the spotlight was being held steady; the beam shone into a palmetto patch from the truck's passenger side. Half-hidden in the illuminated greenery was a deer, staring curiously into the million-candlepower spotlight.

I was thirty feet from the pickup's tailgate when a series of events took place in rapid succession: the truck stopped, a rifle barrel poked out of the passenger side window, orange flames shot from the barrel along with a sharp *crack*, and four men leaped from the truck running pell-mell into the brush.

Things had just gotten complicated.

The hooves of a deer beat against palmetto fronds as it spun round and round. One man shined a flashlight onto the ground, while the rest stood around and watched, waiting for the deer to die. But the deer wouldn't die. It kept thumping and thrashing and bleating as it whirled around in circles. After a couple of minutes I realized it was most likely a spine shot. (A shot from a small-caliber bullet into the vertebra can cripple a deer, but rarely does it kill one immediately.) The deer needed to be shot again or have its throat slit.

Things were about to get even more complicated for me if they didn't put the deer down pretty quick. "Please kill it, you dumbasses," I prayed, "so all four of you can drag it back to the truck together."

I was really switched on now. I wanted to catch them all. My only chance, though, would be if they all walked back to the truck as a group. If only one or two came back by themselves, I'd be out of luck for sure.

They'd left the driver's door open. I crouched down behind it and waited for whatever was going to happen. It would have been too noisy to approach them while they were still in the palmettos. They'd bolt at the first sign of a game warden.

The truck had been left with its headlights on and the engine turned off. After a few minutes, one of the men came back to shut off the lights. He casually walked around in front of the pickup, where he was briefly lit up by the headlights. He was a slender white guy, early twenties, blond hair, wearing a blue-and-white plaid long-sleeved shirt.

I watched him close the last few feet. Still I waited.

Timing was critical. I wanted him within arm's reach when I pounced.

When he was five feet away, I side-stepped around the door and jabbed out with my left hand—like a snake striking a rat—and grabbed hold of his shirt collar. I squeezed hard at the neck and drew him to me.

"Game warden," I hissed. "Don't say a word. Do you understand me?"

His head bobbed up and down in a most satisfactory manner. This was a good sign. It means the suspect is scared, and when they're scared, compliance usually follows. I felt his knees start to buckle and hoped he wouldn't pass out. He hadn't expected the boogeyman to jump out of the dark.

One down.

But I had no clue how the last act would play out. I could only wait and hope that an opportunity would present itself to capture the remaining three men.

My prisoner and I stood silently in the dark. I released the pressure on his neck but kept a firm grip on his collar.

The men in the bushes became quiet, and their flashlight blinked out. I imagined them watching the truck across the tops of jagged-edged palmettos forty yards away, wondering why their friend hadn't returned. Time clipped on for a few minutes, and then sounds of worried whispers drifted out of the bushes. Then it got quiet again.

Suddenly, the palmetto fronds rustled and snapped. One man pushed toward the truck. I wondered if they'd drawn straws.

I bent down behind my suspect and kept one hand latched onto the nape of his shirt collar. When the second fellow saw him, he would see only one person standing by the driver's door in a dim glow cast by the cab's dome light.

The second man timidly stepped up to the truck's hood and peered into the windshield for a few seconds. He gingerly took another step and craned his neck. His eyes swept back and forth, nervously touching all points around the truck. He knew something was afoot.

When he finally inched his way around to the driver's side, I stepped out from behind the door, dragging the first guy in tow, and got in his face. I pressed one finger to my lips and quietly mouthed, "Game warden. Don't say a—"

"Game Warden!"

The bellow rolled out across the fields and through the pines. Someone a half mile away could have heard him.

On that cue, the other two men bounded through the palmettos and vanished into the night. I had my two suspects stand in front of the truck while I got their identifications and checked them and the truck for weapons. Other than some knives, there was a scoped .22 magnum bolt-action rifle lying on the front seat. I shined my light into the truck's bed and saw a mixed bag of opossums, raccoons, and a fox. That would give me more charges to work with when the case went to court.

I unloaded the rifle and pocketed the shiny brass cartridges. I slung it over my shoulder and had the two men walk with me into the palmettos where the deer was.

It was a doe shot midway in the back, barely alive. She tried to lift her head. I drew my service pistol, a Smith & Wesson 9mm, and shot her once through the neck. (Quick and deadly—neck shots are my preferred way to dispatch a wounded animal.)

"Grab the deer and drag it back to your truck," I told them.

The guy who had alerted his friends grabbed it by the hind legs and started to pull, when the deer, in a reflexive death throe, kicked him in the thigh. "Hey, this deer's kicking the hell out of me!" he shouted.

"You ever hear of poetic justice?" I asked him.

"Huh?"

"Never mind.

"This is how it works," I told him. "You shot it, you drag it. When you get it over to your truck, throw it in the bed. Now do it!"

When they reached the tailgate, the two men swung the deer up and over. It landed on top of the other carcasses with a meaty thud.

I gathered up the knives from inside the truck's cab and dropped them into the bed. I told "Weak Knees" to drive the truck and that if he did something stupid, it would mean certain jail time. I cuffed "Big Mouth" and put him in the truck's passenger seat. I climbed up into the truck's bed and sat atop the empty dog box (a box that holds hunting dogs). From this elevated position, I could look down through the back windshield and keep an eye on both men with my flashlight.

As we bumped along, I thought about how tonight's events had unfolded and was reminded of the old English proverb, "A bird in the hand is worth two in the bush." In my case, I'd beat it with two in the hand. And when I got to interview them, I'd know the two in the bush. Given the circumstances, this wasn't a bad night after all.

20

Warden Hank Starling and Buckshot the Decoy Deer

Boom! Boom! Boom!

The shots rang out in a thunderous roll as I watched Buckshot—the decoy deer—get blasted by three rounds from a 12-gauge semi-automatic shotgun in the blink of an eye. Only the firm mud of the creek swamp bottom prevented the mechanical deer from toppling over with each shuddering blast.

What saved the robot deer from total annihilation was the 12" × 12" fluorescent-orange safety flag pinned to its flank, on the blind side to the man sighting down the barrel. On the third round fired by the wannabe Davy Crockett, the colorful cloth was blown into the air, where it fluttered briefly before falling to the forest floor. Stunned and in utter disbelief, the hunter lowered the shotgun and slowly shook his head.

I sat nearby in a patch of thick palmettos, a backup for one of my officers who waited a few yards behind the young hunter. This was the kind of incident we had gotten used to.

I could see the characteristic flush of brilliant pink crawl up his neck and into his cheeks. He was muttering to himself. I couldn't understand the words, but guessed it wasn't flattering.

He knew he'd done wrong, and his body tensed, knowing he wasn't alone. Palmetto fronds shook as Warden Hank Starling stood up. He pulled a golf ball–sized chaw of tobacco from inside his cheek and said in a deep baritone, with the clipped efficiency of a twenty-two-year veteran, "State Wildlife Officer. Drop the gun. You're under arrest." He stuffed the dark-brown wad of masticated leaves back in his mouth and smiled, thumbs hooked in satisfaction over the buckle of his basket-weave gun belt.

* * *

Buckshot's handler was Henry "Hank" Starling. Back then, in 1995, he was forty-eight, stood five ten, and wore a military flattop that bordered on a buzz cut. With his belt cinched high at the waist, he typically stood with both legs locked, hands crossed atop his belt buckle, a posture I likened to a stout fireplug at full attention. Hank, as he preferred his friends to call him, came by his military bearing from a five-year stint in the U.S. Navy as a sonar technician aboard a nuclear-powered submarine. He would have made a career of it had it not been for a serious accident that resulted in a head injury during a North Atlantic sea deployment. After a six-month hospital stay, he was medically retired by the navy.

To this day, Hank proudly wears a black ball cap with gold thread embroidery that says "U.S. Navy Submarine Service." He was, and still is, an ardent believer in God, country, and family with little tolerance for those who view life through a different lens.

In 1973, Hank hired on with what was then the Game and Fresh Water Fish Commission (GFC). His patrol zone was all of St. Johns County, on the northeast coast of Florida, with forty miles of pristine sugar-sand beach, along with thousands of acres of saltwater marsh and lowland pine forests.

* * *

In the mid-1990s, the GFC didn't have any funds to spend on a robot deer. My crew and I would have to fund it ourselves. It was the only way we would ever be able to acquire the valuable play toy that many conservation agencies in the western states were using with spectacular success. A Georgia taxidermist quoted me a price of nine hundred dollars for a full body mount deer—actual fur and hide, all the way down to the original hoofs—with a motorized head and tail that worked from a remote, radio-controlled handheld unit. To come up with the money, I turned to Hank, who had an excellent working relationship with many of the large landowners in St. Johns County. He knocked on doors, begged, coaxed, and cajoled until three farmers kicked in the amount needed for the purchase.

Two months later, a United Parcel Service truck delivered three cardboard boxes at Hank's front doorstep. When he arrived home at three in the afternoon, he hurriedly pulled the boxes into his den and shut the door. A quick glance at his watch told him he had about thirty minutes before his five-year-old grandson, Tyler, would arrive home from kindergarten. Hank locked the door just in case he came home early. He wanted to surprise him.

The deer came in two parts: the main body, with a set of iron spikes at the hooves where it could be stuck in the ground; the second part was the head and upper neck, which slid down onto a square, ⅜-inch metal shaft sticking out from the body's lower neck that connected to a small electric motor. So attached, it could rotate thirty degrees from side to side to mimic the curiosity of a real deer. The head could be made to look like a doe, a spike buck, or a 6-point buck. The change-out of the antlers took only seconds, by plug in or removal of them from metal sockets set into the skull. To round out the lifelike appearance was a tail that flipped up and down. The brains behind the operation were a rechargeable control unit with an antenna and two plastic joysticks.

Starling assembled the deer and set it up in the den, then turned off the lights and closed the door. He settled back into his easy chair in the living room, feet up, with the controls hidden by a towel on his lap—just in time for Tyler, who burst through the door and gave him a big hug.

"What you doing, Pa?"

"Oh, not much. Can you do me a favor?"

"Yes, sir."

"Go into my den and bring me a book lying on my desk."

"All right." Tyler opened the door and reached up on his tiptoes to flip the light switch on. He kept his eyes glued on Grandpa, to make sure he was watching. When he turned back to look in the den he was face to face with the robot deer. Starling jiggled the joystick once and the head flipped around.

"Yoweee!" shouted Tyler. With eyes the size of saucers he backpedaled into his grandpa's arms as fast as he could.

Nearly two decades later, Starling recalled the practical joke he played on his grandson with a chuckle, "I knew when that deer rattled Tyler's tree we had a winner."

*   *   *

On a crisp fall afternoon in the general gun season of 1995, the inaugural debut of our brand-new mechanical deer commenced. It would, as they say, be a "baptism by fire."

Wardens Hank Starling and Tommy Shearer squatted on fold-out stools, hidden inside a strip of brush along a hardwood creek bottom.

Warden Henry "Hank" Starling holds the remote control for Buckshot, the decoy deer. Two plastic toggle switches controlled movement of the head and tail. By permission of Chris Christian.

Sitting in the woods together was nothing new to them. They'd done it for years and were good at it.

From my point of view as their supervisor, I thought them to be an excellent match. With Tommy—the more senior and taciturn of the two—offering a sobering reality, a check and balance, if you will, to Hank's often excessive exuberance, which could lead to a hasty and not always fully developed plan on how to execute a goal (like the night Hank wanted to rappel out of a helicopter to retrieve a deceased drowning victim, even though he'd had no training.)

The warden's view between the airy gaps in the branches and leaves displayed a raised road, a causeway built up of lime rock to form an east-west bridge across the low spot with a metal culvert in the middle. Twenty-five yards beyond the road stood the replica deer, spiked into the edge of the creek, a wax myrtle branch draped in front of a slit in the neck, the only flaw in an otherwise perfect taxidermy specimen.

Hunters know to look for deer in openings within thickly forested areas. Fire lines, meadows, natural glades, timber clear-cuts, and creek bottoms all make excellent places to survey for deer movement. Thus the officers knew that many of the hunters entering the Georgia-Pacific Wildlife Management Area that day would at least slow down— some would even stop—to look for game before they continued across the creek.

The replica deer, set up as a 6-point buck on the south side of the road, presented a classic "shoot, don't shoot" dilemma. That area was designated as a wildlife refuge and closed to hunting; on the north side, it was legal to kill a deer with at least one antler five inches in length. To be fair and to avoid the dreaded accusation of entrapment, the officers had placed the replica directly behind a bold-lettered, white rectangular sign that identified the area as off-limits to hunting. Consequently, the sign would be within the sight picture of anyone who aimed a gun at the robot deer.

*　　*　　*

The faint beat of a country music tune wavered through the pine forests and down into the creek bottom where the wardens waited. "You hear it," said Tommy, into his handheld radio. He sat apart from Hank where he could videotape vehicles crossing the creek. Hank, "the deer man," sat closer to the road with the controls in his lap so he could watch the decoy. Moving the head and neck required a deft touch. If the joystick was tugged too fast, the head would give an epileptic jerk, a dead giveaway that something wasn't right.

"Yep," replied Hank, "I can hear the engine now. Sounds like a four-cylinder baby truck."

"Probably 'Tweedledum and Tweedledee,' don't you think?" asked Tommy.

"Most likely. I doubt they'll take a shot. They've always been squared away when we checked them in the past."

Tweedledum and Tweedledee were twin brothers with scraggly hair, small pinched noses, and close-set eyes, a pair of twenty-something country boys who were low-key and polite, but not the brightest bulbs on the Christmas tree. Hence—for communication between the wardens—the nicknames Tommy had christened them with stuck, from the not-so-swift Disney cartoon characters.

The twins usually wore loose T-shirts over blue jeans that hung from their gaunt frames like empty feed sacks. When it came to deer hunting, their philosophy was simple—one shot, one kill. Something at which they had become very adept.

Part of their success may have come from their choice of firearms: single-shot 10-gauge goose guns loaded with three-and-a-half-inch magnum rounds of No. 4 buckshot. When fired, the propellant pushed fifty-four pellets of .24 caliber–sized shot through a thirty-inch, full-choke barrel at 1,100 feet per second. No whitetail deer could survive a direct hit from a load like that. It would be akin to swatting a fly with a baseball bat.

The truck bumped into view, radio blaring as it slowed to cross over the creek. The driver and passenger scanned the terrain, heads hanging out open side-door windows. "Looks like they're going on," said Tommy. Then the music shut off just as the truck passed out of sight.

"No, wait," whispered Hank. "I think they're going to do it. They've stopped down the road away from the decoy."

The passenger door swung open and Tweedledee stepped out with a long-barreled shotgun. Bent over at the waist, he scooted swiftly along the side of the pickup, then ducked below the underbrush to shield him from the deer. When he reached the culvert, he eased up above the foliage and swiftly shouldered the gun. In his haste, Tweedledee had forgotten to brace his 130-pound frame for the cannonlike recoil.

Booommmm!

The impact knocked him back onto the roadway. He bounced once and landed on his butt. He shook it off and looked up at the deer. Those big brown glass eyes stared right back at him. Unblinking.

The wardens now realized what Tweedledee lacked in mental acuity he more than made up for in grit. With the determination of a spirited gamecock, he flung the empty gun aside and sprinted for the truck. He was going to kill that damn deer.

Tweedledum leaned over and stuck a second goose gun out the open passenger door. His brother grabbed the barrel and whirled to make another run for the replica.

Hank stood up: "State Wildlife Officer. Drop the gun!"

Tweedledee stopped in midstride about thirty yards from the warden, staring at him wild-eyed and shaking. The whites of his eyes showed all around. He was riding a super adrenalin high, in full "fight or flight" mode. He wanted to kill.

"Easy now," said Hank as he drew his 9mm service pistol. "Put the gun down. It's going to be OK.

"Put the gun down," repeated Hank.

"Drop the gun," said Tommy, who by now had eased up to the left flank of Tweedledee with his gun drawn. "Take a deep breath. It's going to be all right. Just breathe." Both wardens knew the man's heart was racing. He hadn't come down from the jolt of adrenalin yet.

Suddenly, he dropped the gun, his eyes relaxed, and the color came back into his cheeks. He was back in the real world again. "Oh, my God. I'm so sorry. I'm so sorry. I don't want to go to jail. Please don't put me in jail."

"We're not going to put you in jail," said Tommy. "Just back away from the gun."

"Yes, sir, Mister Shearer. Yes, sir."

* * *

"Hank and I were writing our citations out on the hood of their truck," recalled Tommy, "when I noticed Tweedledee stick a cigarette in his mouth. He paced around the tailgate of their pickup, nonchalant like, then inched his way back toward the culvert until he could sneak a look at the decoy. His head swiveled back to look at me. He was in shock. Then he said, 'I can't believe it ain't real.'

"I told him, 'Looks good, doesn't it?' Up to that point we hadn't said a word about the deer being fake.

"After we sent them on their way, Hank and I walked down to examine the deer. That 10-gauge had done a number on it. Tufts of hair and pieces of hide had got blown off all over the chest area. So Hank said, 'I guess we should call him Buckshot.'"

Postscript

Hank eventually put together a tool kit to doctor Buckshot after each shooting. Like a doting parent administering first aid to a child's skinned knee, he'd carefully cut out pea-sized patches from a tanned deer hide with a razor-sharp X-Acto knife, then patiently superglued them over the holes, one at a time. When the internal wiring was shot up, he'd bring out the soldering gun. Electric motor destroyed? He'd replace it with a new one. When the eye color for night work wasn't right, he'd mix and match reflective materials until he'd fashioned the perfect luminescent light green—the color a deer's eye reflects when bright lights are shined on it. There was seemingly nothing Hank couldn't or wouldn't do to keep the decoy going.

But even Hank, with all his careful ministrations, couldn't keep the mechanical deer going forever. Buckshot finally retired after seven years—the most underpaid and most often decorated warden of the GFC, if buckshot holes and shredded safety flags could be counted as decorations.

21

Survival Notes

No game warden book would be complete without treating its readers to a few survival stories. Here, I've chosen six commonplace incidents from the many search-and-rescues I worked and condensed them into short, easy reads.

These outdoor mini-dramas reveal my own fascination and frustration with the psyche of hunters and fishermen who abruptly found themselves stranded or lost. I believe all of them thought—at least in the beginning—that their daytrip would be uneventful.

Lost Hog Hunter

I got the call at three in the morning. Warden Daryl Amerson was on the line: "Hey, Sarge, you ready to go?" He was one of my St. Johns County officers, young, intense, and always full of mischief.

"Daryl, I just woke up. How in the hell could I be ready to go anywhere?"

He laughed.

I wasn't in the mood for any humor, at least not at that time of the morning and at my expense. "All right, run it down for me," I said gruffly.

"We have a lost hog hunter up in the river swamp north of Toccoi Fish Camp. I'm here now with his two hunting buddies that reported him missing. They heard a gunshot just before dark and two more a couple of hours later. They figured that he wounded a hog and got lost tracking it, the last two shots were a signal for help."

"Soon as I get dressed, I'll head that way."

"Better wear your long johns. It's about twenty-six degrees out."

An hour and half later I rolled up to the fish camp. A mercury-vapor light lit up one corner of the parking lot. That's where I found Daryl and the two men from the missing hunter's party. I shook hands with everyone and asked the hunters to tell me what had happened. It pretty much followed what Daryl had told me by phone. Except now I knew the missing man's name. I'll call him John Brunton. He was twenty-nine years old, last seen wearing rubber boots, blue jeans, and a summer-weight camouflaged hunting jacket. According to his hunting partners, he carried a double-barrel 12-gauge shotgun and extra ammo.

At dawn, Daryl and I left the fish camp in his eighteen-foot patrol boat. We motored to a spot on the shoreline where the hog hunters had disembarked from their boat the afternoon before. The threesome had split up here, with Brunton walking alone into the swamp. We switched the siren on and off every few minutes to give our missing hunter a consistent sound signal to key on.

Ten o'clock arrived and still no sign of Brunton.

Daryl backed away from the shoreline, then drove us on a parallel track to the river swamp's edge. We rounded a point and saw an object on shore that looked out of place. It was still and blended in with the mottled greens and browns of the trees in the background. As we came abreast of it, I grabbed the binoculars and adjusted the focus dial until a man wearing a camouflage jacket and seated on a concrete block came into full view. He sat immobile, staring at our boat with a blank expression. We were about two hundred yards away.

"Daryl, I can't believe it," I said. "I think that's the guy were looking for, but he's not waving at us." I paused for a moment, gesturing toward the man with one free hand. "I can see a long gun lying in his lap. Why doesn't he wave at us?"

"Maybe he's another hunter who just happens to be out here this morning," replied Daryl, as he leaned against the center console, peering over the Plexiglas windshield with the intensity of a bird of prey.

"Could be," I said. "Let's go talk to him."

What puzzled me was the lack of animation from the man seated on the block, if, indeed, he was Brunton. Most folks, upon spotting a rescue boat, will yell, scream, wave, jump up and down, or shoot off a round or two to attract our attention. Other patrol boats had made several passes by this area earlier in the morning, including a spotter aircraft that likely would have seen him had he stood up and made some gesture to catch their eye.

Amerson pointed the bow toward shore and gently ran the fiberglass hull up on the narrow beach with a sandy scrunch. Fifteen yards in front of us sat the guy, still as a statue on the cinder block, his hands folded across his knees like two limp dish rags. I pointed my finger at him. "Are you the one we're looking for?"

He nodded his head yes.

"Are you OK? Are you hurt?"

"No, I'm fine," he replied, "just trying to warm up out here in the sun."

"What happened?"

"Got lost tracking a hog I'd shot. I didn't have a flashlight or a compass to find my way out."

"How did you stay warm?"

"I rolled up in a pile of leaves. It helped some, but it was still awfully cold last night."

"Don't worry. We'll get you warmed up in a minute. But I have to ask, why didn't you wave to us or fire off a gunshot to get our attention?"

He gave us a sheepish shrug.

I got it then. He was embarrassed. I'd encountered this reaction before in those we had rescued. But I couldn't help being annoyed with Brunton for acting like a knucklehead. He was so close to the finish line and never bothered to help himself across. While my toes curled inwardly, I gathered myself to exude all the professional warmth I could muster: "Hop in the boat and we'll run you up to the fish camp for a cup of coffee."

Overdue Deer Hunter

Even Game and Fresh Water Fish Commission personnel aren't immune from problems in land navigation. One biologist—whom I will not name and who left the agency many years ago—liked to hunt the swamps of Caravelle Wildlife Management Area along the St. Johns River. This particular swamp runs for many miles and is a good mile in breadth. It has an uncanny way of turning people around. After a few hours, every tree looks the same, and at night there is no escape without a compass.

I personally informed the biologist of this salient point before he headed out one afternoon on a deer hunt. I reminded him of a major search-and-rescue in this area only the week before, when a hunter had gotten lost, injured his leg, and had to be cable-hoisted up through the treetops by a U.S. Coast Guard helicopter. Still, the biologist chose not to carry a compass.

Eight o'clock that night the biologist's wife called me. Her husband had not returned home. Why wasn't I surprised?

I had Warden Mike Fischer bring up the heavy equipment backup alarm. The high-pitched warning device is used on all earth-moving equipment when in reverse and can be heard for a great distance. The merits of using it were first discovered when two children became lost in the Ocala National Forest and walked out to the sound of *beep, beep, beep* from a bulldozer working on a new home construction site.

We set the device up where the biologist had left his pickup truck. Mike laid a heavy-duty 12-volt battery on the ground and hooked up two wires from it to the alarm, then flipped on the switch. We backed away. Standing near it for any length of time would have scrambled our brains.

At midnight, the biologist emerged from the swamp. Acting all surprised, he said, "Hey, what are you all doing here?"

"We're here to rescue you is what we're doing," I explained.

"No, no, no," he said. "I wasn't lost. I just walked in a little deeper than I had intended."

"So I guess you didn't hear the sound beacon."

"Oh, I heard it fine, but I didn't need it to find my way out."

"Right."

Overdue Boat

Then there were the overdue fishermen on Crescent Lake. Warden Gator Banks and I received the call just after dark in mid-July. The wife of one of the men told me her husband and a friend hadn't returned home and she was worried. It wasn't like her husband to miss dinner.

We focused our search on the southern end of the 15,960-acre lake, where it made a hard dogleg to the east south of Crescent City. This was where the men were supposed to have gone fishing for largemouth bass. We had about 2,000 acres of water to search. Not a lot if the missing boaters cooperated. I expected this one to wrap up quickly; a still night with no wind meant sound would carry well across the lake—ideal conditions for a search-and-rescue. I figured we could have heard a man yelling for help over a mile away.

Gator drove our patrol boat back and forth, crisscrossing the lake's lower end, while I swept it with a bright searchlight. Every now and then we'd stop, shut the engine off, and call out over the boat's public address system loudspeaker. We identified who we were and asked for the missing men to give us a shout back. Occasionally, we'd turn on the emergency blue lights to identify us by sight just in case they were out of hearing range.

By two o'clock in the morning we still hadn't found our fishermen. I went home and left Gator to stay with it until the sun came up. If he still hadn't found them by then, we would put all hands on deck and bring in the sheriff's department to aid in the search. Situations like this occur often on the river, and many times one or two wardens looking for a few hours can recover the missing boaters.

Gator called me about midmorning. "Well, boss," he said. "I found them. Their battery had gone dead."

"Great. I guess they must have been up in the north end of the lake."

"Nope, they were right where we'd been looking. I was sitting in my boat, watching dawn break, when they materialized out of the gloom about a half mile from me."

"You're kidding me. No way did we miss them."

"Get this—they said they'd seen us, but thought we were drug smugglers and got scared thinking we'd shoot them if they yelled out to us."

"Bullshit!" I shouted. I was apoplectic. This went beyond embarrassed to stupid. They could have ended the whole search by hollering out to us one time.

I found it absolutely maddening that adults in perfectly good health, with all of their wits about them, wouldn't lift a hand, call out, or otherwise signal to us when we were literally right in front of them. I gritted my teeth and told Gator, "I hope you had a little chat with them."

"Apparently they felt kind of bad about keeping me up all night, so they bought me breakfast. I'm good with it," he chuckled.

"Well, Gator, as long as you're happy."

Lost Bowhunter

The late September thunderstorm dumped four inches of rain in a two-hour period. It had started in the afternoon and quit by dark. Warden Tommy Shearer and I got the call an hour later. Two bow hunters had parked their truck on private property near Clifton Road and gone into Green Bay Swamp to hunt for deer. Neither one had returned. Shearer and I drove to the edge of the swamp, turned on our siren, and then shut it off to listen.

"Hey . . . whoa . . . help," echoed a voice from deep in the swamp.

"Walk to the sound of my voice," I said over the truck's loudspeaker. "When you get to the woodline, you'll be able to see the spotlight." This rarely worked, but I always liked to give it a try. People in these situations usually didn't carry a flashlight.

We tried this tack for a few more minutes with no results. Tommy and I decided to go get him. We followed an old logging road into dense hardwoods and soon were slogging through calf-deep water. By the time we had gone another hundred yards, the water was waist-deep and floating branches and logs bobbed all around us. We yelled out, and the hunter answered. Tommy stayed on the logging road, and I waded to the guy.

He was sitting in a tree stand, scared to death. His stand was clamped to a cabbage palm located on top of a tussock, where the swamp water pooled thinly around the base of the tree.

The hunter said the woods had been dry when he first came in and now it was four feet deep in water. He'd dropped his glasses beneath his hunting stand and was afraid a water moccasin might bite him if he searched for them in the dark. He'd failed to bring a flashlight or a compass.

I found his glasses lying in a thick layer of sodden leaves at the base of the palm. I wiped them off, stretched up on my tiptoes, and handed them to him. He was only eight feet off the ground. This was where he had decided to hold up for the night after the water rose and he couldn't find his way out of the swamp. I shined the beam of my flashlight on him while he eased his climbing stand down and strapped it to his back. I carried his bow and arrows.

"Tommy, give me a shout," I hollered.

"Here!"

"Coming to you."

When we reached our patrol truck, the second hunter had already found his way out.

Being prepared makes a difference. Flashlight, matches, whistle, compass, signal mirror, food, and water are necessities no matter how brief the trip is intended to be. In this case, the hunter had only been a mile from his truck. But to him it must have felt like being stranded in an Amazon rain forest. His fear would have been the same.

Details matter.

Commercial Fishermen Make a Bad Choice

Details can also make the difference between life and death. So can the decision not to spend $7.95 at the local super discount store.

At 9:30 a.m., two commercial fishermen left the Paradise Lakes Boat Ramp to run gill nets in the northeast corner of Lake George. As they left the shelter of the lee shore, their fifteen-foot open runabout was pummeled by a February nor'easter, winds of twenty to twenty-five miles per hour pushed up a brutal chop with wave peaks of three to four feet.

Greg Jacobs, thirty-one, and his fishing partner, another man of about the same age, should have turned around then. Instead, they continued southwest toward a net they had left out overnight in the 46,000-acre lake, a mile and a half from land.

The men led a hardscrabble life. Fishing these nets was their job, their livelihood, and the only way they knew how to earn a paycheck. And like most commercial fishermen, bad weather was rarely a deterrent.

The net was set for gizzard shad, a nasty fish that oozes a sweet-smelling slime that can cause the uninitiated to gag. These fish were not being caught for human consumption. Instead, they would be sold as bait to blue crab fishermen. Typically the net is picked of its smelly catch on-site and set again to be run the following day.

Because of the rough water, the men decided to haul the whole net—several hundred yards of webbing—in with the fish and make a run back to shore. Total weight: about 1,200 pounds.

The bow had four to five inches of freeboard, pushed down by the mass of fish and the wet monofilament. The vessel traveled 300 yards before it nose-dived under a wave and rolled over. The smooth bottom of the rounded fiberglass hull offered little purchase as the fishermen anxiously clung to it—an experience not unlike trying to hold onto a greased beach ball.

What the men didn't know was that the homemade vessel had no flotation. It was afloat solely because of an air pocket trapped under the bow. A week earlier they'd made a verbal agreement to buy the boat—along with the 65-horsepower outboard motor—for $150 from another commercial fisherman. Twenty minutes later the air bubble burst and their intended investment sank straight to the bottom in nine feet of water.

Personal flotation devices on board: one red Type IV seat cushion that had been flattened hard as pancake from many years of use.

One man clutched the cushion while the other snatched an empty detergent jug from the float line of the gill net. The jug would act as his surrogate lifesaving device. After an hour, both men had become delirious, struggling to stay afloat in the sixty-degree water. Then the one who had the jug lost his grip, and it blew away into the spume of the waves.

Now the two men faced a harrowing dilemma. Their sole hope for survival rested on one waterlogged boat cushion. Being friends and business partners, they decided to share.

But the longer the cushion stayed submerged, the more water it soaked up and the less buoyant it became. Sewn inside the cushion were vinyl plastic packets filled with kapok, a waxy coated vegetable fiber found in tropical tree pods—the material responsible for buoyancy. One problem with the packets is that they will crack and deteriorate over time from use and exposure to the elements and absorb water—rendering them of little use as a lifesaving device.

Tossed and sloshed by the washing machine–like waves, the men gradually separated until they were thirty yards apart. Jacobs, without the boat cushion and exhausted from treading water, slipped beneath the waves and never surfaced again.

The wind blew the survivor away from shore toward the middle of the lake. If he stayed on this course, it would mean a nine-mile drift before he set foot on hard bottom again. By one in the afternoon, he'd traveled three-quarters of a mile and was in the channel clinging to a crab trap cork for his life. He hoped and prayed someone would come by to rescue him.

He got lucky. A rental houseboat happened by a few minutes later and picked him up.

I investigated this boating fatality in 1990. While the two fishermen committed many grievous errors that day, the one thing I could never forget about was the cushion. Had they spent the money for a new one, better yet for two—Greg Jacobs might be alive today.

*   *   *

Author's note: Boating safety laws back then required one Type IV personal floatation device per occupant of a vessel less than sixteen feet in length. Current laws have changed. Please check up-to-date United States Coast Guard and state boating safety regulations before going on the water.

Nighttime Boat Wreck

Every now and then you meet some folks who embody the "can do" pioneer spirit that makes America great. Take the night I was heading downstream on the Ocklawaha River at one in the morning. I was about a half mile east of the Hwy. 19 bridge when I rounded a bend and my headlight beam swept across the flotsam of a wrecked boat.

Seat cushions, life vests, coolers, and freshly splintered wood swirled all around me in the stark white light. The overturned hull of a black, flat-bottomed wooden boat bobbed up and down with the current in the center of the creek. "This one's going to be bad," I told myself.

I shut my engine off and shouted, "Hey, anyone out there?"

"Over here," answered a voice from the dark. I swung my headlamp onto two men who stood barefoot in ankle-deep mud at the swamp's edge, wearing cutoff jeans and T-shirts. I motored over to them.

"I guess you guys are having a bad night."

"We hit a deadhead log and rolled our boat," one of the men replied. "Two of our buddies swam back to the boat ramp to get help."

"They did what?"

"They swam upstream to the ramp."

"Oh, no," I thought. The alligators in this creek are as real and as fearsome as anywhere on the planet. The toothy bastards inhabit every turn and every straightaway of this narrow, twisting ribbon of water. Swimming upstream meant the two men would really have to churn the water to fight against the current. Frothy water meant noise, which can mimic a swimming deer or hog crossing the creek. Candy to a big gator.

"Jump in my boat and I'll run you both up to the ramp and see if we can find your friends." I said a silent prayer as I edged the throttle into forward gear.

We drove up to the Hwy. 19 ramp, and there they were, backing down a boat and trailer into the water. Apparently, one or both of the men had driven back to Palatka for a rescue vessel.

Once the boat was unloaded, the driver of the truck put it in forward gear and headed up the ramp. *Bam!* Sparks flew as chunks of metal showered out from underneath the frame. The driver put it in park, got out, and crawled underneath the truck with a flashlight.

"Busted universal joint," he said, matter-of-factly, emerging with a metal shard in one hand.

Unfazed by this turn of events, one of the men I hauled in said, "No problem, I'll just drive my truck back to town and yank another one off an old junker I got in the backyard."

I was beginning to like these fellas. In spite of the risky business of a nighttime upstream swim through a gauntlet of alligators, I'd finally met some guys who understood the true meaning of self-rescue.

Country boys "get 'er done."

22

Marsh Hens, High Tides, and Warden Gator Banks

The Ford Bronco's boxy frame settled back on worn springs with a familiar squeak. We had come to a complete stop. Warden Gator Banks put the shifter in park and then folded his hands atop the steering wheel. He turned to me with a big grin: "I guess that's about as far as we can go for now, unless you say otherwise."

Thirty yards ahead, the raised dirt and coquina-shell road we'd been driving down disappeared under a sheet of salt water. The marsh around us had swollen so that only the tips of the reeds showed, bent stiff by a strong easterly breeze. With nowhere to hide, a four-foot rattlesnake casually swam across the flooded causeway, leaving an S-wake in its path.

It was September 15, 1999, and Hurricane Floyd, a category-4 storm, churned 100 miles off the coast of northeast Florida. While the strongest winds had bypassed St. Johns County, a massive storm surge prevented the marshes and lagoons along the Intracoastal Waterway from draining during normal low tide. And now, at one in the afternoon, the water had risen into the yards of low-lying mobile homes, swamped streets, and made public boat ramps inaccessible—ideal conditions for a super marsh hen hunt.

*   *   *

The saltwater marsh hen—or clapper rail, as it is formally known—can be found throughout coastal marshes in North America. In St. Johns County, part of my old patrol area, they live in great abundance along the Atlantic Intracoastal Waterway in vast green flats of spartina grass. A ground-dwelling bird, it seldom takes to the air, and only then with a low, fluttering flight over a short distance with legs dangling. An opportunistic feeder, these secretive, crow-sized birds with brown plumage and short tails can be seen at low tide as they scour sun-baked mud flats, dipping their long, slightly down-curved bill in search of crabs, snails, the fry of fishes, insects, and seeds from water plants. Their clattering calls of *chack, chack, chack* are the most vocal of the region and can be heard day or night.

In Florida, they lead an uneventful life until September 1 rolls around. Then hunting season opens for these migratory game birds and runs until the end of the first week in November. The timing of this season coincides with the astronomical high tides of late summer and early fall, when the full- and new-moon lunar cycles tug hardest on the ocean, flooding the saltwater grass flats to the brim. With little natural cover left, the birds gather on mats of floating dead vegetation and wait for the tide to recede.

Experienced hunters know to watch for offshore storms that will push tides even higher, offering unprecedented opportunities for success or excess, depending on the hunter's integrity. In my experience, greed often rules the conscience of many who pursue marsh hens under these conditions.

*　　*　　*

"Let's get out and listen for a shot," I said. "I don't want to deal with an equipment damage report unless we have a violation out here."

"Well, boss, that's what's so great about working with you today. If something happens to my patrol truck, it won't be my ass on the chopping block."

"Now, Gator, haven't I always taken care of you?" I asked.

"Yeah, boss, you've been a regular knight in shining armor."

Gator, then forty-seven, had green eyes and a wiry head of salt-and-pepper hair that rarely needed a comb. He was of perpetual good nature with a cordial country charm. With a mischievous twinkle in his eye, he could bamboozle just about anyone into believing what he told them, a convivial trait that served him well when interviewing outlaws and poachers who had run afoul of the game laws.

For today's mission, he was the perfect choice. When he and his younger brother, Howard, were still in elementary school, they often hunted in these marshes after the closing bell. Fred Banks, their dad, would drop the two boys off on foot, each armed with a single-shot, 12-gauge shotgun and a pocket full of shells, with the admonition, "I'll be back at dark, and you'd better not miss, or you won't have anything for supper."

With no watercraft to ferry them across the tidal creeks, they swam using a one-arm sidestroke, shotgun held aloft, and a burlap sack full of birds tied to their waists. These mini-adventures forced them to choose their shots wisely and not squander ammunition, and as a result, they became excellent wing shots. But more important, they developed a keen sense of how to read the marsh and the folks who hunted there.

Gator and I walked around to the front of the patrol truck and leaned on the hood. We didn't have to wait long.

Pop, pop, pop ... pop ... pop, pop. Muted shotgun blasts, some faint, others only loud enough to cause a tiny tap within the eardrum, came from the north and on the far side of a finger of land that jutted into the marsh. And that's exactly what Gator and I had hoped to hear when we drove out to this area for a listen. We figured if anyone was hunting in these extreme conditions, it would likely be a man we both knew well. I'll call him Sonny McCoy. He lived on the narrow peninsula at the end of the very road we needed to navigate down.

McCoy was in his early fifties, six foot three, 185 pounds, with blue eyes set deep in the high brow of a bald head leathered by the summer sun. The profile of his spindly legs, bony upper frame, and a soccer ball–sized beer belly made for an image I could distinguish at some distance. He was an affable sort, a longtime resident of the tiny community of commercial crabbers and oystermen who lived on blocked-up mobile homes beneath the shadowy canopies of live oaks and ragged cabbage palms growing on this isolated strand of upland hammock. McCoy had one passion in life—he loved to hunt marsh hens. He'd been raised as a meat hunter, which differed from the sport hunter who would wait for a bird to take flight before shooting it on the "wing," as it is called. Not McCoy. If a dozen birds were rafted together, he'd try to nail them with one round; the same principle as carpet bombing, only done with a 12-gauge shotgun loaded with No. 8 birdshot.

McCoy lived in a single-wide trailer next to a dingy cinder-block and tin-roofed building that at one time operated as a commercial fish house. Scattered about the yard were old boat trailers, rusted and in disrepair, half-hidden by waist-high weeds. On the backside of the fish house, a concrete loading platform led to a wobbly wooden dock that poked out into a narrow saltwater creek. Here, McCoy kept a twenty-four-foot blunt-nosed skiff he used to crab from. Thus McCoy lived the dream of the ultimate marsh hen poacher—unfettered 24/7 access to the saltwater grass flats.

Gator and I came up with a simple plan: park our patrol truck on the front side of the fish house so it was hidden from the view of hunters on the marsh. Then we'd wait for McCoy and his party to come in and allow them to off-load what they had killed before inspecting them. The problem for us—or for me, really, since I would be the one to make the call—was whether or not to drive through the corrosive salt water to get there. If we left the truck where it was parked and tried to wade in on foot, we risked one of McCoy's neighbors finding it.

The temptation to vandalize a game warden truck left out in the open could be overwhelming—it was like asking a cat not to play with a ball of string. Cut tires, loosened lug nuts, and sliced brake lines were just a few of the fun tricks outlaws had played on us in the past. So it was with this thought in mind that I made my decision.

"Let's go," I said with a sigh, resigned to the fact I was about to commit administrative suicide. Any major damage to the truck would be on me.

Gator had a remarkable ability to sum up an adverse situation to his benefit. So I wasn't surprised when he told me: "Let's look at it this way. If we catch these guys, it will improve my stats for the month, and you'll have something to put in the weekly report. Best of all, I can take it easy until the next report cycle begins," he chuckled, immensely pleased with himself.

I refused to take the bait. He knew I was an easy mark and usually went ballistic when an officer talked about taking a free ride on a good run of cases early in the monthly report period. I believed you needed to keep pushing forward. The job of catching poachers was a lot like swinging a two-hand scythe in a thousand-acre wheat field—it never ends.

Gator dropped the shifter into drive and nudged the truck ahead. "Go slow, now," I cautioned. "If we're lucky the water will stay just beneath the undercarriage. The less splash, the better."

Water swirled around the knobby off-road tires, leaving a stream of white foam bubbles in our wake. Except for a couple of minor potholes, we managed to keep the engine and transmission from becoming soaked.

Gator pulled up tight to the south or front wall of the fish house and parked. The door of the mobile home screaked open. Sonny's wife, who looked to be in her early forties, with stringy blond hair and a sun-bitten face, came over to us. "Can I help you all with anything?"

"Not really," I said. "I guess Sonny's doing some bird shooting."

"Yeah, he's out with a couple of friends killing marsh hens. So why are you here?"

"We want to check his hunting license."

"All right, but it will probably be a while." She ambled back to the trailer, and the door slammed shut behind her. When I turned around to talk to Gator, he muttered under his breath, "She's watching us through the kitchen window."

"Figures. She knows exactly why we're here and she's worried. I sure hope Sonny doesn't have a cell phone with him on that boat or we'll be screwed."

Two hours later the drone of a big outboard motor reverberated across the grass flats as it approached from the north. Gator and I couldn't see the boat, but we listened as it came off plane, the frying sound of spray showering under the angled prow until it settled fully into the water and chugged up to the dock. Fiberglass rocked against wood, booted feet clumped, and footsteps swished through tall grass—three adult men and one teenage boy walked around the corner. None of them looked surprised to see us, least of all McCoy, who was wearing white rubber boots, cut-off jeans, and a sleeveless, mud-smeared T-shirt. Apparently, this wasn't going to be the slam dunk I'd hoped it would be.

Gator and I met them at the corner. We checked their hunting licenses, took four shotguns from them, and secured them in our patrol truck for safekeeping. The only thing left to do was check the birds, which filled a wooden crab box at our feet, where two of the hunters had set it down.

The bird math was easy to do. The group, including the teenager, could legally possess one day's bag limit, fifteen birds per person, for a total of sixty. What they had brought in would be close to the limit.

I looked over at Sonny, "How many birds did you kill?"

"We got our limit. Go ahead and count them if you want."

Gator counted the birds—sixty-two. Two over the limit was not something we would cite them for. I still believed they had killed more birds. Hunting conditions were too spectacular for them not to have.

"Sonny, did you kill any more birds today?" asked Gator.

"Only what you see, except for another feller left out earlier with his limit."

"Mind if I check your boat?" asked Gator.

"Go right ahead."

Gator disappeared around the corner with McCoy. I entertained the other men until he came back. While I chatted with them, I heard the drone of a refrigeration compressor click on behind me. It meant one of the walk-in coolers inside the dilapidated fish house was still in use. It would need to be checked.

A couple of minutes later, Gator came back with Sonny. Gator gave me a subtle shake of the head. The silent cue told me he'd come up empty.

"What's in your cooler?" I asked Sonny.

"Not much, just a couple of hogs."

"Do you mind if we have a look?" I asked.

"Naw, go ahead." His eyes cut to the side for just a moment. The flinch gave me hope, like spotting the "tell" from a poker player who gets caught in a bluff.

I'd developed a phobia about cooler inspections from my days of working on the St. Johns River. In fact, I'd had nightmares about being locked in them by some ticked-off commercial fishermen. To avoid being trapped, I never walked in first.

"Go ahead . . . open the door, Sonny," I instructed.

With a clank, Sonny yanked up on the steel lock-bar and swung the eight-inch-thick metal and foam-insulated door open. He waved me inside.

"No, after you," I said.

The blast of ice-cold air felt refreshing after having been outside in the muggy, ninety-degree heat. McCoy pulled down on a string, and a single incandescent bulb lit the space. Gator came behind and propped the door open with a cinder block. Two brown and black hogs lay on the floor, split open from stem to stern, ready to be butchered. Wedged into the far corner of the nearly empty room sat another crab box. Gator walked over to the box and dragged it to the middle of the floor, so it sat directly under the light. I stepped up to the open doorway to keep an eye on the other men who sat on overturned five-gallon buckets, awaiting final word of their fate.

"Why didn't you tell us about these birds?" asked Gator, nudging the box with his toe.

"I didn't think I had to. We killed them yesterday," boasted a smug McCoy, confident he'd taken advantage of a loophole in the law: a single hunter was allowed to possess two days' bag limit—thirty birds—without being in violation. To charge McCoy and his crew, we'd have to prove all of the birds were harvested today.

Gator and I knew without having to say it that we'd have to break McCoy loose from the lie. Before I could come up with a strategy, Gator shoved one hand deep into the middle of the box, pulled a limp bird out, and held it upside down so its head and beak dangled toward the cement floor.

"Lieutenant, you ready to time me?"

I knew better than to ask why. He had a plan, and that's what counted. I would play along as his "straight man." I pushed the buttons on my digital watch until the timer mode came up.

"Ready," I said, with one finger poised.

"Go!" Gator plunged his forefinger into the bird's anus—sinking it up to the hilt. Brown-yellow viscera oozed from around the base of his finger, dripping onto the floor. At that moment, he represented every man's worst nightmare. The thought of him giving a prostate exam sent shivers down my spine.

"Let me know when thirty seconds is up," he called out.

"You're crazy," blurted Sonny. "What in the hell are you doing?"

"Don't bother me," said Gator. "I've got to concentrate." Brow furrowed, he was giving it all he had.

I watched the digital counter on my watch click off until it reached thirty.

"Stop."

Gator pulled his finger out, now sheathed in fresh bird guts. He ran it beneath his nose for a good sniff and held it up in front of McCoy to inspect. "This bird was killed today, Sonny, and I'll testify to that in court."

"That's right," I added, stone-faced. "Gator's been trained by U.S. Fish and Wildlife service agents to determine bird time of death."

"With his finger?" screeched Sonny, who had become near apoplectic at this latest demonstration of game warden science.

"Listen to me, Sonny," said Gator, in the calm voice of a professional bird anal examiner. "You can see for yourself. Pick out any bird from the middle of the box and feel it. They're all warm. No way could they have stayed this temperature overnight in a cooler set at thirty-four degrees. Common sense ought to tell you that."

While McCoy mulled over this latest revelation, Gator counted out the birds in this box. "Sixty-four," he announced.

"Sonny, let's put this in perspective," I said. He took his eyes away from the pile of birds on the floor and looked up at me. "Have you ever robbed a bank?"

"No."

Warden Guy "Gator" Banks holds two boxes filled with marsh hens (clapper rails), an over-the-daily-bag-limit case he and the author made totaling 126 birds, 1999.

"Well, there you go. No one would ever confuse killing a few too many marsh hens with the crime of the century, now, would they?"

"That's the way I've always looked at it."

"Good. We can agree on something then. But I also want you to consider this: picture Gator Banks in court testifying against you, waggling that sausage-sized forefinger all around in the air. You and I both know he's just like his daddy and can talk his way around and through just about anything. By the time Gator is finished, he'll have the jury convinced he sleeps at the foot of the Cross."

"Ain't that the truth," said McCoy, nodding his head in agreement.

"Well, then. I only have one final question for you."

I let a couple of seconds tick by for dramatic effect.

"WERE . . . THESE . . . BIRDS . . . KILLED . . . TODAY?" I asked, enunciating each word like a hammer hitting a sixteen-penny nail.

"Yes."

*   *   *

I stuck my hand out the Bronco's passenger window and gave McCoy and his crew a wave. In the side-door mirror, I could see each of them holding a yellow sheet of paper fluttering in the wind. Gator and I were heading to a local charity to donate the birds, and then on to the nearest car wash.

"Well, Gator, you certainly pulled that one out of the hat." I said. "Perhaps you should consider joining an improvisation group. I think you'd fit right in."

"Does that mean I get to take it easy until the next report cycle begins? I feel like I've done enough work for one month."

"Hell, no!" I shouted.

"Gotcha."

23

Finding Lost Tire Tracks

When most people think of tire-track evidence, their first thought is probably the most recent episode of *Crime Scene Investigators*, the popular television show where actors cast as forensic investigators perform incredible feats of deductive reasoning based on minute bits of evidence. This makes for a good story, of course, but what happens in reality is often more muddled. Investigators frequently have to cast about like a bird dog winding a scent before they find a relevant clue.

A continuous set of tire tracks exiting from a crime scene is easy to follow. The dots line up nicely enough that even a first-grader could cipher out the question of where the vehicle went next. But what if the tire tracks are partially erased from traffic or appear to be entirely lost? Those dots now become much harder to connect.

Putnam County, with more than 1,100 miles of county dirt roads and hundreds more in sparsely developed subdivisions, has provided a virtual vehicle-tracking laboratory for game wardens to hone these skills. The result: highly tuned, keen-eyed wardens who can read tire sign as well as most folks can read the fine print of a Sunday-morning newspaper.

One of the more interesting tire-tracking techniques is the ability to follow a seemingly lost tire track. We call it the four-corner method. All it takes is time, patience, and a little luck.

Deer-Hunting Season, November 2002

On a crisp fall afternoon, Warden Eric Meade and I circled a patch of bare road shoulder like two hungry buzzards. Eyes to the ground, with the sun in our face, we took our time sorting through the clues, always careful not to step on the tire and foot tracks impressed into the dry, dusty soil.

We were examining a potential wildlife crime scene. I use the word "potential" because we weren't sure if a game violation had occurred or not, and neither was our complainant, the president of a 4,000-acre hunt club near the community of Hollister, population 721, in west Putnam County.

We'd met with the president an hour before. He reported that around 8:00 a.m., he'd driven to the west fence line of the club's property to head off a pack of deer-hunting dogs. While he was waiting on them, he heard one gunshot come from a subdivision outside of the club's property. He'd also seen an orange Ford Courier pickup truck parked nearby. He wanted to stay to see if anyone loaded a deer into the truck but had to leave when the dogs changed course. When he came back an hour later, the truck had left. He had a feeling that an illegal deer may have been killed, and so did we. (An illegal deer would have meant any deer with antlers less than five inches in length, or a doe deer.)

Interlachen Lakes Estates, the 10,000-plus-acre subdivision from where the shot had been fired, was an interesting blend of quiet retirees and working families who lived in modest mobile homes mixed in with dopers and thieves and deer poachers laid up in run-down trailers.

Other areas of the "Estates" ran for miles with little or no human habitation. These regions had become a no-man's land, crisscrossed by potholed dirt roads, littered with broken refrigerators and washing machines, tires and roofing debris, and the skeletons of stolen autos burnt to a crisp.

These unattended patches of ground had become a poacher's paradise when surrounded by state wildlife management areas and private hunt clubs.

* * *

I stepped back for a minute to watch Eric work. He patiently studied the tracks on the ground, occasionally scrunching his face up in concentration. I liked to see intensity in a young officer, and right now Eric was totally focused on the task at hand.

He was a great guy and one of my favorite wardens to work with. But there was one thing about him that aggravated me. Apparently he'd been blessed with superior genes because he never seemed to age. Perhaps it was the playful, upbeat personality that made him look younger than the twenty-eight-year-old that he was. But I swear, every time I laid eyes on him he reminded me of a fresh-faced, blond-haired, blue-eyed, college-age wrestler, with a perfect complexion and an easy smile.

The tire tracks from the Ford Courier ran off the main road and then looped back into it again. In about the middle of this half circle, where the tracks came closest to a tree line, were a series of wave patterns cast up by the right rear tire where it had slipped in the soil. This marked the spot where the truck had been parked before it was driven away.

Eric and I probed up to the edge of the tire tracks and around two different sets of foot tracks, but no closer. Once a track is trampled, it can't be taken back or ever examined again.

Tracks always leave a story on the ground. We would stay as long as it took to figure out if a wildlife crime had been committed. Patience was on our side. We had all afternoon and no calls pending.

The area we stood in was clean dirt. No weeds or forest litter. The tracks, other than being bone-dry, had the purity of what one would expect to find at the beach.

"How does it look to you?" I asked.

"Two people got out of the truck," said Eric. "The bigger foot track came from the driver's side, the smaller one from the passenger's side. They walked into the woods, came back out, and walked up to the tailgate of the truck before getting back in the cab."

"Good. That's how I read it too."

Eric took point and followed the foot tracks, walking parallel with them into the woods. He was careful to keep the line of tracks between him and the sun. Using this technique,[1] the viewer can better see the shadow relief of the shoe tread pattern. If Eric had been turned around the other way, with his back to the sun, the task would have been twice as hard.

It doesn't matter if the tracker is viewing tire, human, or animal tracks, this is always the correct position to look from in relation to the sun.

I followed Eric as he left the road shoulder and entered the woods. Twenty yards inside the tree line he paused. "Listen," he said, and held up one hand.

The air was still. At first I could only hear the skittering of small lizards across dry leaves. Then I heard it, a familiar sound that brought a warm flush to me. The buzzing of blow flies. "I hear them," I said. "Going to be blood somewhere."

Blood excites me. It's earthy and prehistoric and visceral. No amount of innovation in modern society will ever change the realness of it, the sickening-sweet smell, the coppery taste, or the candy-apple-red brightness when fresh. The skills required to find and follow blood have not changed since man first hunted beasts with spears. In some small way, I have always felt a connection to those who came before me when on a blood trail.

Eric and I scanned the ground, casting our eyes down and around our feet. Four or five of the turgid flies—their iridescent green heads reflecting in the low-angled light—flew in lazy, erratic circles a few inches above the forest litter. One finally landed, crawled upside down under the corner of a turkey oak leaf, and disappeared. Eric bent down and flipped the leaf over with one finger. Underneath was a thumbtack-sized dollop of wet blood with one white hair. "Bingo," he said, as he held up the belly hair of a deer.

---

1. For those interested in trying out this tracking technique, find a soft, sandy area and leave one good foot track. Stand back from it a few feet and then walk a slow circle all the way around it, never taking your eyes off the track. Upon completing the circle, you should see that the track is most visible when it lies directly between the viewer and the sun.

Warden Eric Meade examines the carcass of a butchered (illegal) doe deer.
Scenes like this are fairly common along Putnam County's back roads during
hunting season, 2010.

We looked up and studied the terrain ahead. A trail of turned-over
leaves created a dark shadow line from where a deer had been dragged
out of the woods. Curiously, the drag marks ended right in front of us.

"What do you think?" I asked.

"They picked the deer up right here," said Eric, pointing to the ter-
mination of disturbed leaves at our feet. "Then carried it to their truck
so they wouldn't leave any drag marks along the road shoulder for
someone driving by to see."

"I agree. Most likely they sneaked out an illegal deer. Let's see what
we've got back in the woods."

Eric took the lead again. The drag sign led us to a kill-site inside
of a sandy clearing, about the size of a large house, where the deer
had "kicked out" in its death throes; flailing the ground and shredding
the low cover with its hooves. Splotches of blood and loose brown
hair were scattered about the scuffed-up area. Twenty-five yards away
stood a homemade ladder stand—a "leaner," we call them—made

from pressure-treated scrap lumber and nailed to a pine tree. A wide, plywood seat, big enough for two, sat twelve feet off the ground, and well above the eye level of a feeding deer. Lying in the pine needles under the stand was a spent No. 1 buckshot, 12-gauge shotgun shell. Eric picked the dark-green hull up with a stick, gave it a sniff, and nodded at me with a smile.

It had been recently fired.

He pulled out a brown paper bag, dropped the shell inside, and stuffed it into his cargo pants pocket.

We returned to the truck and spent a few minutes on wildlife crime-scene investigation work, where we measured and photographed the tire and foot tracks.

The wave pattern spun up by the truck's rear tire showed us the direction it had last gone. Like ocean waves, dirt waves have a crest. One side of the crest falls away at a shallow angle; the other side is steep. Draw an imaginary line beginning with the crest and then across the shallow slope and that will be the direction the vehicle had last gone.

We climbed into our patrol truck and followed the tracks in that direction. These were the freshest and therefore offered a higher probability of a successful follow-up. We pulled onto the main dirt road and immediately ran into a problem. The tracks had vanished, completely erased by passing motorists.

We drove ahead to the next intersection, pulled off to one side, and parked. Eric grabbed a Polaroid photo of the suspect's truck-tire tread pattern off the dash. We got out and walked over to the four-way. We stopped at the first corner of the intersection. A confusing amalgamation of intricate tire-tread patterns—one on top of other—lay at our feet. Our task: to sort through them and find the one design that matched the compressed tire-track image in the 3" × 3" photograph. If we had no luck at one corner, we would move over to the next, until all four had been thoroughly scrutinized.

The intersection corners often offer up the best clues as to where a vehicle had gone because these areas receive less traffic than the straightaways and are more likely to retain a partial track. We found nothing at this crossroads.

Warden Eric Meade demonstrates the four-corner method of finding a seemingly lost tire track, 2010.

We drove to the second and then to the third intersection. We began to wonder if too much time had elapsed. There's a finite amount of time for how long any given tread pattern will hold in the dust before it is completely obliterated by traffic and natural weathering.

So here we were at the third intersection with Eric down on one knee, the Polaroid flat on the ground. Next to it was a likely match. It looked good to me, but with only a 2" × 3" sliver of the tire track remaining, it was hard to judge.

I peered over Eric's shoulder and looked at the picture and then to the ground pattern and back again. "I think we got it," I said, careful not to sound too enthusiastic.

I wanted to hear Eric's honest opinion. We had previously decided if both of us could agree on a match, we would follow that track until it couldn't be followed anymore.

"I feel good about it too," said Eric," as he pointed to outer lug marks in the photo and then to the corresponding grooves left in the dirt.

"All right, then, let's run it down."

We made a right turn just as the truck had done. Over the next two hours we weaved our way through the subdivision from one intersection to the next. It was a lot like following a trail of bread crumbs.

As we went along, patches of the Courier's tire tracks began to appear in the middle of the road and with greater frequency. It felt like we were closing in on the center of a giant spider web. "We're getting close." I told Eric.

Eventually, the tire tracks led us to a driveway that turned into a single-wide mobile home with a blue metal roof and moldy white siding. In the front yard a tattered Confederate flag hung limp from a bent flagpole. Parked next to it was the orange Ford Courier pickup truck. A camouflaged hunting jacket lay crumpled on top of the cab, and a white cooler with streaks of dried red blood sat on the ground near the truck's tailgate. I nodded at the flag and said, "Things are looking up."

"I'm stoked about it too," said Eric, as he eyed the flag and nodded in appreciation.

Putnam poachers were mighty proud of their southern heritage and didn't mind displaying their enthusiasm with a show of support for the Confederacy. The blue-and-red flag tilted the odds in our favor that the fella living inside that mobile home was involved in the killing of an illegal deer.

The kitchen curtain was briefly pulled back, before it fell into place. We had been seen.

A thin aluminum door screeched open and out stepped a forty-some-year-old shirtless man with a bald head, one earlobe laden with triple gold earrings, and a chest full of dragon tattoos. He had a harsh tan, the kind of deep brown that looks like burnt toast. I made him for a roofer.

Indeed, he was rough-looking character. But looks can sometimes be deceiving. He offered up an enthusiastic handshake to Eric and me and asked, "What can I help you guys with?"

"Listen," I said. "I'm going to be straight up with you. You and I both know why we're here. A deer was killed early today and put in this pickup truck"—I jabbed a finger toward the rusting hulk for proper theatrics—"and brought back here where it was obviously butchered, by the look of that bloody cooler. We want the truth about what happened."

"If I tell you what happened, will I go to jail?"

"No, not for an illegal deer."

"My twelve-year-old son killed a spike buck with two-inch horns. He was sitting next to me in the tree stand this morning when he shot it. I guess I should have told him not to shoot."

"Here's what we're going to do. Your son will get a warning, and you'll get a citation for a mandatory court appearance since you were responsible for his conduct. We're also going to seize the shotgun and the deer meat."

"Fine."

Eric and I finished up the paperwork and loaded up a Remington Model 870 12-gauge shotgun, along with the three white plastic garbage bags filled with butchered deer meat, into our patrol truck. I opened the passenger door to get in, when the tattooed man walked up and asked, "Hey, how did you find us anyway?"

"We followed your tire tracks."

"No way! Not with all the traffic on these roads. You all just got lucky."

"Luck it is, then. Have a nice day." I quietly shut the door and gave him a little wave, while Eric cranked the truck and drove us on down the driveway.

I turned to Eric and asked, "So what do you think?"

"He'll be scratching his head for a while trying to figure this one out."

"Exactly, keep them guessing. That's what it's all about."

24

Burn Marks

The constant beeping of the alarm clock jolted me awake. "Please shut it off," my wife begged, throwing a pillow over her head. I reached up to the nightstand and yanked on the electric cord until I was eyeball close to the flashing red digits—3:00 a.m. I thumbed the alarm switch off and collapsed against the soft mattress and hazily recalled why I had set the clock to go off at this ungodly hour.

Tommy Shearer, my senior officer, had asked me to go with him that morning to work a stakeout on Roger Gunter—Putnam County's most elusive poacher and a continual thorn in our side. Tommy believed he'd patterned Gunter by studying tire tracks left by his all-terrain vehicle inside Caravelle Wildlife Management Area. The plan was to catch him as he traveled through the public hunting grounds to poach turkeys on an off-limits, military bombing range.

The management area opened one week each spring for a special turkey hunt by quota only, and now the season had closed. No hunting, no guns, and no ATVs allowed.

I was glad someone had a lead on Gunter because most of us in the wildlife law enforcement business stood as good a chance of figuring him out as we did picking out the winning lotto numbers.

Tommy, then fifty-five years old, was a no-nonsense kind of guy with a full head of close-cropped, wavy gray hair. He stood a little over

Tommy Shearer, 1967. By permission of Tommy Shearer.

six feet and carried 210 pounds on a ramrod-straight frame. Like me, he was a walker and could cover many miles on foot without fatigue, so we were kindred spirits in that regard. During his then thirty-three-year career, he'd caught Gunter a record five times. So it was with some optimism that I crawled out of bed and made ready to try to catch Gunter—one more time.

An hour and a half later, Tommy and I bounced along an abandoned two-track woods road with only the bumper-mounted sneak light to illuminate our way. The nose of the heavy-duty Dodge 2500 pickup truck broke through the dense brush and overgrown palmettos that grew into the trail with the ease of a battle-tested army tank. We'd traveled about two miles from the nearest paved road, when

Tommy turned off the rough path and into a natural clearing ringed by palmetto bushes and parked.

He switched on the truck's interior dome light so we could arrange our gear. "Got room for my citation books in your pack?" asked Tommy.

"No problem." My day pack had plenty of room to hold his citation books. I snapped the top flap shut, stepped out of the truck, and shouldered the pack.

"We need to follow this fire trail," said Tommy. His hand cupped over the lens of his flashlight so only a dim glow illuminated the freshly plowed, foot-deep firebreak. "We'll follow it for a good half mile to a grassy road where there's a cable-gate. I think Roger will avoid the cable by driving into a ditch. We can hem him in there because he'll have to slow down."

Briefing over. Tommy clicked off the light.

"Sounds like a good plan to me," I said. "Lead on." I followed behind him step for step as we kept to the dried leaves, dead sticks, and desiccated palmetto fronds that lay on either side of the freshly churned sugar sand. We didn't want to leave any foot tracks behind. Gunter was obsessive about checking sign and would often inspect side trails along his main route for any hint of a human.

"I sure hope he shows up," murmured Tommy while we paused in the trail to listen for a moment. "The wind is really kicking up and with the sky overcast . . . well, I just don't know. Turkey hunters usually don't come out on a morning like this."

"I know, but Roger doesn't think like most hunters."

"True enough."

We reached the cable-gate by five o'clock and squatted down in the bushes next to a three-foot-deep ditch. Pine trees sighed and palmetto fans rustled in the stiff breeze.

Directly across from us stood two creosote railroad ties—one on each side of the road—with a wire cable stretched between them. We'd stop Gunter as he drove along the bottom of the ditch to avoid the nearest post.

The dim gray of predawn had begun to fill the woods when the *putt,*

putt, putt of a four-cycle engine drifted to us on a steady west wind. Moments later the bike's headlight shone round a bend in the road heading our way. When it swung down into the ditch, I jumped out in front, my flashlight shining into the operator's eyes: "State Wildlife Officer! Hands up! Hands up now!"

Gunter threw up his hands, leaving the bike in neutral. "OK, Cat. You caught me!"

I reached across the handlebars, shut the ignition off, and yanked the key out.

The frame of a large handgun filled a homemade holster fashioned from cotton camo. It lay loosely against Gunter's chest, attached by a thin cloth sling around his neck. The holster setup was vintage Gunter. By hooking one thumb under the sling, he could make the gun disappear with a flick of the wrist should anything spook him on the trail ahead.

Tommy carefully relieved him of the weapon.

"Roger, step off the bike," I told him.

Gunter stood next to his four-wheeler, stiff, arms crossed, watching with keen, pale-blue eyes that evaluated us as we evaluated him. The picture he and his equipment presented—as the long shafts of first light crept between the pines—would have made the perfect advertisement for a hunting commercial. Every square inch of his bike was spray-painted in dull browns and greens and black. He wore faded military-fatigue woodland camo pants and jacket, including a Vietnam-style boonie hat pushed back to reveal a broad forehead.

Tommy reached inside the holster and pulled out a .223 caliber Thompson/Center single-shot pistol, with scope attached. He broke open the long-barreled pistol, removed a shiny brass cartridge from the chamber, and handed it over to me. I hefted the weapon and complimented Gunter on what a fine piece of armament he carried. An unusual choice for most turkey hunters, it was nonetheless a potent round for North America's premier big game bird.

Gunter's thoughts had now turned inward. He seemed annoyed, distracted, and upset with himself. "Gawd dammit," he blurted out. "I knew you all were going to be here. I knew it. I should never have come out this morning." He pointed at Tommy. "You had burn marks on you. That woman up at the bait shop told me she seen you with burn marks."

Tommy and I looked at each other and shrugged. "What on earth are you talking about?" I asked.

"You know . . . burn marks." Gunter bent over and broke the stem off a burnt palmetto frond and rubbed one calloused finger over it. A film of black smut showed on the pad.

"OK, I'm tracking now," I said. "You're talking about the woods having been control-burned a few months back."

"Right. Two days ago I heard Tommy come into the bait shop with his shirt belly streaked with charcoal. I suspected he might have been doing some recon work back here. I know this isn't the only place in Putnam County that's been burnt. But you can't be too careful. I violated one of my own rules by ignoring my suspicions. Not only that, but this was my third time coming here in a row, and I never come more than twice to the same spot." Excited now, Gunter became more animated, gesturing with both hands. "But I got to tell ya . . . there was a big-ass gobbler I needed to kill back in them woods." He nodded behind him. "I couldn't stand it. And I figured the two of you wouldn't be out here on such a rotten day anyway.

"You all do what you got to do, and let me get on out of here. I got things to do."

"Well, Roger," I said, "I'm sure you have a busy calendar, but you're just going to have to work us into your schedule. You'll leave here when we say you can leave."

I slipped out of my backpack and opened the top flap. I pulled out Tommy's citation book and handed it to him. He issued Gunter a couple of citations for management-area violations and sent him on his way.

"He's a clever guy, isn't he?" I remarked.

"One of a kind," replied Tommy. "We hurt his pride a little this morning. But I figure after he sucks down a beer or two, he'll get over it."

Tommy and I headed back to the truck. Only this time we walked in the bare sand, down the center of the fire trail.

Epilogue

By now you should know that I prefer to tell a story as it naturally evolves, without extraneous sidebars that would detract from the narrative. Writers call this "in the moment" storytelling. The goal is to allow the readers to feel they are taking part in an adventure rather than sitting high up on a bleacher seat viewing the action from afar. This particular writing style, however, does leave certain things unsaid.

This book was devoted in large part to the types of poachers one would usually find in the inland regions of northeast Florida. In order to hold a common thread throughout the book, I kept the story lines to my personal experiences and to those of the wardens I worked with. For the most part, I skipped any mention of boating-safety enforcement, which has become the bread-and-butter job for many wardens. While the topic is an important one, it rarely has the story value to justify an entire book chapter.

The act of catching poachers—and, more often, not catching them—was a mixture of extreme emotional swings for me. But whatever the outcome, whether elation or frustration, few people can say they were lucky enough to have spent their entire career chasing Indiana Jones–like characters through the tangled woods and untamed waters of Florida's backcountry.

I remember those experiences fondly.

Back when I still wore the uniform, folks would occasionally approach me on the street and inquire what exactly it is that we do. I'd gather myself, mentally editing out all but the most concise sentences to briefly sum up the job. More often than not, after a few seconds of explanation their eyes would begin to cast about; they'd already lost interest before I'd even warmed up. They just couldn't relate. It is, I think, in part due to "Nature Deficit Disorder," a term coined by author Richard Louv in his 2005 book, *Last Child in the Woods*. Louv argues many children today (and I would add, a good many adults) can't relate to nature and the environment because of an endless appetite for the consumption of electronic media. Nature has become an abstract concept, while "kids' pagers, instant messaging, and Nintendo" are the new reality.

Sadly, I would agree. Call me old-fashioned, but I enjoy those occasions when I can unplug from cyberspace. I like the old reality, where entertainment was less artificial. Like watching a flying hawk suddenly close its wings and plummet from the sky to ensnare a hapless rabbit in its talons.

The contrast between old and new, the void in nature education, and, even more, the lack of understanding about conservation law enforcement work became the primary motivations for me to write this book.

When I look back on my career, I can't help but put a measuring stick to the different types of poachers I dealt with. They came in all manner of stripes, but generally fell into one of several categories.

Some were "weekend warriors," teenagers out for a Saturday-night lark, naively shining deer along a major highway until we busted out of the bushes with blue lights flashing.

Others were driven by the need to decimate the deer herd. "Kill crazy," we called them. They lived to see a deer drop dead in its tracks, like the two young men we caught one night who'd intentionally run over a deer with a pizza delivery truck. Flushed with success and a fresh dead deer, now broken and bloodied in the truck's bed, they decided to double-down. This effort ended abruptly (with what some would call poetic justice) when they aimed their front bumper—nicknamed "12-gauge"—at five deer standing on the road shoulder and T-boned a live oak tree instead. The truck was totaled. The deer escaped unharmed. Final score: 1:1.

A handful of poachers really were in need of something to eat. One morning another warden and I searched a clapboard home in the community of Bostwick for an illegal deer. The shooter had hung the animal from bare wooden rafters in his dining room and butchered it there. Blood and pieces of entrails lay splattered across the dining-room table. The refrigerator was empty except for a stainless pan filled with boned-out venison. In cases like these, we issued a citation, but we'd also slip a note to the judge asking him to take it easy on them.

Then there were the poachers who were real hunters. Careful and meticulous, they devoted a great deal of time to developing a strategy that would circumvent us at nearly every turn. They employed the tactics of lookouts and drop-offs and light signals. And they utilized all manner of electronics, too, like police scanners, Citizen Band radios, handheld GPS navigation systems, cellular phones, and ear bud walkie-talkies. The likelihood of them being caught was remote, unless we received help from an informant or happened to be in the right spot at the right time.

But of all the poachers I encountered, I would have to tip my hat to the outlaw commercial fishermen on the St. Johns River. They were worthy adversaries, indeed. They poached fish to survive and worked at it around the clock, often expending a great deal of mental energy to figure out the best way to avoid the law. Thus stealth and cunning, combined with superb gamesmanship skills, allowed them to stay a step or two ahead of us a good deal of the time.

In the beginning my relationship with the commercial fishermen was, well, rocky, to put it in temperate terms. I was barely a year in Putnam County when forty of them gathered at the Welaka Fire Station—of which I'm now president—one evening for a meeting. Only one item was on their agenda: the best way to get me fired (an informant of mine attended the meeting). In the end, none of them had the nerve to go to management about the problem (me). They were too worried about retribution.

A few years later the issue became more serious when the vandalism began. Two or three times a month my driveway would be tacked with simplex roofing nails. The newspaper lady and the mailman refused to make deliveries; my neighbors were furious. I changed and had repaired dozens of flattened tires, costing thousands of dollars in damage to my personal vehicles and to my state ride. One night, they nailed me, the county judge, Warden Gator Banks, and another war-den who lived down in the Ocala Forest, a one-way trip of over fifty miles.

A few nights later, two wardens worked a stakeout in an abandoned, weed-choked orange grove next to my driveway. They were set up to catch the dastardly nail throwers. By three in the morning, no suspi-cious vehicles had been seen, so they called it quits and headed home. A quarter mile down the highway, however, the signature sounds of metal clicking against hard asphalt pavement vibrated through their patrol truck. My driveway had been tacked, again.

From that experience, we learned that roofing nails could be tossed with extraordinary accuracy by someone passing by in the dark at sixty miles per hour. Until then, we'd always *assumed* the bad guys would have to slow down. There were many more incidents as well, but I mention these only to illustrate that it wasn't exactly a love fest in the beginning.

Over time, though, I began to look at the commercial fishermen in a more mellow light and tried to help them whenever I could. A gradual change in our relationship—for the better—started to take place.

The actual turning point may have been when Gator and I captured two hoop-net thieves who'd moved into the area. They'd taken dozens of hoop nets owned by three local fishermen from out of the river. We found the culprits laid up in a rental house with twenty-five stolen nets stacked up in the backyard. We connected each net to the fisher-man who built and owned them by the unique method of how they tied their own knots. It was a lot like using arches, loops, and whorls to distinguish one fingerprint from another.

Then there were the commercial fishermen who drowned in the river north of Palatka and Lake George, their vessels having capsized in the most horrid weather (you don't have to be in the Bering Sea off the coast of Alaska to find a life-threatening situation on the water). The wardens up and down the river worked day and night until the bodies were recovered. We gave it our all, and I think the fishermen appreciated us for it.

*　　*　　*

For more years than I care to count, I've helped out at the Welaka Fishing Rodeo. It's an annual event hosted by the U.S. Fish and Wildlife Service for three hundred children each spring. The grounds are well maintained and kid-friendly: stocked ponds surrounded by gently sloping grass banks that allow easy access to the water's edge.

The ponds are filled with channel catfish and a sprinkling of bream and bass, and one monster catfish of nearly forty pounds, which offers the ultimate challenge for any junior angler. Who among them would turn down an opportunity to haul in "Mister Whiskers"?

My job is to rally enough commercial fishermen together so we can efficiently clean, ice, and bag all of the fish. Then the parents don't have to mess with figuring out how to shuck a catfish of its hide, a daunting and often painful task for the inexperienced.

Interestingly, at least half of the commercial guys who show up to help are ones I'd chased in my early years as a river-patrol warden.

I never would have dreamed that one day I'd be standing elbow to elbow with former adversaries sweating over a fish-slimed skinning table. Yet we continue to do it every spring.

Acknowledgments

This book could never have reached fruition without the kind help and patient tutelage of a great many folks.

Many thanks to the Ponte Vedra Writers Group, who helped keep me from tacking off course early on; Jerry Teske, retired educator, for pointing out grammatical errors and picking apart the finer points of writerly pitfalls; Jack Owens, a thirty-year veteran newsman, who offered sage advice on openings and closings and everything in between; Joy Hill, FWC public information officer, who inspired me in so many ways; Laurel A. Neme, Ph.D., who became my long-distance cheerleader from the great state of Vermont; Jeff Klinkenberg, veteran *St. Pete Times* reporter, who thought my book would be a good match for the University Press of Florida (UPF); and Chris Christian, an outdoor/freelance writer and longtime friend, who is responsible for kick-starting my writing career and admonishing me to never forget "Joe Six-Pack," the typical reader of everything outdoors.

And to others who gave at least one of my book chapters a hard look—my deep appreciation to Cara Chase, Fred Petty, and Gabriel Smith. And special thanks to Debbie Banks, the wife of the legendary Gator Banks, who worked with me through numerous revisions to make sure her man stood on the good side of the fine line.

To the dedicated wardens and good friends I spent much of my career working with, I can't tell you enough how much I appreciate your help with this project and taking the time to make sure I got the *facts* right. A heartfelt thanks to Bob Raulerson, Hank Starling, Gator Banks, Wilbur Holdridge, Bruce Hamlin, Eric Meade, and Tommy Shearer.

A special thanks, too, to the notorious outlaw Roger Gunter for sharing his stories and allowing me to peek into the mind of a serial poacher. Without his cooperation, this book wouldn't be nearly as interesting.

I am forever indebted to Charlene Nelson for taking the time to dig out old trial transcripts and case dispositions from the basement of the Putnam County Courthouse.

Thank you to Robin Strickler, Dennis Bayer, and John Tanner, the former prosecutors who worked with me on the Amtrak case and helped me with research in other ways.

A special note of gratitude goes out to FWC Lt. Jeff Hahr (ret.) and to business owner James T. "Tom" Mastin, who took on the enormous job of manuscript peer review for UPF. They spent countless hours reading the manuscript and then offered insightful comments that helped fashion it into the finished product it is today.

The staff at the University Press of Florida deserves a special round of applause; professional, efficient, and inspiring are the first adjectives that come to mind when thinking of them. Thanks to my editor, Sian Hunter, who has a fine eye and a deft hand for manuscript critique, and to Meredith Morris-Babb, Shannon McCarthy, Sonia Dickey, Marthe Walters, Susan Murray, and all the unnamed souls I will likely never hear of but who toil daily behind the scenes.

Finally, to my friends and family, whose encouragement was heartfelt and welcome. Thanks to my sister-in-law and her husband, Lisa Hall and Michael Grina; to my wonderful son, Jason; and to my lovely bride of thirty-seven years, Karen, who put up with endless late-night critique sessions over stories she's heard a hundred times before.

Portions of chapter 1, "Meeting the Enemy," were previously published in *Folio Weekly*, August 18, 2009.

Index

Bob H. Lee is a former lieutenant and thirty-year veteran of the Florida Fish and Wildlife Conservation Commission (FWC). Prior to his retirement in 2007, he was the lead man-tracking instructor at the FWC Academy. He has also taught classes in commercial freshwater fishing equipment and regulations, as well as night driving (without lights). He writes freelance articles for law enforcement and outdoor magazines. He lives with his wife, Karen, and their two Labrador retrievers, Dixie and Sweetie Pie, in northeast Florida. This is his first book. Connect with the author online at bobhlee.com.

*   *   *

The University Press of Florida is the scholarly publishing agency for the State University System of Florida, comprising Florida A&M University, Florida Atlantic University, Florida Gulf Coast University, Florida International University, Florida State University, New College of Florida, University of Central Florida, University of Florida, University of North Florida, University of South Florida, and University of West Florida.

The Florida History and Culture Series
Edited by Raymond Arsenault and Gary R. Mormino

Paradise Lost? The Environmental History of Florida, edited by Jack E. Davis and Raymond Arsenault (2005)

Frolicking Bears, Wet Vultures, and Other Oddities: A New York City Journalist in Nineteenth-Century Florida, edited by Jerald T. Milanich (2005)

Waters Less Traveled: Exploring Florida's Big Bend Coast, by Doug Alderson (2005)

Saving South Beach, by M. Barron Stofik (2005; first paperback edition, 2012)

Losing It All to Sprawl: How Progress Ate My Cracker Landscape, by Bill Belleville (2006; first paperback edition, 2010)

Voices of the Apalachicola, compiled and edited by Faith Eidse (2006)

Floridian of His Century: The Courage of Governor LeRoy Collins, by Martin A. Dyckman (2006)

America's Fortress: A History of Fort Jefferson, Dry Tortugas, Florida, by Thomas Reid (2006)

Weeki Wachee, City of Mermaids: A History of One of Florida's Oldest Roadside Attractions, by Lu Vickers (2007)

City of Intrigue, Nest of Revolution: A Documentary History of Key West in the Nineteenth Century, by Consuelo E. Stebbins (2007)

The New Deal in South Florida: Design, Policy, and Community Building, 1933–1940, edited by John A. Stuart and John F. Stack Jr. (2008)

The Enduring Seminoles: From Alligator Wrestling to Casino Gaming, Revised and Expanded Edition, by Patsy West (2008)

Pilgrim in the Land of Alligators: More Stories about Real Florida, by Jeff Klinkenberg (2008; first paperback edition, 2011)

A Most Disorderly Court: Scandal and Reform in the Florida Judiciary, by Martin A. Dyckman (2008)

A Journey into Florida Railroad History, by Gregg M. Turner (2008; first paperback edition, 2012)

Sandspurs: Notes from a Coastal Columnist, by Mark Lane (2008)

Paving Paradise: Florida's Vanishing Wetlands and the Failure of No Net Loss, by Craig Pittman and Matthew Waite (2009; first paperback edition, 2010)

Embry-Riddle at War: Aviation Training during World War II, by Stephen G. Craft (2009)

The Columbia Restaurant: Celebrating a Century of History, Culture, and Cuisine, by Andrew T. Huse, with recipes and memories from Richard Gonzmart and the Columbia restaurant family (2009)

Ditch of Dreams: The Cross Florida Barge Canal and the Struggle for Florida's Future, by Steven Noll and David Tegeder (2009)

Manatee Insanity: Inside the War over Florida's Most Famous Endangered Species, by Craig Pittman (2010)

Frank Lloyd Wright's Florida Southern College, by Dale Allen Gyure (2010)

Sunshine Paradise: A History of Florida Tourism, by Tracy J. Revels (2011)

Hidden Seminoles: Julian Dimock's Historic Florida Photographs, by Jerald T. Milanich and Nina J. Root (2011)

Treasures of the Panhandle: A Journey through West Florida, by Brian R. Rucker (2011)

Key West on the Edge: Inventing the Conch Republic, by Robert Kerstein (2012)

The Scent of Scandal: Greed, Betrayal, and the World's Most Beautiful Orchid, by Craig Pittman (2012; first paperback edition, 2014)

Backcountry Lawman: True Stories from a Florida Game Warden, by Bob H. Lee (2013; first paperback edition, 2015)

Alligators in B-Flat: Improbable Tales from the Files of Real Florida, by Jeff Klinkenberg (2013)

CPSIA information can be obtained
at www.ICGtesting.com
Printed in the USA
BVHW032116131120
593007BV00005B/21